Creative Accounting Exposed

Creative Accounting Exposed

Ignacio de la Torre
Translated into English by Bartus Hamilton

First published in Spanish as *Ingenieria Financiera* in 2006 by LID Editorial Empresarial, S.L.

English translation published 2009 by
PALGRAVE MACMILLAN

Palgrave Macmillan in the UK is an imprint of Macmillan Publishers Limited, registered in England, company number 785998, of Houndmills, Basingstoke, Hampshire RG21 6XS.

Palgrave Macmillan in the US is a division of St Martin's Press LLC, 175 Fifth Avenue, New York, NY 10010.

Palgrave Macmillan is the global academic imprint of the above companies and has companies and representatives throughout the world.

Palgrave® and Macmillan® are registered trademarks in the United States, the United Kingdom, Europe and other countries.

ISBN-13: 978-0-230-21770-6
ISBN-10: 0-230-21770-2

This book is printed on paper suitable for recycling and made from fully managed and sustained forest sources. Logging, pulping and manufacturing processes are expected to conform to the environmental regulations of the country of origin.

A catalogue record for this book is available from the British Library.

Library of Congress Cataloging-in-Publication Data
Torre, Ignacio de la, 1974-
  [Ingeniera financiera. English]
  Creative accounting exposed/Ignacio de la Torre; translated into
  English by Bartus Hamilton.
     p. cm.
  ISBN 978-0-230-21770-6
  1. Financial statements   2. Corporations—Accounting.   I. Title.
  HF5681.B2T6713 2008
  657'95—dc22   2008021140

10   9   8   7   6   5   4   3   2   1
18   17   16   15   14   13   12   11   10   09

Printed and bound in China

To my parents, Amparo and Fernando

Contents

List of Tables and Figures

Tables

Figures

Acknowledgements

As a Professor of Creative Accounting I insisted my students (some of them chief executive officers) should enhance their creative accounting skills when the economic cycle was in the boom period so that they would be able better to understand accounting practices once the bubble burst. The bubble burst in the summer of 2007, and we soon saw how the main Western banks has kept billions and billions of dollars out of their balance sheets. Creative Accounting, like History, is cyclical; this makes its study imperative for the professional of the financial markets.

In the writing of this book I have to thank my Spanish editor, Marcelino Elosua, for giving me the idea of writing a book on the subjects I was teaching (by the way, I always hated professors who would force students to buy their own books, so this book, *Creative Accounting Exposed*, keeps being an optional reading on my course). I would also want to thank my students, who since 2002 have constantly challenged me to look into more and more cases of creative accounting. Interestingly enough, as the reader will be able to observe, most of the cases follow common patterns. My academic institution, the IE Business School, supported the study and promotion of creative accounting as a relevant field within its expanded offering of a master's in finance.

Having worked in the investment banking industry for over ten years, I am also grateful for the privilege of having been able to learn from the excellent people in that sector. Having enjoyed acess to excellent equity research (especially that of the UBS valuation and accounting team) of the main banks (which I have employed to illustrate some of the cases that the book exposes) has been a great advantage. Now that the banking industry is suffering in reputation I would like to honour most of its employees for their sharpness, hard work and client-centricity. Finally, I express my gratitude to my parents (to whom this book is dedicated), Amparo and Fernando, my wife and my three children (and a fourth, under way). It is not easy to explain to all of them how amazing creative accounting can be...

IGNACIO DE LA TORRE

List of Abbreviations

CDO	collateralized debt obligations
EBIT	earnings before interest and tax
EBITDA	earnings before interest, taxes, depreciation and amortization
EITF	emergency issues task force
EPS	earnings-per-share
ETD	exchange traded derivative
EURIBOR	Euro interbank offered rate
EV/EBITDA	enterprise value/earnings before interest, taxes, depreciation and amortization
FAS	Financial Accounting Standards
FASB	Financial Accounting Standards Board
FIFA	International Federation of Football Association
FIFO	first in, first out
GAAP	generally accepted accounting principles
GDP	gross domestic product
IAS	International Accounting Standards
IASB	International Accounting Standards Board
IFRS	International Financial Reporting Standards
IPO	initial public offering
LIBOR	London interbank offered rate
LIFO	last in, first out
OFHEO	Office of Federal Housing Enterprise Oversight
OTC	over the counter derivative
PER	price earnings ratio
REITs	real estate investment trusts
ROE	return on equity
SEC	Securities and Exchange Commission
SFAS	Statement of Financial Accounting Standard
SIV	structured investment vehicle
SOP	statement of position
SPE	special purpose entity
SPV	special purpose vehicle

Introduction

Corrupt executives are no better than common thieves when they betray their employees and steal from their investors.
John Ashcroft, US Attorney General
August 2002

One week ago General Motors restated its accounts since 2000, reporting 2.2 billion dollars more in losses than those announced in 2005, 2.3 billion dollars relating to the possible bankruptcy of its subsidiary Delphi, 500 million to its financing subsidiary GMAC, and 400 to staff restructuring charges. General Motors incorrectly recorded payments and accounts payable received from suppliers.
The Wall Street Journal, 20 March 2006

General Motors recognises accounting errors that caused its shares to collapse 4.5% to a 13-year-low of 23.5 dollars. General Motors admitted losses in 2001 of 1.07 billion dollars, four times the amount reported previously.... Until 1981 General Motors used more conservative accounting techniques, but the changing climate in the automobile sector prompted it to use more aggressive accounting techniques, such as prematurely recording future payments as income.
Expansión, 22 March 2006

The French Judicial Police searched the office of the Minister of Economy, Thierry Breton, for evidence linking him to an accounting scandal when Breton was president of the Audit Committee of the chemical company Rhodia, in April 1998. Rhodia, which had been floated on the stock marked in June 1998, informed the market that its earnings would be below those forecast in September 2000, and in June 2003 it underwent its first investigation for fudging accounts.
Financial Times, 19 January 2006

Nortel has reached an out-of-court agreement to pay 2.4 billion dollars in compensation in two lawsuits brought against if for fiddling earnings figures. It will also pay half of any amount it receives in open litigation against its ex Managing Director Frank Dunn and former financial directors Douglas Beatty and Michael Gollogly, all fired in 2004 after it was revealed that they had manipulated the company's accounts to maximise their personal bonuses in 2003, the result being a 41% reduction in reported net 2003 earnings.

The Wall Street Journal, 9 February 2006

According to the US Attorney's General's Office, American International Group (AIG) infringed criminal law by performing transactions to boost reported reserves and conceal losses. Consequently, AIG agreed to pay a $1.6 billion fine. AIG unlawfully increased its earnings by 500 million dollars in 2000 and 2001 through transactions performed with General Re, a subsidiary of Berkshire Hathaway ... AIG will pay 800 million dollars to the SEC and 819 million dollars to the US Tax Department.

Financial Times, 10 February 2006

The Bank of Spain has fined CajaSur 350,000 euros for fiddling its 2003 and 2004 accounts and for irregular accounting practices. The Bishop Miguel Castillejo and Fransisco Jurado, former Chairman and General Manager of the Cordoba Savings Bank, respectively, have also been fined 50,000 euros each. ...Spain's regulatory body has inspected the accounts for those years and has discovered transfers of funds from credit lines to current accounts that were made twice a year, at the end of each quarter. CajaSur used these operations to pretend it had more customer assets than it really did.

Expansión, 17 May 2006

The accounting scandal of the Japanese securities agency Livedoor and its auditors Koyo & Co. arose due to the company's failure to use objective accounting criteria to consolidate special purpose vehicle companies (SPVs). In 2005 the following companies were delisted for breaching securities market law on counts of financial fraud: Associant Technology, Surugaya, Kanebo, Zecoo and North.

The Wall Street Journal, 26 January 2006

The Scandinavian airline SAS detects accounting errors in Spanair valued at 44 million euros, generated between 2002 and 2005. SAS owns 94.9% of Spanair, the subsidiary it acquired in 2002.

Expansión, 25 January 2006

These newspaper extracts show that companies have used creative accounting for many years and in many different economic sectors.

However, what is striking about this line of reasoning is that many of these scandals could have been foreseen by investors with a modicum of basic knowledge in the forensic analysis of financial reporting, a discipline that studies the quality of financial information. In fact, many of the accounting scandals that came to the public eye after 2001 had already been predicted in 1998 by Arthur Levitt, then President of the SEC,[1] in his speech entitled 'The Numbers Game', in which he severely criticized the creative accounting practices used by North American companies to meet the earnings forecasts promised to the market and highlighted the main accounting hocus-pocus behind much of this abuse.[2]

This book offers an analytical insight into the procedures used by reporters of financial information to fiddle accounting information. However, we cannot assume outright that such alterations are illegal. Accounting leaves room for a great deal of interpretation on the part of reporters of financial information, and this subjectivity, taken to an extreme, might mean that financial information does not reflect the real situation despite complying with the law. That would be creative accounting. Different chapters in this book look at the areas where creative accounting is most common, using numerous case studies to give readers hard facts to investigate the impact of such practices. Whenever possible, we have tried to relate creative accounting practices to the impact any abuse could have had on company value, accompanied by modest tips on how to identify cases of creative accounting. With the interests of readers in mind, we have focused on topics of current importance and sacrificed more academic classifications.

Why do companies engage in creative accounting? In the short term, creative accounting when employed to improve earnings might have a positive effect on share prices or give companies access to lending or even allow them pay larger bonuses. However, our analyses should make us reconsider the extremely harmful mid-term consequences of financial reporting: manipulation on corporate value and, consequently, on employees, shareholders and, ultimately, basic ethics. The book therefore seeks to inform and educate recipients of financial information so that, in the future, they can limit such obscene cases of accounting prostitution that have tragically ruined so many investors, left so many workers jobless or behind bars and emotionally devastated so many managers obsessed with fraudulent short-term gains.

1

Revenue Recognition

When investors try to predict future cash flows and profits,
past performance becomes the foundation of credible forecasts.
Timothy M. Koller
McKinsey on Finance, summer 2003

Introduction: Lucent Technologies

In June 2004, the Securities and Exchange Commission (SEC) fined the telecommunications equipment company Lucent US$25 million after determining that, in 2000, it had incorrectly recognized sales valued at US$1,148 million and earnings before taxes of US$479 million.[1] In its report, the SEC estimated that the company had inflated revenues to complete certain internal sales increase objectives on which the variable remuneration of its executives depended. To achieve these objectives, 'some employees had violated and circumvented the company's internal accounting controls'[2] and had recorded certain products sent to distributors as revenues, despite the fact that these were never sold to end-consumers due to the significant deterioration of the balance sheets of telecommunications operators at that time. A verbal arrangement had been reached whereby distributors were allowed to return these products to Lucent, hence these could not be recorded as revenues.[3] Figure 1.1 shows the evolution of the company's stock price and the negative impact the investigation and subsequent penalty had on its value.

In this chapter, we will look at how this type of aggressive *interpretation* of when a sale is a sale is one of the most commonly used mechanisms in creative accounting, and describe the most common techniques used to manipulate company sales figures. The reader should keep in mind that, despite the fact that in some cases these techniques are clearly illegal, in other circumstances such mechanisms might be legal because

1

Figure 1.1   Lucent Technologies stock price during the SEC investigation (25 March to 9 April 2004)
Source: Bloomberg.

they belong to so-called *grey areas of accounting* that can be interpreted in different ways when it comes to recognizing revenues.

To begin this chapter, we will describe in detail the most common areas in which *doubtful* sales are generated, in reference to acts such as recording revenues received in year 1 that actually correspond to future years, recognizing revenues without transferring the sales risk, recording cost reductions as sales, treating financial revenues as operating revenues and recognizing as revenues taxes collected for payment to the Inland Revenue Services. Examples will be provided of real companies that have engaged in such practices.

We will then provide a more detailed and concise list of other legal techniques for recognizing revenues followed by a list of illegal techniques for increasing sales revenues. Most of these techniques are also presented in a schematic chart outlining the main problem areas associated with revenue recognition. After this list of examples, we will approach the problem by focusing on two practical cases: one relating to revenue recognition in the software industry and another concerning the treatment of sales in the Dutch semiconductor company ASML. The chapter concludes with a guide on to how to detect possible irregularities in sales figures, details of applicable accounting regulations and some reflections on the impact that the heterodox recognition of sales can have on a company's stock market value, illustrated by a practical case study. Finally, there are some short conclusions on the reasons why companies manipulate revenues and a possible solution to the problem.

Improper revenue recognition is one of the most important but, at the same time, least studied aspects of creative accounting. In fact, between 1997 and 2001, 126 of the 227 enforcement matters brought by the SEC regarding the quality of the financial statements of listed North American companies – that is, around 40 per cent of the total – involved the manipulation of revenue figures.[4] The Treadway Commission, in its 1999 report on fraudulent accounting, established that more than 50 per cent of the cases of accounting manipulation between 1987 and 1997 were due to aggressive revenue recognition.[5]

Revenue recognition methods and associated problems

Two fundamental aspects must be borne in mind when considering revenue recognition: timing, and the transfer of risk.

- *Timing* Imagine a grocer who purchases and pays €1,000 for some lemons on 31 December and sells them in January for €1,250. If cash-basis accounting is used, the expense is incurred in December (and therefore a loss, because no revenues are recorded that month) and the revenue (which is all profit) is generated in January. If the most common accrual-based accounting method is used, the payment received for the merchandise does not prevent the recognition of the corresponding expense from being deferred until the following month and that therefore in January: sales are €1,250; costs €1,000; and profits €250. Since cash flow and net profit are not the same over the years, an increase in revenues recognized in the short term will improve profit margins and, consequently, net profit in the current year, at the expense of reducing future margins and profits.

  Thus, the policy on timing of revenue recognition is crucial for determining the future. Let us look at an example to illustrate this: a kindergarten that offers nursery schooling for children aged one to four charges €300 a month plus an enrolment fee of €900 when a child enrols at the school. Let us assume that some parents enrol their one-year-old baby on 1 January and pay the €900 enrolment fee and the €300 corresponding to the first month. Should the kindergarten recognize €1,200 of revenues in January or should it only record the monthly instalment of €300 and record the other €900 according to the average period during which the baby is enrolled at the kindergarten? In other words, if most children spend an average of two years at the kindergarten, should the kindergarten recognize €50 of the €900 enrolment fee as first-year sales and the other €450 as sales in year 2? Over two years, recognized sales are exactly the same: the monthly instalment of €300 during 24 months plus a €900 enrolment fee gives a total of €8,100. Nevertheless, if the first method is used, in the first year sales would be €300 × 12 months = €3,600, plus the €900 enrolment fee, giving a total of €4,500; and in year 2 this would only be €3,600. If the second method is used, in year 1 the kindergarten would recognize €3,600 plus half of €900 (€450) – that is, €4,050 – and in year 2, €4,050 once again. Although aggregate profits in both years are the same with both methods, obviously with the second method the same profit would be obtained in year 1 as in year 2, hence, with the former, profits recognized in year 1 would be higher and lower in year 2.

- *The transfer of risk* This concept implies that every sale in which the merchandise risk has not been transferred is simply not a sale. For example, if a newspaper sells its copies to kiosks and these have the option to return unsold copies to the publishers at the end of each day, the latter is not permitted to record copies distributed in the morning at the kiosks as revenues but only those sold to end-consumers, since the risk of no sale remains with the publishers and not the kiosk.

One way to approach the problem is to consider the company's operative cycle when a sale is generated. This cycle normally involves the following:

(a) Receipt of the order;
(b) Production of the good;
(c) Delivery of the good or service to the client;
(d) Invoicing the client and collection of payment;
(e) Sometimes, after-sale service.

The accounting principle of accrual implies that revenues generated from the sale of goods or services must be recognized when the actual flow of the related goods and services occurs, regardless of when the resulting monetary or financial flow arises. Therefore, one way of bringing revenues forward is to increase or bring forward deliveries of products or services to clients. Hence, the sooner a sale is recognized – the times closest to point (a) – the more aggressive the company is; the later the sale is recognized – that is, closer to point (e) – the more conservative it is.

Using this approach to compare the revenue recognition policies of different companies operating in the same sector can be very useful. For example, in the Spanish construction sector civil buildings were treated as sales when construction work had been technically or economically approved but before it had been certified. However, the application of international accounting standards has brought about important changes in practices within this sector because it is no longer sufficient for construction work to have been completed, it must be *certified* – that is, accepted by the customer – and this could have a serious impact on accepted revenue volume. To complete the example, the recognition of the revenues of the insurance company providing civil liability cover for the building is also highly subjective. Let us assume that the insurance is contracted for a period of ten years. If the insurance company recognized 10 per cent every year, it might be committing an error – either intentionally or unintentionally – because the likelihood of claims occurring normally increases as the building ages, so most of the premium should really be recognized in these final years.

It is important to remember that the timing of revenue recognition might depend on the accounting method applied by the company.[6] In the following sections, we will look at the most common methods.

Critical event method of revenue recognition at points of sale. Revenues are generated at a specific moment: for example, when an ice cream seller gives a strawberry ice-lolly to a buyer. This system is mainly used in the automobile, chemicals, consumption, distribution, media and electricity sectors. For example, Renault recognizes its sales when it delivers cars to its dealers.

Having said that, the critical event method of revenue recognition, despite its simplicity, could give rise to subjective interpretation: My Travel Plc, who sold package holidays for a price that included the holiday and travel insurance, decided to recognize, at the time of the transaction, the percentage of the package holiday sale price corresponding to travel insurance and to defer the rest of the sale price to the moment when the holiday was actually taken; Rolls-Royce recognized subsidy payments – also called 'launch aids' for the development of future products and normal payments in the aerospace industry – as revenues.[7] This accounting treatment could be incorrect; the problem lies in the fact that other companies in the sector recognize such payments as liabilities and only record them as sales once the product in question has been delivered; this makes it very difficult to compare companies in the sector in terms of stock market multiples.[8]

Percentage-of-completion method[9]. This method is used for long-term contracts and consists of calculating the percentages of estimated costs that will be incurred to manufacture a good or render a service; these percentages of the global amount of the contract are then applied to recognize the corresponding revenues in every year. This method is only applied in some companies with long-term production periods such as construction companies (for example, in the construction of tunnels or motorways) or airplane manufacturers. As well as these two sectors, this method is also used in the electrical engineering and telecommunications equipment sectors. Nokia, for example, applies this method in the construction of mobile telecommunications networks. The subjectivity resulting from the lax interpretation of the percentage-of-completion method is broad. There are companies that, despite having short production cycles, apply this method to recognize prematurely revenues that are actually deferred revenues that should be recorded, for accounting purposes, in future years. The other technique is when companies are too aggressive in their quantification of percentages of completion.

Gamesa and the percentage-of-completion method

The Spanish engineering company Gamesa, when preparing its 2004 financial statements, applied the percentage-of-completion method to recognize revenues obtained from its wind park sales aeronautical structures manufacturing activities, for which purpose three requirements had to be satisfied: the duration of the operations generating the revenues had to be more than one accounting year; sufficient means and controls had to have been implemented to enable reliable estimates to be made; and there had to be no risk of the operation being cancelled.[10] Until 2003, Gamesa used the policy of recording margins obtained in wind park construction projects when these were actually sold, while costs incurred in wind parks under construction were recorded in the 'Inventories' category. The company's 2004 decision to adopt an alternative method for recognizing revenues was geared to reducing assets and softening results in order to present a sustained growth of revenues, perhaps in order to reduce share volatility.

Revenue allocation method. This is a combination of the two methods described previously. One firm that employs this method is the German software company SAP. When it concludes a licence sales agreement that incorporates maintenance, it applies the critical event method to recognize the sale price of the licence, and the percentage-of-completion method to recognize the amount received for maintenance and integration services. When the critical event and percentage-of-completion

Figure 1.2   Gamesa's stock price during the accounting change between October 2004 and May 2005
Source: Bloomberg.

methods are combined, the revenue figure calculated using the critical event method is often inflated and the figure obtained with the percentage-of-completion method reduced; this method is used very often to increase short-term revenues and profits, as we will see in the case of Xerox.

FIFA and the cash-basis accounting method

In 2003, the International Federation of Football Association (FIFA) decided to adapt its accounting methods to the International Financial Reporting Standards (IFRS).[11] Until then, it had used the Swiss bookkeeping system of recognizing revenues and expenses on a cash basis; in other words, it recognized sales when cash was received and expenses when cash was paid. By switching to the IFRS standards, FIFA began recognizing revenues in accordance with the accrual-basis accounting method.[12] FIFA was collecting revenues from the Word Cup that was to be organized in Germany in 2006. Most of these revenues corresponded to television broadcasting rights payable by different channels in the form of royalties, which were fixed and determinable, plus a percentage of the profits to be obtained by these television channels. This percentage might vary according to the volume of advertisers. Switching to the IFRS standards meant that FIFA began applying the percentage-of-completion method, allowing it to recognize revenues corresponding to the percentage of profit and not to the royalty, if this was quantifiable and probable. Notwithstanding the foregoing, the risk inherent in this method is evident since it is conditioned by many highly volatile factors. In particular, it is important to bear in mind that television channels apply the critical-event method; they would only recognize revenues and profits when the World Cup takes place. FIFA, on the other hand, is already bringing revenues as yet unrecognized by the payers forward to current years.[13]

In this brief introduction, we have looked at the problem of revenue recognition and the impact that more conservative or more aggressive interpretations might have on corporate financial statements. Let us now look at the different revenue recognition policies that can be used to manipulate revenue figures.

Premature revenue recognition

A multi-element contract is one in which a company undertakes both to pay an amount for the purchase of a good and to render services in the future or to make future improvements to the purchased good. For example, the purchase of a car with a three-year guarantee is a multi-element contract. Part of the price received by the seller is used to purchase the car and the other part to cover the guarantee in the agreed years: this type of contract can be easily manipulated by companies that increase the value of the good and reduce the value of the service, thus maximizing profits recognized when the contract is signed. In general, these contracts are normal in the software, systems integration and telecommunications equipment services industries. As we have seen, this method might be open to subjective interpretation, which, in some cases, could be abusive or improper. Now, let us look at some examples.

Dixons

In 2004, the British distributor Dixons changed its policy for recognizing revenues in respect of guarantees. Imagine a customer who purchases a television set for £140 (real cost £80) and pays another £60 for an extended guarantee for years 2 and 3 after the purchase of the product (the first year is covered by the sale price of the television set). Let us assume that the cost of this Dixons guarantee is £10 pounds per year and that if it were to ask a third party to insure the risk, this would cost £15 per year. In this scenario, it has three options:[14]

- It can recognize the £60 as income in year 1 (Dixons' policy before 2004), and record a provision that year for the costs it expects to incur in years 1 to 3; thus, all profits from the transaction are generated in year 1.
- It can defer the full amount of revenue obtained in respect of the guarantee (Dixons' policy after 2004); thus, the sales corresponding to the £60 guarantee and the corresponding profits are recognized in years 2 and 3.
- It can recognize, of the £60 of revenues relating to the guarantee, £30 in year 1 and defer £15 in each of years 2 and 3; that is, deferring the amount that Dixons would have to pay when transferring the risk.

Thus, with the first method, the company would recognize sales of £200 in year 1, £100 in costs (including £20 of provisions), giving a profit of £100. If it were to use the second method, it would obtain year 1 sales of £140 (£60 profit) and £30 in sales in each of years 2 and 3, with £20 pounds. If it were to opt for the third method, year 1 sales would be £170 (a profit of £90 since the cost of the guarantee would be deferred), and £15 in revenue and £10 in costs in each of years 2 and 3 (£5 profit in each year).

The new bookkeeping method applied by Dixons in 2004 reduced equity by £357.5 million (21 per cent of the total); in the year prior to the year in which the aggressive bookkeeping technique was used, profits were inflated by £357.5 million and operating revenues by £510.8 million.[15]

Xerox Corporation

On 6 February 2001, *The Wall Street Journal* published a long article that analyzed the abusive accounting practice of Xerox, which had the habit of recognizing leasing payments as sales. In April 2002, after an investigation by the SEC, the American company was forced to reclassify its financial statements for the years 1997 to 2000 and reduce recognized revenues by US$3,000 million and profits by US$1,500 million, with equity being reduced in the same amount.[16] As a result, the SEC fined Xerox US$10 million. By that time, the price of the company's shares had plummeted from US$62 to US$4.5.[17] How did this company manipulate its revenue figures?[18]

Xerox sold customers photocopiers under long-term agreements, in which the customers paid a sum of money to Xerox, part of which

Figure 1.3   Evolution of the Xerox's stock price
Source: Bloomberg.

was to purchase the machine and the other part to cover repairs and maintenance on a long-term basis. This was not problematic in itself from a bookkeeping perspective, provided that the amount corresponding to the sale price of the machine was recognized as revenue in the first year, plus revenues corresponding to maintenance services in the current year, transferring the rest of the received amount to deferred revenues, which, in turn, were recorded as sales in the year in which the repair services were rendered.

So, if a photocopier, for example, is valued at US$100, and five-year maintenance costs US$50, the customer would pay Xerox US$150 when purchasing the machine. The correct accounting method for recording this operation, if the transaction were performed on 1 January, would be to recognize US$110 of sales in year 1 and US$10 of sales in each of the following four years. Accounting malpractice on the part of Xerox consisted in recognizing US$125 of revenues from the sale of the machine, thus undervaluing the amount of future repair services, recording US$130 as revenues in year 1 and deferring only US$20 over the remaining four years of the contract. In this way, it increased year 1 profits substantially and reduced future profits. The total amount of the transaction in sales remained the same (US$150); the problem is simply the timing of the recognition of these sales.

Vodafone

Let us now look at another problematic case of premature revenue recognition. A customer visits a department store and contracts a mobile telephone with Vodafone, paying €150 to register. Does this €150 correspond to sales that should be recognized immediately or should they be deferred over the average estimated life of the customer relationship? Under Spanish or British accounting standards, Vodafone España and its parent company Vodafone Plc are required to recognize the €150 as sales in year 1. However, their revenues under North American accounting standards would be lower than those presented under British or Spanish accounting standards since North American bookkeeping standards require companies to defer revenues corresponding to customer registrations over the average estimated life of the customer relationship.

In 2002, Vodafone declared revenues of US$32,554 million according to British accounting standards.[19] Since the company is listed on the New York stock exchange, it is also required to file accounts in accordance with American bookkeeping standards. Surprisingly, in its American accounts it reported US$25,136 million in revenues, almost 20 per cent less than in its British accounts! Why did Vodafone's sales differ according to the accounting standard applied? Well, on the one hand, British accounting standards allow the company globally to consolidate subsidiaries whose boards of directors are effectively controlled by the company, even if it does not own more than 51 per cent of the subsidiary. However, under American accounting standards the company can only fully consolidate subsidiaries in which the company has more than a 50 per cent shareholding. Since the scope of consolidation varies, the consolidated revenues figure also varies. On the other hand, under British accounting standards, registration fees must be recognized when the customer is registered; that is, the date he/she pays the registration fee or on a nearby date. The reason for this is because registration fees are not considered to be sales. Under US GAAP, they are recognized as revenues according to the average expected life of the customer's relationship with the company. In the case of Vodafone, this is assumed to be an average of four years. Without attempting to determine which of the two solutions is correct, it is interesting to note that the impact on cost allocation might also vary depending on which method is applied.[20]

Telefónica Móviles

The same accounting effect applies to the Spanish mobile telephony operator Telefónica Móviles. When the company switched to the IFRS accounting standards, this did not only entail a change in the accounting of registration fees but also equipment sales, which under Spanish accounting standards were recorded when they were sold to distributors. Under the IFRS, they were only taken into account when the equipment had been sold to the end-consumer. As result of this switch, the telephony operator's profits would have been reduced, in 2004, by €7.1 million, and the impact on the values recorded in the company's balance sheets would have been a reduction of €30.8 million.

Recognition of bank revenues (Banesto and Bankinter)

It is very common for financial entities to perform interest rate swap transactions (by paying fixed interest and receiving variable interest, or vice versa) or foreign currency swap transactions. Sometimes, these types of contracts generate revenues if the underlying risk is transferred to the financial entity. The problem is the point at which these revenues should be recognized. Banesto recognizes them at the end of the accounting year, regardless of when the contract ends. Bankinter waits until the contract ends before recognizing these revenues. Both systems are perfectly legal; in the case of Banesto, the bank uses this method to bring forward the recognition of income.

The recognition of revenues without transferring the sale risk or payment obligation: Sunbeam

Sunbeam, a company that sold gas grills, recognized sales invoiced to distributors with which it had no risk commitment as revenues; that is to say, these distributors would return to Sunbeam all goods not sold at their establishments within a given period. Technically speaking, such deliveries of goods should not have been recognized as sales because the risk was still assumed by Sunbeam and not the distributor. If the risk of the merchandise had been transferred to the end-consumer, it would have been correct to recognize these sales as revenues. Hence, when distributors returned unsold products to Sunbeam, the latter proceeded to cancel these sales. In 1998, the SEC discovered that rights of return existed in the case of US$24.7 million of sales recognized in the fourth quarter of 1997; that is, they were sales without any economic impact that should not have been recognized.[21] The charismatic Managing Director of Sunbeam, Al Dunlap, was fined US$15 million by the SEC for endorsing and instigating such practices, and he was prohibited from occupying an executive position in any North American company for the rest of his life. Sunbeam is now a subsidiary of American Household, Inc.[22]

Recognition of cost reductions as revenues: Ahold

In the Ahold supermarket chain, a series of irregularities in the revenue figures of a North American branch led to accounting manipulations. The supermarkets receive discounts – in cash or in credit, to purchase more merchandise *free* – from suppliers when they achieve certain sales targets. These discounts should have been treated as reductions of sales costs. However, the branch incorrectly recognized these discounts as revenues.[23] Furthermore, they were also recognized before they should have been. The Financial Accounting Standards Board (FASB)[24] has established that these types of discounts must be treated as follows:

- If they are received at the beginning and in cash, the costs of the purchased materials have to be reduced by the amount of discount at the time of the sale; in the meantime, they have to be deferred
- If the cash amount is received after the sales target has been reached, the cost of the materials must be systematically reduced according to the percentage of purchases made from the seller
- Only if the cash amount is received at the beginning and is irreversible (it does not have to be returned) can it be recognized immediately as a reduction in sales costs.

In the case of the Ahold subsidiary, the discounts were not irreversible because they depended on the attainment of the sales objective but were nevertheless recognized immediately instead of being deferred.[25]

Recognition of financial revenues as revenues of sales: Parmalat

Revenues generated in financial operations, such as securities purchase operations, or even profits obtained in derivatives transactions, should always be recognized as financial revenues and must not be recorded with operating profits. However, some companies have recognized these revenues as 'other revenues' in the same sales bracket. The impact of this fraudulent recognition of revenues is enormous because financial revenues, if recognized as 'other operating revenues', inflate operating margins artificially. Thus, if a company with sales valued at €100 and operating profits of €20 fraudulently recognizes financial revenues in the amount of €10 as 'other revenues', sales would amount to €110 but operating profits would increase to €30, so the margin would rise from 20 per cent to 30 per cent!

Let us look at an example to illustrate the problem. In 2003, Parmalat recognized €40.7 million in financial revenues as 'other sales', equivalent to the first payment received as part of a financial swap deal. In 2002, the company recorded as 'other sales' revenues generated from the sale of products such as ice creams, water, chocolate, sports activities, fruit juices, butter and cheese.[26] However, the financial difficulties experienced by the company in 2003 prompted it to reclassify the supposed financial revenues obtained under the swap deal as operating revenues in the third quarter of 2003, giving an operating margin of 8.3 per cent, when it was really 7.6 per cent.[27] As we will see later, Parlamat's former Financial Officer and former Chairman were sentenced to prison for engaging in such accounting practices. This showed that their actions were not just illegal and unethical but also violations that were punished as criminal offences (imprisonment) and with penalties that affected equity (heavy personal and corporate fines).

Recognition of taxes as sales: Heineken

The brewer Heineken changed its revenue recognition policy when filing its accounts for the first six months of 2003. It no longer treated sales collected as taxes on alcohol as revenues.[28] This reduced revenues by 12 per cent, obviously without affecting net earnings. In 2001, the Belgian brewer Interbrew recorded the same entry, which is a requirement under international accounting standards, reducing its sales by 30 per cent to €5,600 million.[29]

Other techniques for recognizing revenues[30]

- *Sending goods to clients without these having been ordered beforehand.* The accounting entry is corrected when the 'error' is discovered, but the error is normally notified in the accounting period after the one that concerned the company.
- *Renting warehouses to send products there and recognize them as sales.* Returning to the case of Sunbeam, this company convinced its distributors to purchase grills six months before the season was due to begin in exchange for important discounts. The merchandise was not

delivered until six months later and the price would not be collected before that date. In order not to wait half a year to recognize the sales, Sunbeam sent its merchandise from its Neosho factory in Missouri to different third-party warehouses rented by the company where the merchandise would be stored for six months until delivery. Thus, Sunbeam recognized US$35 million as sales; later, however, independent external auditors declared that US$29 million of these sales were fictitious.[31]

- *Recognizing, as revenues, orders received from customers for certain products when these have not yet been sent.*
- *Keeping the sales order book open in January but recognizing these sales in December* by recording invoices issued previously.
- *Manipulating the end-of-quarter figure* (Sunbeam decided to postpone closure from 29 March to 31 March).
- *Selling products through loans granted to clients on a recurrent basis* to pay for products, with these sales accounting for a high percentage of total sales. At the end of 2000, telecommunications equipment companies granted US$15,000 million of financing to operators so that they could continue buying their products. What they were really doing was buying their own products from themselves.
- *Accelerating sales by offering extended payment periods* if new products are acquired by means of third party financing to obtain cash revenues in less than twelve months.
- *Recognizing revenues despite having serious doubts about the solvency of customers* due to their financial situation or repayment capacity, or to the lack of a sufficiently solid source of financing. It is important to remember that under the new international accounting standards, revenues can only be recognized if the customer is deemed to be capable of repaying the loan (or when the customer has received the correct type of financing). In other words, it is not permitted to recognize revenues and record an insolvency provision. If there are serious doubts regarding the collectibility of the sale in question, the sale must not be recognized.
- *Carrying out bilateral transactions between strategic partners*. The revenues reported by the Spanish satellite TV company Sogecable for the first quarter of 2005 were up 4 per cent to €396.4 million. When Telefónica – in turn one of Sogecable's two major shareholders – was awarded the contract to broadcast the Spanish Soccer League on its pay-per-view ADSL television platform Imagenio, Sogecable obtained around €25 million in revenues. This contract increased revenues dramatically by 37 per cent to €107 million and compensated for the 6 per cent downturn in subscriber revenues, Sogecable's core

area of business.[32] The North American company Healtheon signed a five-year collaboration agreement with Microsoft under which it undertook to purchase software packages from the software giant for US$162 million; in return, Microsoft would pay Healtheon the first US$100 million in advertising on three of Microsoft's thematic channels.

- *Recognizing inflated revenues corresponding to consideration with additional economic value* (for example, by selling something worth US$100 for US$200, by inviting customers to overpay US$100 for a *gift* or *consideration*). Broadcom, before completing an acquisition, would convince the acquired company to obtain purchase commitments from customers in exchange for warrants on Broadcom's stocks. When the warrant stocks were issued, the resulting goodwill was redeemed over 40 years while generated revenues were recorded in the following year. Thus, if Broadcom received orders for the value of US$1,000 and it committed a warrant valued at US$250, the real amount of revenue was US$750 and not US$1,000. What customers were actually doing was only paying for the net portion of the warrant.
- *Recognizing extraordinary revenues as ordinary revenues*, such as profits from property sales recorded by a non-real estate company. Once again, the impact of this fraudulent practice on operating margins is enormous.

Seven techniques for recognizing fictitious revenues[33]

- *Invoicing false customers.*
- *Recognizing sales without the customer making a commitment to pay* for the delivered product.
- *Sales conditioned by future events*. This can be achieved by invoicing the product sent to a customer where full approval of the purchase still depends on an additional formality. This formality is established in so-called 'side letters'. For example, HBO & Co. sold software to hospitals by issuing an additional letter that established a condition for the sale: approval by the hospital's board. However, the company recognized the revenue despite North American accounting standards requiring all the conditions to have been fulfilled before such revenues could be recorded. Bausch & Lomb used a similar technique. On 19 December 1994, *Business Week* revealed the accounting tricks used by this contact lenses firm, which persuaded distributors to purchase a total volume equivalent to two years' worth of stocks, at inflated prices, before 24 December 1993, the date on which it closed its

books. The company generated orders valued at US$25 million, yielding US$7.5 million in profits, the same as those obtained in 1993. In 1994, this practice produced an inventory excess at distributors, which reduced orders substantially. As a result, that year's income also fell sharply, with stocks falling from US$50 to US$30. Eventually, Bausch & Lomb only collected 15 per cent of the sales generated at year-end 1993, since these were conditional upon the lenses being sold, in turn, by the distributors and this did not happen.

- *Recognizing, as revenues, discounts offered by suppliers linked to future purchase undertakings.* These are contracts under which customers agree to overpay for certain goods now if the seller agrees to repay this extra amount later in the form of a cash payment. This cash payment is not a sale but a purchase refund; thus, the costs of materials are reduced by diminishing the value of stocks. However, some distributors treat these as sales in order to thus increase their turnover.
- *Recognizing sales that are incorrectly deferred during a merger process.* When a merger is announced, one of the companies is instructed to defer the recognition of sales until after the merger has been concluded in order to improve comparisons and achieve the promised revenue synergies; in the merger between 3Com and US Robotics, US$600 million of sales were not recognized for two months so that they could be recorded after the merger had taken place.
- *Distributing goods to other company warehouses* that are invoiced as customer revenues by *mistake.*
- *Selling goods to participated companies with an agreement to repurchase* these goods in the future. This practice is particularly relevant in the case of strategic partners.

Case study: recognition of revenues from sales of licences in the software industry

The revenues of software companies normally include licences, maintenance (technical support and licence renewals with state-of-the-art packages or upgrades) and service (integration and training). The sale of licences and the rendering of services and maintenance during the first year are normally recognized in the quarter in which the transaction is performed; the rest is recorded as deferred revenue, against which an obligation must be recognized as established in the signed agreement.

Receivables must also be considered since many software companies lease their products to customers under financial leasing arrangements through third parties, normally financial entities, in without-recourse

Table 1.1 Problematic areas in the recognition of sales[1]

Area	Recommendation
Sales returns	The invoiced sales figure must be reduced.
Non-recurrent fee obtained for a recurrent risk	If the recurrence of the risk corresponds to a fixed period, the fee must be recognized as deferred revenue in this period. If it corresponds to an indefinite period, the fee may be recognized as year-1 revenue if the company does not have to provide any service in the future; if it does have to render services, then the recognition of this revenue must be deferred. If the customer has to pay the fee, the regular payments and future revenues also cover future costs; then, the initial fee may be recognized as revenue.
Cash discount (prompt payment discount)	These discounts do not affect the value of the sale unless they appear on the invoice since the payment conditions do not alter the invoiced amount. The discount is normally a financial cost.
Exchange or barter transactions (transactions performed by similar companies exchanging products; for example, two newspapers that exchange adverts)	For these transactions to be recognized as revenues (for example, in the case of two newspapers), there must be persuasive evidence that, if the advertising had not been exchanged, it could have been sold in cash in a similar transaction with another client. This rule applies to all exchanges in general.
Delivery costs invoiced to customers	These costs may be recognized as revenues provided their associated costs are recognized in the same accounting period.
IRUs (indefeasible rights of usage) on telecommunications sector assets	These are normal arrangements that affect unused fibre optic capacity with regard to the acquired total. Problems arise when these rights are resold to the same company that had initially sold them without any cash exchanging hands (these arrangements are known as 'hollow swaps'). The accounting principle applied in such cases should be similar to the one applicable to barter transactions. If the contract is equivalent to a long-term lease, total revenues may only be recognized in the case of a capital lease and not an operating lease; that is, a lease in which the risk and profits resulting from ownership of the asset have been transferred.

(Continued)

Table 1.1   (Continued)

Area	Recommendation
Gross or net sale (excluding fees) by an agent	An agent may only recognize, as revenue, the fee obtained from the sale of a good if the agent assumes the risks associated with not selling the good. The gross amount of the sale, and not just the fee, may only be treated as revenue if the agent does not sell the good and assumes the risk of owning that good. According to this rule, a travel agency cannot record the total amount of an air ticket sold to a private customer as revenue, only its fee, because the risk of the airplane taking off with empty seats must be assumed by the airline and not the agent.
Defaulted credit	Under international accounting standards, a provision must be recorded for any defaulted credit detected and the corresponding amount will increase the sales cost.
Long-term receivables	The logical thing to do is to recognize the current value of these accounts in the balance sheet and not the total value, and, in each accounting period, to increase the amount corresponding to this asset with the financial revenues account in the profit and loss account.
Transactions without physical entry of the item ('channel stuffing' and 'billing and holding'): a customer agrees to buy a good but the physical owner is still the seller until the place where the item is to be delivered is specified	In the case of trial products with a right of return, the sale cannot be recognized. For sales to be recognized as revenues in such cases, the following requirements must be satisfied: • The risk must have been transferred (that is, there is no right of return) • The purchase commitment is strong • The customer has a reason for ordering the item and it has not yet been delivered to the customer • The shipment date is fixed • The sale is complete and is not subject to any future condition • The goods are finished products.

[1]Peter Suozzo *et al.*, 'Can You Trust the Numbers?', *UBS Investment Bank*, March 2002, p. 27.

transactions; that is, if the customer does not pay, the financial entity cannot lodge a claim against the software company, but it can in transactions in which a defective software package might give rise to liability on the part of the manufacturer.

Two methods can be distinguished in this case: the sell-in revenue method, in which the product is delivered to a distributor; and the sell-through revenue method, in which, as its name suggests, the products are delivered to the end-consumer. Both methods are permitted, but the second obviously implies better-quality revenues because these correspond to sales to end-consumers, whereas the first method only implies sales to an intermediary, in this case a distributor. In the software sector revenues can only be recognized if the fee is fixed, and this is presumed not to be the case if the payment has to be made at least twelve months after the software is delivered (FAS).[34]

To limit abuse of the lax accounting regulations, the United States issued Statement of Position (SOP) 97-2, *Software Revenue Recognition*, which established the specific requirements to be satisfied by software companies for recognizing software revenue. This standard, which was introduced in 1997 and modified in 1999, not only established these requirements but also later served as the legal framework regulating the recognition of sales in general.[35] SOP 97-2 established that four criteria must be met prior to recognizing revenue; persuasive evidence of an arrangement; delivery must have occurred or the service rendered; the vendor's fee must be fixed or determinable; and collectibility must be probable.[36] In any case, constant abuse within the sector through the use of multi-element arrangements forced the issuance of another accounting standard, the EIFT 00-21 (Revenue Arrangements with Multiple Deliverables),[37] specifically applicable to the software sector. This standard prohibits the recognition of sales between associated companies (related parties), the recognition of revenues from licences deemed to be premature (not yet terminated) and sales transactions in which payment has been guaranteed by the actual seller.[38] This standard prohibits the application of the percentage-of-completion criterion to the sale as a whole. Instead, it stipulates that these contracts must be divided into separate transactions, thus reducing accountants' discretion (one transaction accounting for the sale of the software package and another one accounting for the maintenance service); once both elements of the contract have been distinguished, the criteria established in accountancy standards for recognizing revenues can be applied. Moreover, the standard does not initially allow revenues to be recognized in respect of services rendered until the systems or services have been completed. This method even prohibits companies from recognizing unbilled receivables, although, to compensate, it does permit the amortization of costs incurred in long-term arrangements. Lastly, the standard makes it obligatory for companies to provide details of the accounting policy used in these types of arrangements and the clauses established in the corresponding contracts. As a consequence of the application of this standard, in the fourth quarter of 2002 Perot Systems was forced to reduce its expected profits for the year by US$14 million; that is, 50 per cent.[39]

After American firms were obliged to adapt to this accounting standard, which produced more losses at the beginning of contracts than with the percentage-of-completion method, while European companies were not so obliged, the latter were able to capture market shares in contracts that generated profits under international accounting standards and losses under the American system.[40]

We will now look at three case studies to exemplify manipulation in revenue recognition.

BAAN

The Dutch software company BAAN enjoyed great success in the mid-1990s. When its sales started dropping off, BAAN decided to apply more aggressive revenue recognition criteria. It started invoicing new products that had not yet been completed that were sold to customers, who obviously received them much later than agreed. It also recognized US$43 million in revenues from the sale of systems to its own distribution company, basically an intra-group sale. In April 1998, the auditors refused to sign BAAN's accounts, forcing the company to issue a profit warning to the market that it would not be able to meet its profit estimates. These events prompted customers to abandon BAAN for more rigorous companies and eventually marked the end of BAAN as an independent company.[41]

EDS

In January 2003, the SEC began investigating the accounts of this North American technology company. In October that year, as a result of this investigation, EDS was forced to reduce revenues recognized in 2001 and 2002 by US$2,900 million corresponding to non-invoiced sales and US$400 million in incurred losses and to defer US$1,100 million in system construction costs. In net terms, EDS had to face a charge of US$2,240 million of losses before taxes as consequence of this accounting regularization brought about by the improper use of the percentage-of-completion method.[42]

Microstrategy

On 20 March 2000, as consequence of the application of the restrictive SOP 97-2 statement applicable to software companies, Microstrategy was obliged to reduce its 1999 sales by US$50 million (25 per cent of the total); as a result, its declared profits for the year of 15 cents per share were transformed into a loss of 44 cents per share, meaning its shares dive-bombed 60 per cent that day. Microstrategy was listed on the stock exchange in 1998 and had applied very aggressive criteria in 1999 to support the operation, prematurely recognizing revenues corresponding to services that were to be rendered in the long term, or even recognizing revenues on contracts that had not yet been signed. The directors were hit with a US$11 million fine.[43]

Finally, we will compare three British companies that sell software licences. London Bridge Plc carries out short-term contracts (about six months) and recognizes revenues at the beginning of each contract, an aggressive but nevertheless legal approach to recognizing revenues. Marlborough Stirling Plc adopts a neutral policy; its contracts are long-term (24 months) and it recognizes part of the arrangement as revenue when the contract is signed, invoicing the rest over the term of the contract. The third company, Alphameric, employs a very conservative approach by recognizing all revenues six months after the software licence is implemented to ensure that any problems arising after this date are resolved correctly (with the corresponding costs clearly valued).[44] The three companies apply perfectly legal accounting criteria but obviously the quality of their revenues is extremely diverse.

Case study: revenue recognition in the semiconductors sector: ASML

ASML is a Dutch company that manufactures semiconductor equipment. It reported revenues of €1,960 million in 2002, up 23 per cent on the previous year. However, of that increase 9 per cent (€138 million) was due to a change in its accounting criteria. ASML makes a distinction between revenues from *new* and *tested* technology, adopting different criteria to recognize revenues from each type of technology. For *tested* technology, it recognizes revenues when the product is sent to the client since the latter becomes the owner when it has accepted the system unconditionally during a test performed at ASML's factory prior to delivery. *New* technology, however, is not recognized as revenue until the equipment has been installed and accepted at the client's factory. Once the equipment has been operating normally for a certain period, this *new* technology is recognized by reclassification as *tested* technology, and any revenues perceived for such equipment, recorded in the balance sheets as deferred income, are then carried over to sales. In the second half of 2002, ASML Twinscam's technology, which had previously been classified as *new* technology, was reclassified as *tested* technology, increasing 2002 revenues by €138 million. This reclassification in itself was not abusive (it affected 13 of Twinscam's 70 installed systems), but it should be studied in depth by analysts since it accounted for a large part of the company's increase in turnover that year (specifically 9 per cent of 23 per cent; in other words, without the change in accounting criteria, the company would have increased its revenues by 14 per cent, and not 23 per cent).[45]

How to detect doubtful revenues in company accounts[46]

- *Identify variations in returned sales accounts*; the percentage of returned sales with respect to total sales should be stable in ordinary circumstances.
- *Calculate whether operating cash is much lower than net income.*[47]
- *Look for changes in accounting policies without the appropriate adjustments having been made in previous years*, since this hinders organic comparisons.
- *Determine whether receivables have increased in a larger proportion to revenues*. If long-term revenues receivable increase dramatically, this means that the company is recognizing revenues payable more than twelve months later, which might suggest it is recognizing revenues prematurely.
- *Determine whether unbilled receivables*[48] *increase much faster than billed receivables.*[49]
- *Make sure that the product has been delivered before the end of the accounting period and that it cannot be returned.*

In general, increases in unbilled receivables with respect to billed receivables suggest that there is a high risk that the company might issue a profit warning to the market, since such increases are normally the result of the company prematurely recognizing revenues using very aggressive criteria, without replacing these with better revenues in the future. This system allows the company to resolve the current year at the expense of disappointing shareholders and investors the following year.[50] The same can be said of receivables. A sharp increase in receivables could imply that the company is unable to collect its sales; this might occur because the company, in its desire to boost sales, provides services or sells goods to clients who are unlikely to be able to meet their payment commitments. It might also be a sign that the company is using the so-called 'jockey stick' effect, which consists of bringing forward sales from the following year to the current year. Clients are normally asked to place orders today instead of tomorrow in exchange for discounts. This allows the company to reach its sales objectives for the current year, at the expense of profits. Once again, if future sales are not replaced, the risk of disappointing the market in the mid-term is enormous.[51] The problem is that, in practice, it is virtually impossible to detect such accounting behaviour.

Applicable accounting standards

The North American accounting system (US General Accepted Accounting Principles (GAAP), or accounting standards) establishes that revenues 'must not be recognized until they are realized or realizable', and later stipulates 'that revenues are considered to have been earned when the entity has substantially accomplished what it must do to be entitled to the benefits represented by the revenues' and that 'if services are rendered . . . reliable measures based on contractual prices established in advance are commonly available, and revenues may be recognized as earned as time passes'.

Since these standards are fairly vague, in December 1999 the SEC introduced the SAB 101 standard, applicable as from the fourth quarter of 2000, which developed the GAAP through practical cases (10 case studies). It established four principles that had to concur in time in order for a sale to be recognized as such:

- *Persuasive evidence (oral or written) that the sale- purchase agreement has been concluded* (to avoid excessive deliveries of products to customers, or channel stuffing, as we saw in the case of Sunbeam or Bausch & Lomb).
- *The item must have been sent or the service rendered*; this means that neither registration fees nor initial payments can be recognized as revenues but must be spread over the useful life of the contract; hence, Telefónica or Vodafone cannot recognize registration fees as revenues in the United States. Nevertheless, in transactions in which the customer has ordered the product but prefers to wait to receive it – that is, bill and hold – such fees or payments can be recognized as revenues, in accordance with the strict conditions explained above. Following the introduction of this rule, under American accounting standards

the French pharmaceutical company Sanofi was forced to stop recognizing as revenues the payments it received as rights for the use of its technology for medical research.
- *The price must be fixed or objectively determinable* (to avoid barter or exchange transactions in which, as we saw earlier, companies exchange similar goods – for example, adverts between two newspapers, without the exchange ever taking place, in order to increase revenues).
- *The collectibiity of the good or service must be reasonably guaranteed*; this prevents the recognition of sales that are still due after more than twelve months, or payments from customers who are unlikely to be able to meet their payment commitments, meaning that they are granted exceptional invoicing conditions).[52]

In contrast to North American accounting standards, which are very focused on practical cases, international accounting standards, specifically Standard IFRS[53] 18 of 1982, which was revised in 1993, are more conceptual. This establishes that revenues can only be recognized if there is sufficient evidence that there has been a change between assets and liabilities – that is, that the item has been delivered or the service rendered – and also that such changes can be measured objectively.[54] Following the application of these standards, Spanish property companies – which, under the Spanish accounting system, were allowed to recognize revenues from new constructions when sale–purchase agreements were realized and 80 per cent of housing construction costs incurred – could now only recognize, as revenues, housing that had been signed with and handed over to buyers, prompting substantial reductions in revenues recognized by these companies.

Given the current scenario, North American and international accounting institutions are currently working on the idea of issuing a common global accounting standard to ensure greater coherence with a view to a future merger of both accounting systems.

Impact of revenue recognition on the value of companies: priceline.com

We have seen how the subjectivity of revenue recognition does not normally affect sales or profits from a long-term standpoint. Seen from this perspective, one might think that such practices would not have any impact on the value of companies, but that is incorrect. Let us see why.

make their cash flow forecasts based on current year figures; 'restimating margins in a given year in which a company .., say, an operating margin of 15 per cent, could prompt the analysts who failed to picked up on this aggressive recognition of revenues to issue similar projections in future years, and particularly indefinitely when making cash flow discounts. Such errors might inflate the value of the company we wish to analyze.

The impact on market multiples can also be extremely significant. Thus, if we were to compare two companies by applying the mean price earning ratio (PER) for the sector in the current year to each company, and if one company recognized revenues – and, therefore, profits – more aggressively than the other company, and if we did not exclude extraordinary income produced by accounting manipulations, we would be prejudicing the more conservative company. Despite falling into disuse, multiples that measure the market value[55] of companies according to their turnover – or, even worse, multiples that measure market capitalization based on turnover, which are even more inappropriate and vulgar in nature – can be altered by manipulating revenues figures.

The case of Priceline (priceline.com) is well known. This was one of the first online travel agents to be listed on the stock exchange. Aware that there were hardly any other travel companies operating on the Internet in 1998, Priceline determined its accounting criterion for recognizing revenues. Instead of recording the commission the agencies charged on air tickets sold to customers as revenues, and before the company was listed on the stock exchange, it decided that its sales would correspond to the total sale price of tickets, the cost of the sales being the percentage that was collected by the airlines. This had no impact on profits. However, this simple procedure allowed Priceline to multiply its revenues, thus increasing the IPO proceeds since these were based in a capitalization multiple for sales. It is always important to remember who assumes the inventory risk (the transfer of the good or service). If the agency does not sell the ticket, its accounts will not be adversely affected. However, this is not true in the case of the air carrier because the seat remains empty when the airplane takes off. This risk transfer criterion, also mentioned in reference to Sunbeam, should provide us with a solid reference for recognizing when a sale is really a sale.

These problems mainly arise when the person handling figures at a company is unaware of the different accounting methods that can be applied in order to recognize revenues. Strong increases in sales, better profit margins and high income growth could prompt users to compare those figures incorrectly with others published by more conservative companies, or to project them at the same margins and growth rates.[56]

Conclusion

Why do companies choose to recognize revenues aggresively? Sometimes, when young companies that have enjoyed rapid growth in sales
mature, they refuse to accept stagnating revenues and, confident that
they will be able to return to growth in the future, decide to adopt
more aggressive accounting policies that will allow them (fictionally) to
maintain the organic rates of growth they enjoyed in the past. On other
occasions, the boards of directors of listed companies provide the stock
market with results forecasts (sales and profit per share) on either an
annual or a quarterly basis. The pressure directors are under to achieve
these targets is enormous, especially since the appearance of hedge
funds that, with their leveraged strategies, can increase the volatility
of share prices if companies fail to achieve their sales and profit targets.
To respond to such pressure, directors might adopt aggressive revenue
recognition policies to achieve the figures announced to the market, or
simply reach a point somewhere in the middle with respect to the expectations of the company's analysts. Nevertheless, they could have even
more villainous intentions. Hence, if the directors consider that failure to achieve analysts' estimates might destabilize share prices, which
would in turn affect the value of their options on stocks or variable
remunerations, they might decide to use aggressive revenue recognition techniques to somehow 'save the year' at the expense of reducing
the future volume of revenues and profits.

Finally, there have been cases in which companies did not recognize
revenues by allegedly aggressive means for crooked reasons but, as we
indicated at the beginning of this chapter, because accounting standards
leave a lot of room for interpretation, and creative accounting does not
necessarily have to be illegal accounting. In this case, the problem is not
the type of interpretation but rather the fact that this interpretation and
its impact on a company's financial statements might not be sufficiently
explicit in the annual report. In this regard, the improvement of regulations governing the information to be presented in financial statements
would be an important step towards avoiding nasty surprises. What better example of the inherent subjectivity of revenue recognition than
the case of the Spanish utility company Endesa. When subjected to a
hostile takeover by Gas Natural, which was approved by the Spanish
regulatory body, Endesa reclassified its revenues in order to declare one
third of its activity outside of Spain. In this way, it managed to get the
European Union to authorize the operation and not the Spanish regulators. Endesa eliminated revenues collected from operations between
generators and distributors, which were suddenly treated as *intra-group*

operations. It excluded from its accounts the revenues obtained from its mobile telephony subsidiary AUNA, which was in the process of being sold. It worked on consolidating its French subsidiary Snet during the whole of 2004, despite taking control in September, and recorded €200 million in revenues corresponding to costs associated with the transition to competition in Italy. With the new figures, Endesa reduced its revenues in 2004 by €4,401 million to €13,317 million, with international activities exceeding the 33 per cent required for Brussels to intervene.[57]

as expenses, it declared earnings
which also reported sales revenue
sonnel expenses of €30 million a
decided to issue stock options,
granting these options to its emp
market, obtaining the net amoun
among its employees as addition
and Gamma's employees received
However, Delta declared profits c
declared €40 million. Common
information provided, and assum
in all other respects, both should
Delta declared higher profits tha
lower price/earnings (P/E)[1] ratio
Delta records monetary inflows tl
going against all logic.

This anecdote illustrates the
whereby employee compensatior
reflected as a cost. This practice,
tors of large companies (to the d
shareholders), created the illusio
of €100,000, he/she would be wi
a salary of €80,000 and succuler
doxically, although the employe
company's profit and loss accoun
than when with his/her former
compensation in the form of stoc
obtained if the stock options wer
in other words, the company w
being granted to the employee,
amount obtained from this sale
stock options. Hence, failure to
a breach of accounting transpar
mental to shareholders and pot
term, would undermine the co
confidence, which are factors th

What are stock options?

Stock options are used by compa
tors by granting the receivers
obligation, to purchase compa

efore taxes of €50 million. Gamma,
s of €100 million and identical per-
nd other costs of €20 million, also
he difference being that instead of
oyees, it decided to sell them on the
of €10 million, which it distributed
l salary compensation. Both Delta's
compensation valued at €40 million.
€50 million, whereas Gamma only
ense suggests that according to the
ng that both companies are identical
be worth the same. However, since
. Gamma, the former would have a
an Gamma, which could mean that
at make it worth more than Gamma,

ng-standing accounting aberration
in the form of stock options was not
artly fuelled by the interests of direc-
criment, as we will see later, of their
that if an employee earned a salary
ng to jump ship to a competitor for
stock options worth €30,000. Para-
would be better paid, in the new
he/she would appear to be paid less
mployer. The economic value of this
options is equivalent to the total sum
sold by the company on the market;
uld issue options which, instead of
ould be sold on the market and the
vould be the economic value of the
cord these stock options constitutes
cy regulations; this would be detri-
ntial investors and, in the medium
pany's risk premium and business
concern the economy as a whole.

es to compensate employees or direc-
these options a right, but not an
shares as from a specific moment

Table 2.1 Types of employee remuneration

Compensation	Description
Stock options	These operate in the same way as normal options. The receiver is entitled to purchase shares in the future at a price defined in the present. The receiver makes a profit if the share price rises above the predefined purchase price. If the option is exercised, the option holder receives the shares and may make a profit by selling them on the market.
Stock appreciation rights (SARs)	Similar to traditional options, except that the intrinsic value of the option is received in cash if the option is exercised. No shares are issued or received.
Employee stock purchase programmes	Employees can purchase company stock at a below market price.
Granting of stock	Employees receive company stock directly, usually with a deferral period in which they cannot be sold.
Conditions	Any of these forms of compensation can become conditional if certain criteria are fulfilled. The conditions make it harder to determine the market value of the compensation and the moment when it is recognized.

Source: 'Industrials and Materials: The Art of Accounting', *Deutsche Bank*, 7 January 2003.

(exercise date) at a fixed price (exercise price). If the company's shares are listed at a price above the option exercise price when the options are exercised, the employee will exercise his/her right and obtain a profit. If the value of the share is equal to or lower than the exercise price, the employee will have made neither a loss nor a profit.

There are different forms of compensation that are referenced to company equity instruments. The best-known form of compensation is stock options. Compensation can also be paid in the form of 'stock appreciation rights' (SARs), which are basically options on virtual stock that are paid in cash when exercised. There are also 'employee stock purchase programmes', in which companies offer their employees the chance to purchase company shares at a discount on the price at which they are listed when granted. Finally, employers can also establish conditions on each of these remuneration methods. Thus, companies can grant stock options to employees on the condition that they do not jump ship to a competitor within a specific period of time.[2]

For example, in 2002 the German software company SAP issued 3.8 million SARs (called 'STARs' by the company) at a price of €158.8, while the 3.6 million stocks issued in 2003 had a reference price of €84.9. Employees received deferred cash payments calculated as the difference between the share price and the SAR reference price.[3]

How to value stock options

Stock options can be valued in three ways:

- *Historical cost*: the price paid by the company for a sufficient amount of own shares (in treasury stock) to convert the options into stock. The problem with this method is that the value obtained is not equivalent to the economic value of the issued stock options.
- *Intrinsic value*: the difference between the option exercise price and the listed share price. It is therefore assumed that the options are exercised immediately. The problem is that it does not reflect the time value of the options, which is determined by their volatility. A company whose shares are traded at €100 each can issue stock options that mature in three years and at an exercise price of €100. If the intrinsic value is applied, this will be zero. However, the value of the option is greater than zero, since the chances of the shares being priced at more than €100 after three years are substantial, and these possibilities have an economic value.
- *Market value*: this is equivalent to the intrinsic value plus the time value, the latter being the value corresponding to the possibility of the share being worth more than the exercise price during the option exercise period, a possibility that will increase the more volatile the share.

In the eyes of accounting institutions, it is clear that the correct way to value options is the third option; that is, the market value method. One possibility would be to identify listed options similar to those issued, and use these to value the employee stock options. However, this solution is complex because it is normally difficult to find listed stock options similar to those issued to employees, since the latter normally have much longer maturity periods than listed stock options. Given this situation, it is best to use option-pricing models such as binomial trees or the Black–Scholes formula, named after Fischer Black and Myron Scholes, who invented the formula in 1973. Before that, nobody had succeeded in developing a formula to value call options. Dividends were not paid under the original Black–Scholes formula, although these are envisaged in the modified version of the formula. The formula requires variables such as share price, option exercise price, expected option maturity, expected share dividends, share volatility (see further discussion of this concept in the conclusion of this chapter) and risk-free interest, which the formula uses to value options. The only drawback of applying the Black–Scholes formula is that it assumes options are permanently available for sale, which is not the case with most employee stock option programmes, under which options can normally only be exercised during a specific period of time, whereas listed stock options can normally be exercised from the moment they are purchased. In any event, the operating cost of issuing options for employees can be accurately valued using this formula.

There are numerous examples that highlight the importance of option valuation: as a result of applying market value to options issued in 2000, AT&T's profits were reduced by 15 per cent, Lucent's profits by 63 per cent, Cisco's losses would have been 167 per cent, and Microsoft's profits in its financial year ending in June 2001 would have been cut by 31 per cent, from US$7,346 million to US$5,084 million.[4] More recently, in 2004, the average earnings of companies on the Standard & Poor's 500 Index would have been 5 per cent lower if they had recorded options as expenses, and the average profits of one North American technology company would have decreased by 25 per cent.[5]

A brief history of stock options

During the period 1995 to 2002, North American companies could account for stock options in two ways.

The first option was to use APB 25, which determines the value of options according to their intrinsic value and exercise price. However, the problem with this method, as we have seen, was that companies chose to issue options with exercise prices similar to the prices at which shares were listed; hence, their intrinsic value was zero, even though their actual value was much higher, due to the option time factor. In any event, since the value was accounted for when the share was issued and did not vary in time, regardless of share performance, companies could issue huge numbers of options without this affecting their profit and loss accounts.

The other alternative was provided by FAS 123 in 1995, the result of many years of studies on stock options carried out by the FASB[6], which concluded that:

- Options are compensation that must be expensed because these options have a value

- Options should be valued at market and not intrinsic value
- Market value must be determined by applying option valuation models such as the Black–Scholes formula.

FAS 123 also required companies to conduct sensitivity analyses based on the assumptions considered in the option valuation model, which is particularly useful, especially given the importance of the volatility assumed to value the option.

Unfortunately, FAS 123 was not made mandatory due to the army of lobbyists that North American industrial companies, especially those from Silicon Valley, deployed to Capitol Hill in Washington. The lobbyists threatened to curtail the accounting supremacy of the FASB if the application of FAS 123 was made obligatory – arguing, for example, that the accounting of options would limit the enterprising character of the new economy, which used this method to remunerate talent, essential for the booming North American economy and its technological superiority; hence, a compromise was reached whereby its application would be voluntary.

If FAS 123 had been made obligatory, it would have reduced the profits of the main North American stock market index, SP 500, by 21 per cent in 2001 (US$71,000 million) and by 11 per cent in 2000 (US$57,000 million). This reduction has a particularly strong effect on sectors such as technology, where 48 per cent of options were not being expensed.[7]

Following the accounting scandals that shook the US from late 2000 to mid-2002, FAS 148 was approved at the end of 2002, making it obligatory for all companies that did not apply FAS 123 (that is, companies that continued to use the intrinsic value to calculate the price of stock options) to include footnotes in their annual reports on the impact that the application of FAS 123 would have on their earnings and earnings per share (remember that this standard required companies to use the market value and not the intrinsic value).

In the first quarter of 2003, many North American companies decided to switch from using options to using restricted shares to compensate their employees. Restricted shares were offered to employees as salary compensation, normally conditioned by certain criteria such the obligation not to abandon the firm for a given period, although these shares could not be sold until a specific date. Companies that began to use this method included Microsoft, Apple, Exxon and Amazon.[8] Since the tax-deductible expense does not arise until the cost is recognized, which in the case of these shares coincides with the date as from which the shares can be exercised (purchased at the established price), in the meantime a tax asset is generated that is eliminated when the tax-deductible cost is recognized. For example, Microsoft paid US$800 million in taxes on awarded stock options in 2000, but it recognized €5,000 million as costs, generating a tax asset of more than US$4,000 million.[9] Before 2002, 498 of the companies on the Standard & Poor's 500 index decided to apply APB 25 and not FAS 123. However, at the end of 2002, many large companies decided to switch and began recording options at market value instead of at intrinsic value. These companies included General Electric, General Motors, Coca-Cola and Procter & Gamble.

The situation in Europe was similar to that in North America, since under most national accounting systems companies were not required to expense options at market value. However, the smaller presence of the technology sector in Europe compared with North America diminished the impact of a potential change in accounting standards. International Accounting Standard (IAS) 19 offers hardly any explanation of the accounting method for recognizing stock options. As a result, ED 2 was issued on 1 January 2004, which applied the conclusions of FAS 123, making it obligatory for companies issuing international figures to value options using an option valuation model and account for values obtained by this method as personnel expenses for the lifespan of the options (mandatory for all European listed companies since January 2005). This meant that Europe was six months ahead of the US in making it obligatory for companies to recognize stock options as an expense, since this obligation was not established in the US until the first quarter of 2006. The companies responded to the imminent obligation to recognize options as costs by increasing their exercise periods, thus amortizing these options before it became obligatory to account for these options as expenses, thus reducing their current earnings to facilitate future growth.

This expense can be recorded at different moments: when the option is awarded ('grant date'), when the employee has fulfilled the necessary condition to receive the option if this condition exists ('service date'), when the option can be vested ('vesting date') or when it is exercised ('exercise date'). Normally, accounting standards require this expense to be recognized when the options are granted.

The value of options can be recognized as a personnel expense in two ways. The value can be distributed over the number of years until the option matures; this method is followed by the American and international accounting systems. Alternatively, the entire cost can be recorded in the year the options are issued.[10] Part of the investment community prefers the second method, when the cost is recorded as soon as the option is issued, using the principle of prudence and due to the fact that variable cash remuneration is not deferred by more than one year.[11]

The transition from not expensing options to expensing options at market value can be retrospective/backdated or prospective. The retrospective/backdated transition is achieved by revising all past years in which options have been issued, identifying their value on the exercise date, deferring that value over the years in which the option is valid and applying this value in the years in question.[12] The prospective transition is achieved by only recording options issued from the date on which the decision was take to record them as expenses (only the 30 options issued in 2003). Obviously, the latter method increases earnings in some years until the options issued before the transition are completely exercised. Thus, it is sometimes impossible to compare two companies completely for the simple reason that one company might apply the prospective method and the other the retrospective method, as in the case of Novartis and Roche (the latter only recognizes options issued after November 2002). Roche's P/E ratio multiple in 2004 was 29.5, compared to Novartis with 20.6; nevertheless, if both accounting policies were standardised (by applying the retrospective method to both), Roche's P/E ratio multiple would have been 31.6 times.[13]

Why companies issue stock options

It could be said that options are designed to be incentives for employees, aligning their interests with those of shareholders. However, this explanation is somewhat false, especially in the case of stock option issues, since what management is doing is providing incentives to maximize the value of these options in order to reduce or eliminate dividend payouts. Dividend payouts diminish the value of their options since such payments proportionally reduce the price of shares, thus reducing the intrinsic value of the options, and this could clash with shareholder interests. Additionally, the value of options increases the more volatile the shares; hence, any high-risk decision will increase share volatility and, therefore, the value of stock options held by directors. Shareholders, however, would be interested in avoiding this greater volatility generated by artificially high-risk decisions.

As we have seen, the main advantage of options is that they are not treated as expenses for financial accounting purposes, in contrast to their treatment for tax purposes when they are treated as expenses. Therefore, the more the price of shares increases, the lower the taxes will be. This characteristic made stock options very popular from the mid-1990s onward. A lower tax burden improves free operating cash flow, which should, in turn, improve the price of shares. This would, in turn, increase the value of options, resulting in lower taxes, thus closing the vicious circle. Tyco used this system and increased its free cash flow during the period 1998–2001 by an average of 9 per cent, and General Electric achieved a 6 per cent increase.[14]

Why stock options are an expense

Stock options have a dual economic effect: on the one hand, they are a form of employee compensation that should increase the company's personnel expense account and thus reduce earnings; on the other hand, if the options are exercised, their value for shareholders is diluted, which means that the number of company shares must be adjusted according to the prospects of those options being exercised in the future. This larger number of shares consequently reduces the company's earnings per share.

Accounting practice has defended the accrual principle of accounting as one of the fundamental pillars of accounting. The non-application of this principle to compensation in the form of stock options, on the grounds that this compensation does not directly involve an outflow of cash, is an aberration; the amortization of fixed assets or the past service of a company pension fund are items that do not involve cash outflows but are nevertheless recognized as expenses.

Critics of the practice of expensing stock options normally argue that recording them as personnel expenses, and at the same time increasing the number of shares to reflect the corresponding dilution effect if the options are ever exercised, is simply a case of recording the same event twice. This argument is incorrect, since stock options have a dual accounting impact:

- The employee purchases an option from a company for a value 'x' and the company pays the employee the value 'x' as compensation when awarding the options
- The dilution effect depends on the employee's investment decision, and it is therefore different in nature to the compensation perceived by the employee when he/she is awarded the options.

Impact of stock options on valuation

In the period 2000–2002, the impact of having recognized stock options as expenses would have reduced the reported earnings of the French pharmaceutical company Aventis by 16 per cent, and those of another French pharmaceutical firm, Sanofi, by 2 per cent. If we look at the P/E ratio of both companies in 2003, Aventis shares seemed to be 14 per cent cheaper than those of Sanofi. However, by recording stock options as expenses, the decrease was reduced to a mere 2 per cent.[15]

If you agree with our argument that options should be recorded as a cost at market value, a company's profits would have to be adjusted before applying the multiples of comparable companies in order to ensure that all of them report stock options as costs at market value. This adjustment affects the EV/EBITDA, EV/EBIT and EV/OpFCF multiples and particularly the P/E ratio multiple. For example, reported earnings for the semi-conductor industry in 2004 would have been 45 per cent lower if options had been recorded as expenses, and companies would have increased their P/E ratios – Altera by 126 per cent from 46 to 105 times, Maxim Integrated Products by 109 per cent from 39 to 81 times, Xilinx by 86 per cent from 35 to 64 times and ST Microelectronics would have increased its P/E ratio by 79 per cent: National Semiconductor's earnings per share of 0.71 would have been transformed into a loss of 0.64 and its P/E ratio would have rocketed out of orbit![16]

The tangible impact of applying accounting changes is easy to perceive: investment funds tend to use profit figures agreed by analysts, such as those provided by First Call. When this firm decided, on 1 September 2005, to include the costs of options issued by Microsoft in the company's profit and loss account, the estimated profits of the software giant for 2006 fell 9 per cent; in a matter of days, Microsoft's shares fell 11 per cent. When Apple announced that it had recognized options during the fourth quarter of 2005, its profit forecasts were cut 6 per cent and the company's shares dropped 7 per cent.[17]

In cash flow discounts, this would have a double impact. The value of a company's debt should increase by the market value of any option granted and not yet exercised, and thus adjust the dilution effect; by increasing debt, we emulate the repurchasing of all these non-exercised options, thus guaranteeing the right to receive all free cash flow. When forecasting a company's operating margins, we should ensure that personnel costs include the market value of the options, which are simply a source of salary. This precaution is particularly important for determining perpetual operating income.

American Express's annual report for 2000 explains that the company had issued 114.5 million options as of 31 December 2000, of which 39.3 million were issued during 2000 and valued at their intrinsic (rather than market) value. Thus, although the company reported earnings-per-share of US$2.07, if it had valued its options at their market value, its profits would have been US$1.92; that is, 6.9 per cent less. When calculating American Express's market value ('enterprise value'), stock market value, debt and other sources of financing, the value of existing options issued by Amex would also have to be included.[18]

The legally binding condition to record stock options as an expense in the US as from 1 January 2006 is a real challenge for the stock market due to the effects that this obligation could have on earnings and, therefore, on P/E ratio multiples. Let us look at three examples of how this affects technology companies:

- The stock options of Micron Technology were estimated to represent 79 per cent of its earnings in 2006; hence, the application of these regulations would increase its P/E ratio from 87 to 328.
- Sun Microsystems' options represent 68 per cent of its estimated profits in 2006, therefore, its adjusted P/E ratio would increase 36 to 112.
- Siebel Systems' options represented 56 per cent of the firm's profits in 2006, and its P/E ratio multiple would therefore increase from 133 to 353.

These figures give us an idea of the impact that stock options can have on the value of a company.[19]

Backdating

Recently, stock options have been back in the news due to the scandals associated with options issued to directors based on past reference prices. These prices generally coincided with periods in which the value of shares was lower than when the options were issued, a phenomenon known as 'backdating' and which lead to the intervention of the North American stock exchange authorities, who considered this practice to be an illegal transfer of value from shareholders to directors without this fact actually being reported. Such operations are actually no different to the granting of options 'in the money'; that is, granting options at an exercise price below market value, but without acknowledging this. Since 1972, North American accounting regulations require companies to recognize such options as a cost. However, the scandal was caused by the fact that companies were not recognizing these options as expenses, pretending that options were 'at the money'; that is, at an exercise price equal to market. The mechanism consisted, for example, in issuing options with an exercise price dated 28

February (when shares were US$50) on 15 March (when shares were trading at US$65); hence, they were not recorded as a cost. The problem was that on 15 March the shares were already trading at US$65 and this caused the scandal.[20] In the words of Lynn Turner, the SEC's Chief Accountant from 1998 to 2001, 'It's like allowing people to bet on the horses when they've already crossed the finish line.'[21]

On Friday 4 August 2006, the North American technology firm Apple announced that it was withdrawing its 1998–2001 financial statements for review. This announcement prompted its shares to fall 2 per cent. For example, on 17 January 2001, the company granted options to four directors before announcing results that showed how the company had managed to reduce its computer inventories with distributors, prompting shares to increase 11 per cent and earning the four directors profits of US$7.5 million.[22] The reason behind this decision was simply to award stock options to the directors on dates when the shares were particularly low, and indicating a false date on the document granting the stock options.

This type of practice could entail two irregularities: on the one hand, forging the date is a criminal offence on the part of the company, since it seeks to create wealth for its directors at the expense of shareholders. On the other hand, if options are issued – for example, at US$50 when the shares are valued at US$65, making it appear that these options were granted when the shares were US$65 – according to legislation in force at the time the company should have recorded an expense of US$15 at that point, which it did not do; hence, this practice also represents an alteration of balance sheets. Section 403 of the Sarbanes–Oxley Act requires any issue of stock options to be announced to the market within 48 hours. Such scandalous conduct must therefore be eradicated in the future.[23]

Unfortunately, it would appear that 'backdating' has been used much more frequently than expected. This practice was uncovered by the Norwegian academic Erik Lie, a professor at Iowa University, who published an article in which he proved, without mentioning any names, that when stock options were not granted on a fixed date, the price of the shares tended to increase on the days after the grant date: these accusations were later levelled at six companies by *The Wall Street Journal* in March 2006. Since then, more than 80 companies have been investigated in relation to this phenomenon, including the following:

- HealthSouth, whose Managing Director, Richard Scrushy, was made redundant in 2003 after the emergence of an accounting fraud of US$2,700 million[24]

- UnitedHealth, whose chief executive, William McGuire, had US$1,800 million in options issued on dates he seemed to have picked himself, a scandal that lead to the destruction of US$17,000 million in stock market value after its announcement[25]
- The antivirus company McAfee, forced to sack its top lawyer, Kent Roberts, for a similar incident.[26]

Other companies also being investigated for backdating incidents including the Internet job-seeking company monster.com, the processor manufacturer Analog Devices and the education company Apollo, which owns the University of Phoenix.[27]

Conclusion

Stock options have had a serious cancerous effect on financial systems and market economies. This is because stock options granted to directors, with the right but not the obligation to purchase shares, increase in value as share volatility increases. In other words, directors are encouraged to take very high-risk decisions. This produces a clear conflict of interest between the director and the shareholder. By taking very risky decisions, such as spectacular mergers and acquisitions, the director and shareholder can make millions if the operation is successful. However, if it fails the director is not exposed to falling share prices, while the shareholder could become bankrupt. In our opinion, this fact partly explains the unprecedented boom in failed merger operations between 1998 and 2000, which in turn prompted a dramatic increase in share volatility and boosted the value of stock options. This phenomenon is crucial for understanding the recession that hit Western economies in the following years.

Directors' remuneration in the form of stock options, when compared with their salaries, has often been abusive. Between 1998 and 2000, compensation – including stock options – paid to Enron's top 200 executives multiplied sevenfold from US$193 million to US$1,400 million two years before the company went bankrupt.[28] Other scandals associated with abusive salaries at companies such as Enron, WorldCom, Tyco, Adelphia and HealthSouth have meant that public confidence in chief executives fell from 73 per cent before Enron to 45 per cent in 2006, according to the Pew Research Center.[29]

Stock option remuneration created another conflict of interests since directors were encouraged to reduce dividend payouts to shareholders because these reduced the value of options, and the retention of huge business-generated cash flows not distributed through dividends made this squandering all the more easy in that period. Today, given the scepticism with which the market views mergers and acquisitions, directors prefer to increase share buy-back programmes substantially because such operations are well received by markets. At the end of the day, all that glitters is not gold since the purpose of these stock buy-backs is not always to amortize the number of shares in circulation, a measure that is well-received by shareholders; it is, rather, more often to do with having a sufficient amount of treasury stock to cover the eventual conversion of stock options into shares if these options are exercised. Thus, between 1991 and 2000, Microsoft issued 1,600 million shares in the form of stock options and repurchased 677 million shares to partially compensate for the dilution effect caused by the issue of options. This buy-back cost Microsoft US$16,200 million. For example, if Microsoft had recovered the options in 1998, its profits of US$4,500 million would have been transformed into a severe loss![30]

All in all, the obligation to record options at cost and their poor reception by investors, deriving from the agency conflicts that they cause, have changed companies' policy with respect to stock option remuneration. In the global software sector, recognizing options as a cost would have reduced average earnings-per-share by 68 per cent in 2003, 46 per cent in 2004 and 35 per cent in 2005, illustrating companies' change of heart with respect to stock option remuneration.[31]

Nevertheless, although the current framework is much more restrictive, we should not forget that there is always room for subjectivity when it comes to valuing stock option issues. A key factor for valuing options is the implicit volatility of shares during the option exercise period; changes in share volatility could lead to important variations in the recognized cost of these options, since there are no listed options with similar maturity dates, when implicit volatility is determined by the market. In fact, hypotheses regarding the volatility of the 50 North American firms with sales revenues over US$20,000 million fell by an average of 13 per cent in the period 2003–2005. For example, the technology company Analog Devices reported a cost of stock options issued in 2005 at 60 per cent below the value recognized in 2004, mainly due to lower volatility estimates.[32]

Today, the most favoured method is remuneration through restricted shares, which consists of granting workers a specific number of shares at a discount with respect to the trading price. For example, General Electric's CEO, Jeffrey Immelt, no longer receives options but, rather, shares at five years depending on a series of objectives. This means that shareholder and employee interests are aligned; both share the increases and decreases in the value of shares. At the beginning of 2004, the Finnish company Nokia announced that it was changing the way it accounted for stock options. In this announcement, it stated the following:

On January 22, 2004, the Board of Directors approved a new equity based compensation for 2004. Under this program, Nokia will introduce Performance Shares as the main element of its broad based equity compensation program to further emphasize the performance element in the employee' long-term incentives. As part of this change, Nokia will grant significantly fewer stock options in 2004 compared to 2003.[33]

3
Off-balance-sheet Financing

Do you need financial flexibility? Our Fair Market Value lease can provide for off-balance-sheet financing for equipment acquisitions, upgrades, and expansions, allowing you more control over your balance sheet position without tapping debt resources. You may be able to expense your monthly rental payments rather than depreciate the equipment cost, allowing you to order new equipment as you need it.
http://www.sun.com/sales/leasing/options.html

As quarter-end approaches, many companies look for ways to present a more liquid balance sheet for their financial statement. That is why they turn to CIT. Other companies need to liquefy their accounts receivable to meet short-term obligations. They, too, turn to CIT. Companies of all sizes use CIT's bulk sale of accounts receivable programme to turn their accounts receivable into cash.
http://www.citcommercialfinance.com/commcms/
products_servicesCmF.dsp_bulkPge.html

Off-balance-sheet financing refers to transactions that give rise to obligations not reflected on company balance sheets. Sometimes these transactions correspond to justified operations performed by the company to take advantage of good economic opportunities. For example, a firm might decide to give company cars to its executives and to finance these cars by means of operative leases, and undertakes to make these lease payments but without recognizing the cars or the aforementioned payment commitments on its balance sheets. Failure to recognize assets and their corresponding obligations is not problematic from an accounting standpoint if no interests are harmed and when exposure to the risk has actually been transferred. However, the off-balance-sheet concealment of assets and obligations does not constitute the effective transfer of risk. Such practices are potential accounting time bombs.

Back in 1986, the North American accounting body, the FASB, expressed its concern about the growing variety of instruments designed to conceal off-balance-sheet debt.[1] A study the following year reported that limited partnerships for financing research and development were being used more and more to conceal debt. Of the sample of 103 companies studied, half used these limited partnerships to fudge financial statements and thus avoid infringement of precautionary clauses or covenants, which are conditional clauses imposed by banks participating in syndicated loans.[2]

Given this new scenario, in 1987 the FASB ordered listed companies to provide information on all off-balance-sheet financial instruments and obligations, including information on credit risks resulting from this off-balance-sheet financing. The FASB defined a financial instrument as 'a contract that gives rise to a financial asset of one entity and a financial liability or equity instrument of another entity'. The information that had to appear included the maximum possible credit risk resulting from the financial instrument, expected cash flow (positive and negative) of the transaction, other information of interest relating to the financial instrument and the estimated market value of these instruments, including the evaluation of defaulting loans.[3]

The case of the banks

Undoubtedly, the FASB, as revealed by the 1987 regulation, was mainly concerned about the banking sector, particularly banks that used off-balance-sheet financing more aggressively. The reason was to avoid regulatory pressure that would force banks to maintain a certain level of capital in order to operate. If this was insufficient, banks would be required to increase capital in order to continue operating, but this increase would dilute existing shareholders' stakes or force them to contribute more capital. As an alternative, the banks developed a complex system of off-balance-sheet financing to trick the regulator and avoid having to increase capital, for example by issuing preferred stock. This allowed them to obtain considerable returns on equity actual value with relatively low levels of equity, but at the cost of not reflecting in their financial statements the true risk to which the bank was exposed, for example, the moment when the bank had to repay preferred stock.[4]

The existence and the frequency of off-balance-sheet financing as a consequence of the changes in the economy and in the types of transactions have developed rapidly, outpacing the evolution of accounting standards. For example, aspects such as the growing importance of intangible assets and new forms of asset-linked financing[5] have not been incorporated fully in traditional accounting standards based on the concepts of material assets and debt. Generally speaking, many of these contracts separate legal ownership (the title conferring ownership) from economic ownership (exposure to fluctuations in the price of specific goods), and companies skilfully take advantage of this to alter their balance sheets. Let us look at an example.

If a company that has signed a leasing contract to obtain cars for its directors reaches an agreement with the financing entity on the acquisition and maintenance of the cars, whereby these must be used for five years (a period similar to their useful life) and also that the company undertakes to purchase the cars in year 5 at their residual value, then although the owner of the car is legally the financial entity, in economic terms the owner is the company that has leased the cars for its executives, since, for practical purposes, it is exposed to fluctuations in the value of these cars (sooner or later it will become the owner of the car, with the corresponding gain or loss).

The concept that gives priority to the economic substance of operations over their legal form would allow companies to present clearer balance sheets, but it would also require auditors to dig deeper to determine whether specific transactions have been interpreted and accounted for correctly. Fortunately, many of the accounting changes implemented since 2002 have narrowed the playing field for these transactions by applying an economic and non-legal criterion to determine their accounting treatment. In any event, since sophisticated financial instruments are continuously being renewed, these accounting standards will soon be obsolete and will have to be continually reinvented.

Companies are driven to alter balance sheet debt because they need to present certain figures to investors and lenders; for example, in order to avoid breaking certain rules. Thus, earlier we mentioned that covenants are precautionary clauses that restrict the freedom of action of companies that have become indebted, with conditions – in the form of financial ratios – that, if breached, could entitle the lender to recover his/her principal. Written or unwritten clauses of this nature normally impose limits on the total debt a company can assume, and this might put directors in more than one predicament. These alterations of real debt figures entail risks that are sometimes concealed and sometimes insufficiently explained in annual reports. They appear in the notes to financial statements, but obviously lack the clarity and informative impact they have if presented in the balance sheets.

This chapter will examine the methods used most by companies to conceal debt: the alteration of working capital, financial leasing, sale and lease back, factoring, securitization (through 'special purpose vehicle' companies that issue debt secured with the assets of companies, which retain the 'first loss risk'), obligations or commitments, non-consolidated entities and hybrid instruments. We will now look at these in more detail.

Factoring and credit sales in general

One way in which companies can obtain more immediate liquidity is by selling short-term assets, such as accounts receivable, in exchange for a commission from the company acquiring those assets; this commission would vary according to the transferred risk. The accounting of these operations is reflected by a decrease in short-term asset receivables, thus increasing cash in the assets and reducing net debt, defined as gross debt less cash. Sometimes, since the methods for transferring the debt risk to the factoring company are not reflected in the balance sheets but only in the notes to financial statements, such operations might diminish the perception of risk of companies and consequently be used to alter information presented in the financial statements.

Changes in working capital: ACS

Imagine a grocer who reports a bank debt of €6,000 on 15 December. On 20 December, he has to pay another €6,000 corresponding to a receipt for fruit he purchased one month earlier from a supplier, and which he decides to pay using another bank loan. The grocer expects his wife to be shocked when she sees this large amount (€12,000) in the accounts for the year ending 31 December. To resolve this, he reaches an agreement with the fruit supplier. The fruit supplier agrees not to collect the receipt on 20 December but one month later, on 20 January. In return, the grocer will pay an additional 5 per cent on the previously agreed price. In this way, only €6,000 will appear as bank debt on 31 December, but the accounts receivable account (part of working capital) will be larger than normal, and the company's operating margin will decrease due to the 5 per cent surcharge. The supplier will have benefited by obtaining more profit, equivalent to an annual interest of 60 per cent!

The alteration of working capital is one of the oldest methods used by companies to make their debt positions more flexible. However, it becomes abusive when companies use it on a recurring basis to close annual company accounts, offering investors a distorted image of the company's real debt situation, thus fudging debt ratios.

In 2004, the Spanish construction company ACS improved its working capital by 15 days compared with the previous year. According to the company, this was achieved thanks to its successful working capital policy, based on a substantial reduction in its trade receivables and an increase in its suppliers' balance, in spite of the fact that the fourth quarter is a particularly strong period in the construction business (27 per cent of the total). What is unusual about this is that the company substantially increased its working capital in the first, second and third quarters and then reduced it in the fourth quarter; it increased its working capital in the first three quarters of 2004 by €200 million each quarter, and then reduced this entry in the fourth quarter by €456 million.

The successful working capital policy depended on reducing trade receivables through factoring operations without recourse and through securitization operations, performed in the fourth quarter to improve year-end financial leverage ratios.

It is also common for companies, and the sector at large, to use debt without recourse to finance projects. If we add to the 43 per cent financial leverage (debt divided by equity) in 2003 the debt without recourse for shareholders who finance projects, leverage would increase to 64 per cent. Although it could be argued that debt without recourse cannot be claimed on ACS's total assets, it can be claimed on the project assets, which could be consolidated in the balance sheets, as well the consolidated free cash flows.

Obligations

On 23 February 2002, the North American cable company Adelphia acknowledged that it had guaranteed the debt of the company Highland Holdings in the amount of US$2,280 million. Therefore, if Highland went bankrupt, Adelphia would pay that amount. What is unusual about this transaction is that Highland belonged to the Rigas family, which just happened to own a controlling stake in Adelphia, precisely through Highland. In other words, Adelphia was incurring an off-balance-sheet obligation that benefited its main shareholder at the expense of minority shareholders. As we will see, the father and son of the Rigas family ended up behind bars.[6]

There are many ways in which companies can assume obligations that are not reflected in the balance sheets from the outset. The most common method is by means of unconditional purchase obligations: the company commits itself to a series of future long-term payments in exchange for a series of products or services. If the company cannot cancel the contract, there is a risk that it will be accountable for the payment of those products or services even though they are no longer necessary, nor will it be able to benefit from market price reductions if it has not agreed the corresponding review clauses. It is also important to remember that acquisitions that are announced but not materialised can be converted into off-balance-sheet debt if the company to be acquired has assumed investment obligations with authorities. For example, AT&T's mobile telephony subsidiary declared a net debt of US$2,100 million at year-end 2001, and planned to report a much higher debt as a result of the integration of Next Wave, which had network investment commitments in Alaska of at least US$2,800 million, as well as the integration of Telecorp, with its debt, plus the commitment to inject cash to refloat this subsidiary. Both operations meant that the debt of AT&T's subsidiary multiplied more than fourfold in less than one year.[7]

Ericsson

Another type of obligation that companies use to remove debt is debt guarantees in favour of third parties. For example, as indicated in Ericsson's 2000 annual report, the company helped its clients purchase company equipment by providing guarantees (guarantees in case of non-payment) that Ericsson gave on customer debt (telecommunications operators to pay for equipment). These off-balance-sheet guarantees totalled 9,600 million Swedish crowns.[8] This mechanism is only dangerous if it is used abusively. The aeronautical company Raytheon offered its clients loans with recourse totalling US$1,800 million in order to capture sale contracts, but which in periods of economic difficulty could generate high volumes of debt.[9]

Sogecable

A third, more sophisticated type of obligation is derivatives. According to Sogecable's 2001 annual report, the company sold a share in one of its subsidiaries, Sogepaq, to the company Studiocanal S.L. It obtained €40 million from this sale and a non-recurring profit was generated. This amount had a dual effect: on the one hand, obtained cash flow allowed the company to reduce its debt, to avoid the barrier of €620 million on 31 December, a huge figure bearing in mind that the company's equity totalled €349 million. Moreover, the generation of an extraordinary profit allowed the company to cancel out losses that it had generated that year and, consequently, any decrease in corporate equity that this loss might have entailed. The operation in itself was not illegal, but it is revealing: closer examination of the Sogecable's annual report shows that the company Studiocanal was 49 per cent owned by Sogecable. In general, operations with atypical earnings between investee companies are good accounting alarms. The annual report also reveals that Studiocanal had capital totalling €1 million and losses amounting to €300,000, which is perplexing because it suggests that a company with losses equivalent to 30 per cent of its reduced capital stock is able to purchase a share package in another company that is 40 times its size. Furthermore, the annual report also indicates that Sogecable's recognized shareholding of 55 per cent in Sogepaq after this operation was €4.8 million; that is, with a book value of just over €9 million, it sold a share package of 45 per cent for €40 million when the book value of its stake in this company was worth €4.5 million. In other words, in the sale the company was valued at nine times its equity, a multiple that makes the nature of this operation even more surprising. What is the purpose of purchasing something at nine times its book value? Why did Studiocanal agree to purchase a share package in a company of its second shareholder at an exorbitant price? The answer lies in derivatives, since Studiocanal can reserve a sale option to return this percentage of Sogepaq to Sogecable within a specific term and at the same overblown price. Presumably, by that time the parent company's financial position will be more buoyant and it will be able to repurchase the shares at the exaggerated price. Regrettably, the details of these derivative contracts are not presented in the annual report (this information was not obligatory, in spite of its relevance for the presentation of the company's true financial position), but they must be shown to auditors. This situation indicates that Sogecable's auditors in 2001, Arthur Andersen, issued a qualified opinion on the accounts relating specifically to that transaction and to the potential consequences of the termination of the derivative contracts to which the auditors had access. This qualification was maintained by Deloitte, which absorbed Arthur Andersen in Spain in 2002.

Ahold

Another similar example is the Dutch distribution company Ahold. When Ahold acquired 50 per cent of ICA in April 2000, it granted a sale option to its associates (ICAF and Canica) in the joint venture (ICA), which gave them the right to sell their shareholdings in ICA to Ahold. The sale price included a premium on the estimated listed value of ICA if the company were listed on the stock market. On 12 July 2004, Ahold announced that Canica had exercised the sales option on its 20 per cent shareholding in ICA, at a price submitted to arbitration between both parties. The commitment undertaken by Ahold when it granted this sale option in 2000 can be accounted for in different ways. Under Dutch accounting regulations, it was not required to record this commitment as a liability, but simply include a note referring to this commitment as a contingency. However, if Ahold had applied North American accounting standards, it would have been required to recognize this option issued as a liability equivalent to the options' estimated market value, calculated to be €459 million on the grant date, offsetting this liability by increasing the goodwill on the asset side of its balance sheets. The accounting treatment of the application of international accounting standards would have been the same. If Ahold is forced to acquire these packages, it must issue debt to cover this payment obligation; hence, it is more realistic to recognize the obligation as a liability and not as a note.

The problem common to all acquired and off-balance-sheet obligations is basically their cost and their term, which might negatively influence company competitiveness and solvency. Although the existence of such obligations is reported in the informative notes to financial statements, their capacity to explain the overall value and corresponding risks of the company is not the same as if they were included in balance sheets. Nevertheless, this fact should make us reflect on the importance for investors of reading the complete annual report and not just the financial statements.

Capital leases v. operating leases: synthetic leases

The financial manager of an airline has an aircraft on the company's balance sheets at €100 million. Since the aircraft is already ten years old, it has to be replaced but the airline noted in the past that interest on bank loans varied enormously according to market conditions. Thus, the interests paid by airlines varied continuously according to the price of petrol, terrorist attacks, labour disputes, and so on. To remedy this uncertainty, which could negatively affect the company when the aircraft has to be replaced, the financial manager decides to arrange an operating lease contract, under which the airline will receive a new aircraft within one year, awarded by GE Capital for a ten-year period in exchange for a given annual payment. By means of this operation, the airline has wisely avoided being exposed to interest rate fluctuations. However, the question is whether this aircraft and the airline's payments obligations with GE Capital should be reflected in its assets and liabilities? Paradoxically, the financial manager can use both options.

A company that uses a good (for example, a company car for five years with annual payments of €6,000) under a leasing operation can decide whether or not it wants the good and the corresponding payment to appear on its balance sheet. If it decides that it wants both to appear, it will use a capital lease. The value of the car would be included in assets and the €30,000 corresponding to the current value of the car would be recorded as a liability. Basically, the capital lease is similar to a sale–purchase operation because the company purchases a car using debt. The car appears as an asset and the debt appears as a liability. However, there is one clarification that should be made; namely, that a capital lease can be accounted for in two ways:

- *Right of use.*   Only the right to use the asset is capitalized and the obligation is to make future payments in return for use of the good. For example, if an asset has a useful life of ten years, a value of €100 and the lease contract has a term of three years, assuming an annual payment of €15, then $3 \times €15 = €45$ will be capitalized as the current value (say, around €40).
- *Whole asset approach.*   In this approach, 100 per cent of the asset and the payment obligations are recognized. The difference is recorded as an obligation to deliver the good to the lessor at the end of the contract.[10] This is the method most similar to the recognition of sale–purchase operations.

In both cases, the item would appear on the balance sheet with its corresponding debt; the item would be depreciated and the corresponding debt payments treated as a financial expense.

For many years, there have been calls to rationalize the accounting treatment of operating leases. As early as 1963, accountants were calling for regulators to refrain from treating such leases according to the existence or absence of legal title of ownership: what was important, in their opinion, was the right to use a specific asset, or a percentage of capacity, which created an obligation to pay for the use of the asset, an obligation that had to be reflected in balance sheets.[11]

If a company does not want either the car or the associated financial commitments to appear on its balance sheet – either because it wants to keep low operating assets and thus report higher returns on capital, or because it does not want the payment obligations to be added to existing balance sheet debt – then it will use an operating lease. In this way, neither the car nor the payment commitment will appear on the company's balance sheet. Instead, they will appear on the balance sheet of the entity supplying the operating lease service (by keeping the car on its balance sheet, the entity can write if off and thus obtain a valuable tax shield). In this case, the lease payments made by the company will be operating payments; that is, above operating income, and not financial expenses (yet the total amount of the commitments – future payments of the operating lease – will appear on the footnotes in the annual report).

Capital leases are reflected on both the asset and liability sides of balance sheets, whereas operating leases only appear as expenses incurred for use of the asset in question. In capital leases, risks are transferred to the company that wishes to acquire the asset (similar to the transfer of ownership rights on the good), whereas in operating leases these risks remain with the owner, who is often responsible for the maintenance of the good.

The decision to keep debt off or on the balance sheet, depending on whether the lease is an operating or capital lease, is directly related to whether a company wishes to obtain greater or lesser financial or operating leverage. If the lease is an operating lease, debt does not appear, thus reducing financial leverage, but the expenses are fixed, increasing operating leverage. If the company opts for a capital lease, the expenses are financial and therefore the fixed costs determining operating leverage are not taken into account, but debt is taken into account for financial leverage. In any event, the differences between both types of leases can alter the profit and loss account.

Let us consider the example of a ten-year lease with an annual cost of €100. If this is treated as an operating lease, net operating income (EBIT), gross operating income (EBITDA) and earnings are reduced by €100 per year.[12] If the lease were treated as a capital lease, at 6 per cent interest, the asset and liability would initially be recorded at €736 (current value of 10 payments of €100 less 6 per cent). Annual depreciation would be €73.6 (€736 distributed over 10 years), while the financial expense in the first year would be €44.2. Therefore, the expense before tax would be €117.8.[13]

Naturally, operating leases can be very shrewd operations for company business in terms of both costs and risks. But they become dangerous when they are used as operations to conceal part of a company's debts at the cost of very high operating expenses and long-term or even perpetual commitments. However, some operating lease contracts include a commitment to purchase the asset at the end of the contract, sometimes in the form of 'side letters', which, in economic terms, really makes them capital lease contracts. In such cases, the company would be concealing its commitments; that is, part of its debt.

The differences arising from the use of operating or capital leases within the same industry are very significant. One study revealed the different degrees to which the airline industry made use of operating leases, ranging from zero per cent in the case of Singapore Airlines to 42 per cent in the case of UAL. In general, the capitalization of operating leases makes it easier to compare companies from the same sector. Thus, if an airline decides to use capital leases and another firm opts for operating leases, the odds are that the former will report lower returns on capital. This difference is simply the consequence of an accounting decision. Since the company that decides to use operating leases is obliged to provide information on the obligations assumed under the operating lease, these obligations are easier to capitalize and this makes it easier to compare the returns on capital of both companies. If these leases are capitalized and lower returns are obtained on the capital than the capital costs, the company's business model might be questioned, and this would go unnoticed if this adjustment were not performed. This technique also makes it easier to evaluate real leverage ratios. For example, to analyze the coverage of net operating income (EBIT) operating lease expenses should be added and capital lease expenses would have to be added to financial expenses in the denominator. Leases are best capitalized by using the cost of debt before tax, and capitalizable payments will depend on whether the total asset or right of usage method is used.[14] Using this technique, the net debt of American Airlines, including operating leases, would have ranged in 1998 from US$4,000 million to US$10,000 million, that of UAL from US$6,000 million to US$25,000 million, and that of Delta from US$2,000 million to US$9,000 million.[15]

Nowadays, to determine the classification of a lease (operating or financial), it will be classified as a capital lease if one of the following four conditions applies:[16]

- The title of ownership is transferred to the lessee at the end of the contract
- The lessee has a call option at a lower price to market to acquire the good
- The term of the contract is longer than three quarters of the useful life of the good
- The current value of the lease payments is equivalent to more than 90 per cent of the market value of the good.

Another type of operating lease is the so-called 'synthetic lease', which is used to buy real estate on markets in which prices are rising rapidly (as with Silicon Valley during the technology bubble), when the buyer does not want to assume a financial commitment at the time of acquisition. A financial entity creates a special purpose vehicle (SPV) company (or 'special purpose entity' (SPE)), which acquires the real estate, and this is leased to a lessee for a period equivalent to the maturity of the loan taken out to finance the real estate purchase operation. The lessor also establishes a guarantee for the residual value (around 85 per cent of the cost of property). The lessee is the owner of the property from a tax standpoint but not from an accounting standpoint; therefore, it can only write the property off on its tax returns. It is treated as an operating lease and its payments are treated as a deductible expense. This type of financing offers much lower costs than other types of leases. When the lease contract expires, the lessee can: (i) extend the contract; (ii) purchase the property at 100 per cent of the original cost; or (iii) sell the property to a third party. If the sale price is lower than the acquisition cost, the residual guarantee covers the loss; if the sale price is higher, the lessee keeps the profit.[17]

Iberia

The price of an aircraft ranges from between €30 million and €150 million, and an aircraft has a useful life of between 15 and 20 years. At the end of 2005, Iberia reported liquid assets of €2,012 million and debt of €800 million, prompting the company's CEO, Fernando Conte, to state in his letter to the company's shareholders that year that 'We have in cash 1,142 million Euros more than we owe'.[18] However, is that statement correct? Iberia's fleet at the end of 2005 consisted of 46 owned aircraft, 14 aircraft under capital leases, 89 under operating leases and 5 under other types of leases. The large number of aircraft under capital lease contracts gave rise to many commitments that did not appear on the company's balance sheet, since the leases were arranged so that the aircraft manufacturer guaranteed the residual value of the aircraft at the end of the contract. Since these leases did not fulfil the conditions established for other types of capital leases, they were classified as operating leases, which continued to give rise to important future payment commitments that are broken down in the notes to financial statements.[19] For this reason, Iberia needs to maintain a very strong cash position. Therefore, the statement that Iberia had in cash €1,142 million more 'than we owe' was, in our opinion, reckless.

In February 2005, the Spanish airline completed a brilliant synthetic lease operation to renew its fleet of short and mid-range aircraft. From an accounting standpoint, the aircraft were acquired under operating lease contracts; hence, they did not appear on the balance sheet. From a tax standpoint, the aircraft did appear on the balance sheet; as a result, the airline benefited from the tax shield created by writing off those assets. At the end of the contract, Iberia can decide whether to exercise its right to purchase the aircraft at a residual value or sign a lease contract. In the

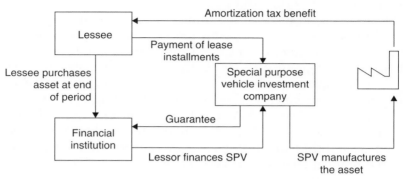

Figure 3.1   Leasing structure
Source: Peter Suozzo *et al.*, 'Can You Trust the Numbers?, *UBS Investment Bank*, March 2002, p. 37.

aviation industry, lease contracts are also arranged that include aircraft operating expenses such as maintenance or crew, allowing airline costs to be reduced.[20]

Iberia also issued a bond valued at US$933 million in December 2004 to finance an operating lease. At the time, it paid 4.26 per cent interest on this lease, below LIBOR, which was 4.29 per cent. Why? Well, the bond included an operating lease with the entity NBB, a subsidiary of Nomura, at an interest rate of 3.2 per cent. This was, by any reckoning, low and justified by the low interest rates in Japan at the time, and also because Nomura was able to write off the aircraft using the tax shield resulting from offsetting the earnings of other group units.[21]

Sometimes, eliminating assets and liabilities from the balance sheet reflects the real nature of an operation that is beneficial for a company. For example, the use of fixed assets such as company cars under operating leases is sometimes the best way to use assets without incurring in the risks associated with their ownership or without having to become indebted in order to own such assets. The problem arises when lease contracts are arranged to maintain all assets and liabilities under certain levels at the expense of higher operating costs, or when the contract is structured in a manner that enables favourable accounting treatment by preventing the assets and liabilities from appearing on the balance sheet, but which contract does not reflect the real nature of the operation or the associated risks. The main risk of operating leases for recipients of the accounting information is the undervaluation of obligations and debts.

Sale and lease back operations

Companies might decide to sell assets to third parties and immediately lease them back to the third party under operating or capital lease contracts. These types of operations are advantageous because the company is able to improve its current liquidity, thus reducing the level of net debt without relinquishing the use of the assets in question. The problem arises when the profits from such operations – consisting of non-recurring income obtained from the sale of assets (typically, real estate) above their book price – are immediately recorded in books, insofar as the obligations under that contract normally include a commitment to lease such assets/buildings for a pluriannual period, and are not recognized as a liability.

Such operations might be a completely justified but they are sometimes used to manipulate the values that appear in company accounts; namely, to reduce debt and assets (when the repurchase commitment is concealed) at the expense of higher lease back periods (in order to present the operation as an operating lease) and thus avoid the item being seen as an asset, with its corresponding debt on the liability side of the balance sheet. Its impact consists of the undervaluation of the company's commitments if an operating lease is arranged after the sale of the asset to avoid having to recognize the operation as a capital lease. International accounting standards recommend the deferral of earnings obtained from sale and lease back operations.

This mechanism has been used very often in the hotel sector. Between 1997 and 2001, the French company Accor disposed of property valued at €3,267 million and then immediately leased this property back – in more than 90 per cent of cases, with fixed payments revised according to inflation. Accor's financial leverage (net debt on corporate equity) in 2001 was 67 per cent, a reasonable figure. However, this ratio does not reflect the future commitments that Accor had assumed when it concluded these sale and lease back operations, transactions that gave rise to average payment commitments of 20 years. If these commitments were capitalized as increases in debt, financial leverage would have been 229 per cent and interest coverage would have fallen from 7.1 to 1.9.[22] This instrument has also been used by distribution companies such as Carrefour, Metro, KarstadtQuelle AG (which sold 174 properties to Goldman Sachs for US$4,500 million to improve its liquidity), or the El Árbol Group (which sold its properties to General Electric, in 2005, for a total of €75 million). Banks have also found this type of operation very useful for selling branches, as in the case of one operation concluded by Bank of America, in 2004, for US$535 million.[23]

Vía Digital

Extract from Telefónica's 2001 annual report

The commitments in connection with this investment are as follows:

1) Certain of the commitments acquired with regard to the acquisition of audiovisual rights by the investee DTS Distribuidora de Televisión Digital, S.A. (Vía Digital) are guaranteed by Grupo Admira Media, S.A., through the provision of a guarantee of €9.02 million plus the related variable consideration.

2) As a result of the loan granted by a syndicate of banks to DTS Distribuidora de Televisión Digital, S.A. (Vía Digital), Grupo Admira Media, S.A. has undertaken to contribute or guarantee the contribution of funds to Vía Digital for a maximum amount of €500 million as a participating loan or capital increase if:

   i)   Vía Digital could not draw down any amount against the loan as a result of non-compliance with the terms of the loan agreement;
   ii) Vía Digital could not settle the loan repayments or the related interest; or
   iii) The borrower entered into any of the situations whereby the loan became repayable early. Through December 31, 2001, Grupo Admira Media, S.A. had paid €271.4 million in this connection.

3) Telefónica has provided to third parties, including other stockholders of DTS Distribuidora de Televisión Digital, S.A. (Vía Digital), guarantees of the liquidity of the investments made which grant the beneficiaries a sale option and Telefónica a purchase option, which can be exercised if certain conditions are met, including that relating to the statutory limitations of percentage of ownership of the capital stock.

4) As a result of the agreement for the acquisition of the audiovisual rights relating to the Soccer World Cup in Japan and Korea in 2002, Grupo Admira Media, S.A. has assumed commitments totalling Swiss Francs 248,246,800.

Figure 3.2   Extract from Telefónica's 2001 annual report

Unconsolidated entities

Vía Digital, the pay-per-view satellite television company, has the dubious honour of being one of the Spanish companies to have lost the most money in the history of business in Spain. This accumulation of losses produced an exaggerated volume of debt. Let us look at Figure 3.2, which presents an extract from Telefónica's 2001 annual report (the Admira Media Group was a Telefónica subsidiary).[24]

Naturally, banks were reluctant to provide financing to a company (Vía Digital) of these characteristics. In order to resolve the situation, Vía Digital's shareholders – led by Telefónica – gave guarantees to banks that if Vía Digital were unable to pay its debts, its shareholders would cover these payments in proportion to their shareholdings (the second point in the extract from the annual report shown above). This decision generated a clear risk for shareholders (Telefónica and others), and yet it was not reflected in the financial statements of any of the companies providing this guarantee. The Spanish State does something similar when it guarantees debt issued by entities of questionable profitability, such as RTVE (*Radio Televisión Española* – Spanish State Television and Radio Corporation) or RENFE (*Red Nacional de los Ferrocarriles Españoles* – Spanish National Railway Network), without these guarantees or the implicit debt appearing in the accumulated debt of the Kingdom of Spain. Therefore, if Vía Digital were unable to fulfil its commitments, its partners agreed to inject money into the subsidiary in the form of loans. This money was used to pay off debts and interest, and, when the company found itself facing liquidation, the shareholders cancelled these debts on its behalf and transformed them into capital to strengthen its balance sheet and avoid the company going into liquidation. The perverse aspect of this matter was that this practice was especially difficult to identify in the accounts of both the parent company and the holding company. The best trick is to look at the notes to financial statements on the net debt of the analyzed company: if debt guarantees exist, these must appear in the notes to financial statements.

Finally, this also highlights another heterodox practice: if the holding company in question were a machine created to lose money and accumulate debt (think Vía Digital for example), then despite there being a clear shareholder of reference (Telefónica, officially with 48 per cent of its capital), the parent company, in order to avoid the consolidation of the holding company – which could cause a considerable negative contribution of EBITDA and operating profit, as well as add the total debt of the subsidiary to the parent company's debt – could declare its holding company to be 'uncontrolled', and then propose 'independent' members of the board of directors. This would avoid any suspicion of effective control over the holding company, consolidating the latter by means of the equity method. In this way, only its percentage of pre-tax earnings would appear – losses, in this case – but, since analysts focused on more operative aspects such as EBITDA, the major problem of consolidating Vía Digital's negative EBITDA was avoided, and its debt was not consolidated in any case. Had Vía Digital been a profitable and healthy company, one wonders whether Telefónica would have prepared to have effective 'control' of Vía Digital by appointing the majority of the board and juicily consolidated the theoretical operating profits of Vía Digital with those of the parent company.

Parking of shares

What happens when, due to political or regulatory pressure, a parent company owns more than 51 per cent of a holding company that accumulates losses and debts? Accounting regulations are clear on this subject: the subsidiary must be fully integrated. How can this be avoided? A percentage of shares, required to reach 49 per cent, is sold to a company based in the West Indies where it is difficult to trace the real owner of the company, and the company grants the enterprise a purchase option so that, when it is worthwhile consolidating the holding company, it can return to the scope of the parent company. This is vulgarly referred to as share 'parking'.

The ideal way to prevent abusive accounting practices is proportional integration, which consists of multiplying the parent company's shareholding in a subsidiary by each of its financial magnitudes. Thus, Vía Digital's 48 per cent of debt would be transferred to Telefónica's balance sheet. Theoretically, it would be feasible to reconcile subsidiaries consolidated by the equity method as integrated by proportional consolidation; the parent company's stake in the subsidiary can be determined using information on the earnings contributed by the subsidiary consolidated by the equity method as a percentage of the latter's total earnings. This is simple to determine by multiplying this percentage by each magnitude on the subsidiary's balance sheet and adding these amounts to the items corresponding to the parent company. Nevertheless, we would need the subsidiary's financial statements, and these are sometimes difficult to obtain because they could be published abroad. This difficulty would decrease considerably if the companies were obliged to include information in their annual reports with details of the key items of the subsidiaries consolidated by the equity method (financing debt, EBITDA, financial expenses, and so on).[25]

This simple example shows how playing with the scope of consolidation is a very simple method of avoiding having to consolidate debt (and also losses). In spite of everything, non-consolidation techniques are very sophisticated, as we will have the opportunity to see later.

Equity swapping

Sometimes, if the holding company is listed on the stock exchange, the company performs such operations through an equity swap contract with an investment bank. In this way, the parent company can 'sell' 2 per cent of its share package of 51 per cent in the holding company to the investment bank; hence, its participation is reduced to 49 per cent, thus justifying deconsolidation. However, to remain economically exposed at 51 per cent, under the contract the investment bank pays the parent company any increase in price on the delivered shares during the term of the contract, or the parent company can pay the investment bank the money resulting from losses in value of the holding company. When the contract terminates, the investment bank resells the 2 per cent to the parent company and consolidates the holding company once again but, by that time, the subsidiary no longer has worrying losses or debts.

The key to understanding whether or not deconsolidation is justified is to determine who is exposed to the risks and rewards relating to the asset or liability in question. For example, if company A guarantees company B that it will assume any debt incurred by company C on behalf of B, company A is clearly exposed to a risk, which is not recognized on the balance sheet. Or if company B is obliged to pay a certain amount if the company B's shares do not reach a specific price on a given date, this is another economic fact that is not reflected on the balance sheet but one that clearly generates an important risk. For that reason, the substance of the contract must prevail over its legal form. A securitization programme with a first loss risk entails an enormous level of risk, but it is off the balance sheet. Thus, as reported by Allan Cook from the UK Accounting Standards Board, a principle-based accounting system (such as the international or UK accounting systems) would have avoided Enron.[26]

Special purpose entities

Many non-consolidated entities are created by parent companies with specific functions to manage risk more efficiently. These entities are normally called special purpose entities (SPEs) or special purpose vehicles (SPVS), and they are very common in certain industries such as biotechnology, where SPEs are set up to deal with the financial risks of research into specific compounds.

Thus, a company might find it appropriate to have a minority holding in a company set up to carry out a specific project. For example, if a society with specific 'know-how' needs financing to perform an R&D project, it can associate with another company that can provide the necessary funds. The latter maintains the option to purchase the product if the project is successful, but the cost and the risks associated with the company in the event of failure do not appear because the company is not consolidated. This is because the finance company uses the equity method of consolidation, given the small size of its participation. By using the equity method of consolidation, only these adjustments independent of the annual accounts reflect the additional commitments and risks of the minority holding companies. With the global consolidation method, this information would be much more visible since it would be included in the accounts that appear in the balance sheet reflecting the specific commitments.

Sometimes these types of ventures are created for legal or tax purposes to carry out specific projects. When a project is carried out for a specific purpose and independent of the company's main activity, and when the latter is not actually exposed to the corresponding risk, it is best to account for the project off the balance sheet in order to provide a true and faithful view of the situation. For example, chemical companies use this type of mechanism to finance their plants through project finance, where finance entities contribute high volumes of debt to joint ventures with petrochemical companies, which guarantee the payment of debt without consolidating the joint venture until several years later when the initial volume of debt has been considerably reduced. Dow Chemical participated in these types of joint ventures with debt amounting to US$1,300 million at year-end 2001, while Dupont had US$1,200 million, of which more than US$700 were guaranteed.[27]

SPVs are not bad in themselves; they are useful instruments for isolating the main activities of projects shared with other associates that involve a particular risk. However, their abusive use could give rise to accounting disasters, as in the case of Enron, which concealed debt in dozens of SPVs, formally pretending that it did not control them to avoid having to consolidate their debt, although a more economic analysis would have revealed that Enron effectively controlled these companies.

In fact, these SPVs or joint ventures become indebted with finance entities, and often finance entities guarantee the corresponding loans, but these are not reflected in the balance sheet. Sometimes, financing companies transfer assets to SPVs, which normally use them as guarantees to request debt (in this case, the risks are limited to the value of the asset used as a guarantee – securitization that is described in more detail in another part of this chapter), or act in the first person as guarantors of the loan. In this case, as well as when the assets used as guarantees do not have sufficient value (shares that have lost value since they were accepted by banks as guarantees), the company that has created the SPV actually has a risk that it is not reflected in the balance sheet, just as a concealed purchase (or part of such purchase) by the SPV would not be reflected on the balance sheet even if the project were unsuccessful. Therefore, additional amounts of debt and risks could be issued without being clearly identified by those affected by this accounting infamy.

In order to react to the vulnerable situation created by the Enron scandal, the North American accounting authorities, following the criteria established in the Sarbanes–Oxley Act, introduced FASB 46. This came into effect on 1 July 2003, and related to the consolidation requirements applicable to SPVs and other similar instruments, such as collateralized debt obligations (CDOs) or synthetic leases. The key element to consider is who is exposed to the risks and gains of the assets in question ('variable interests'). Entities exposed to such risks and benefits are required to consolidate the SPV. Two criteria are proposed for analyzing this question: first, it must be determined whether or not the shareholders' investment in the SPV in question is sufficient for financing the latter's activities without additional support from the parent company and, if the funds are insufficient, then the SPV will have to be consolidated; if the company complies with this requirement, in order not to consolidate the SPV the parent company must make sure that it does not have any control over decision-taking in the SPV ('absence of control'), no liability for the SPV's losses and no right to receive the SPV's 'residual gains'.[28] In short, since the application of FASB 46, accounting follows a system of determining whether effective or economic (risk) has been transferred, and not legal risk, in order to determine consolidation.

Moreover, since then the SEC requires companies to present additional information on non-consolidated entities, particularly information on their nature and corporate purpose, their relevance for parent company liquidity and their credit risk, the financial impact of agreements concluded between the parent company and the holding company, the risk exposure of the parent company's holding company, the possible participation in first loss risks, and known incidents that might affect the results of the contract.

In general, the criteria defended by the SEC in relation to SPVs are based on providing information on these instruments and must include the nature and corporate purpose of the SPVs, their importance for company liquidity and credit risk, the financial impact and exposure of risk to retained interest (possible participation in the initial losses of the SPV) and known incidents that could affect profits under the contract.

Certain sectors use specific types of SPVs. The North American real estate sector, which has listed real estate companies called REITs (real estate investment trusts), uses entities called 'limited life partnerships' to transfer debt to non-consolidated companies. In 2003, it was calculated that the 10 most important REITs in the US had an average debt-to-capital ratio of 62 per cent, a percentage that would have increased to 68 per cent if debt concealed in limited life partnerships had been consolidated. The North American accounting standards board issued a standard (FAS 150) with similar effects to those achieved with FASB 46 in order to limit such abuse.[29]

It must be added that it would have been harder for an Enron-type scandal to happen in a European company that followed international accounting standards at the time, since Parmalat was still using Italian accounting standards. That was because IAS 27 established the principle of effective control and risk as the principle for determining consolidation, rather than the legal ownership of a specific shareholding, as the North American system did.[30] The main risk of abusing consolidation policies is the undervaluation of forward commitments and debts.

Case study: off-balance-sheet financing in the systems integration industry

Systems integration companies have undergone strong growth in their *outsourcing* business. By using certain doses of financial engineering, contracts were divided into an operative component and a capital component. Third parties with strong balance sheets were approached to provide financing and thus improve returns on equity resulting from these transactions, always assuming that customers had strong credit positions. A trust was created through which the financial entity would pay the client for assets and securitize these for sale to investors. Systems integration firms operated the assets and served the customer. The latter paid for the services received by the systems integrator and the trust for the right to use the assets. Risks arose because the systems integrators tended to be exposed to contractual obligations pursuant to which they might be obliged to purchase certain assets if services were not paid for, thus giving rise to fairly substantial contingent liabilities. Resulting off-balance-sheet commitments in the North American systems integration industry totalled US$2,500 million in 2002. The great advantage for integration companies was that these structures reduced the costs of the operation, allowing them to capture more contracts. The assets were also kept off the integrator's balance sheets. For the customer, the advantage was evident because, by transferring the assets, less capital was used and therefore their returns on capital used increased and their fixed costs were converted into variable costs. For their part, finance entities obtained structured financing business and were able to take advantage of the amortization of assets as tax shields.[31]

Guarantees

We will now look at Figure 3.3, which presents an extract from Telefónica's 2001 annual report (the Admira Media Group is a subsidiary of Telefónica).[32]

Audiovisual Sport

Extract from Telefónica's 2001 annual report

Grupo Admira Media, S.A. has provided a bank guarantee to secure payment of 40 per cent of the syndicated loan of €300.51 million granted by several finance entities to Audiovisual Sport, S.L., a 40 per cent-owned investee of Gestora de Medios Audiovisuales Fútbol, S.L., a Grupo Admira Media subsidiary.

Figure 3.3   Audiovisual Sport

Debt guarantee instruments are simple to understand: in order to carry out large investment projects, an investee company is created by two or three partners so that none of the partners controls more than half the capital stock, and thus none of the partners is obliged to consolidate this new company by the global integration method. The new company requests a large syndicated loan to carry out the investment projects. The banks grant the loan, even if the company is not yet operative and has few tangible assets but, in return, they require the partners to guarantee these debts. These guarantees do not appear on the liability side of the balance sheets of the partners; they are only mentioned in a note in the annual report – precisely the extract shown above.

The importance of debt guarantees as financing instruments must not be played down as off-balance-sheet financing instruments. If banks provide guarantees and control is lost over these guarantees, they could put the entire financial system at risk. In Thailand, it was calculated that the level of guarantees issued by Thai banks in 1997 was equivalent to 200 per cent of their book value. This was a real accounting time bomb that was decisive the following year when the economic crisis caused many emerging Asian economies to collapse.[33]

Securitization

Securitization refers to the process of selling to an investor an asset that can generate cash flow in the future. This process includes a wide range of assets such as lease rights, mortgages, credit card receipts, taxes receivable, and so on.

The sale process consists of the creation of a specific SPV to which the asset in question is transferred. The SPV issues different debt instruments that are purchased by the final investor and guaranteed by the transferred asset. Debt instruments are structured according to their quality (greater or lower risk of bankruptcy) to cover all investor risk profiles.

Altadis and Seita

In December 2000, Seita assigned its receivables to a Common Credit Fund (CCF), through the issue of short-term corporate promissory notes at a lower cost than bank loans. As a result of this transaction, receivables were retired and cash was obtained instead. In this way, the company obtained a fixed line of FRF 3,000 million (€457,346.17 thousand); a second tranche can be drawn down, if necessary, as a consideration. SEITA is responsible for management of said balances granted by the CCF. To cover the risk of customer bad debts, a guarantee was provided taking into account the customer's collection risk (financial bad debt, litigation ...). This guarantee was calculated at the beginning of the securitization transaction following more conservative methods than the historical cost method. The guarantee will foreseeably be updated on the basis of actual bad debt experience. This transaction is expected to last 5 years.

As of December 31, 2000, the effect of the securitization transaction was: a decrease in accounts receivable of FRF 3,371 million (€568,779.83 thousand), an increase in cash, in short-term investments and in investments in associated companies of FRF 3,000 million and FRF 273 million (€457,346.17 thousand and €41,620.09 thousand), respectively, and the booking of a deposit in 'Sundry Accounts Receivable' of FRF 497 million (€75,763.59 thousand).

Figure 3.4   Altadis and Seita

Isolating the assets in a deconsolidated SPV prevents the bankruptcy of the parent company causing the company's creditors to reclaim the assets that now appear in the SPV.

Normally, a company's accounts receivable are securitized if they are recurrent and if there is low risk of non-payment. This is an innovative instrument compared with the historical practice of discounting these collection rights commercially with financial entities, thus enabling the company to approach the financial market directly without having to go through intermediaries and reduce their cost.

Now look at Figure 3.4, which presents an extract from the 2000 annual report of the tobacco company Altadis and its subsidiary Seita, which describes a securitization operation that allowed the company to improve its cash balance as at 31 December 2000.

From the point of view of the company, there were only two parties involved, although as indicated later the structure of the securitization programme was more complex: the selling company was the company that sold the accounts receivable but continued to control those balances as if they were its own, without any change in the management of the customer portfolio; the buying company was the SPV mentioned previously, which obtained financing from a third entity in the form of a bridging loan.[34]

The company sold the assets to the SPV but continued to manage these assets by virtue of a contract under which the SPV designated the company as the administrator of the sold asset. Therefore, the accounts receivable were left off the balance sheet but were still managed as normal. The programme did not require complicated procedures or take up much time in the daily management of the company. The latter simply supplied summarized information on its accounts receivable portfolio that had to be sold through the securitization programme each month. The programme administrator was responsible for monitoring and managing all programme transfers and expenses. The company continued to collect its account receivables in the normal way and to create new accounts in the same way as before securitization.

The advantage of securitization is that it is a form of off-balance-sheet financing. Income from sales of accounts receivable is not recorded as debt on the balance sheet, thus improving all management ratios. These can also be used to reduce more expensive financial debt or to finance business growth. Securitization is also a competitive source of financing because, despite the large start-up costs, and due to the long time horizon, the overall financing cost is attractive if the volume to be securitized is sufficiently large. Moreover, there are no limitations or precautionary measures[35] on balance sheet and financial ratios; only the evolution of accounts receivable is analyzed, specifically the debt rate and dilution (due to customer, volume or other discounts). Finally, it enables better management of important company assets when direct value is attributed to the good management of accounts receivable. The better an 'accounts receivable' asset is managed, the higher the price at which it can be sold.

Securitization entails risks such as the undervaluation of the risk associated with short-term assets, the reduction of balance sheet assets and the improvement of corporate efficiency rates that could be unreal. Nowadays, the IAS standards allow securitization structures to be deconsolidated provided that it can be shown that the parent company is not significantly exposed to the risks and benefits of the cash flows of the deconsolidated company.

Case study: off-balance-sheet financing in the banking sector

At year-end 2001, it was calculated that the leading North American banks had open derivative positions taken up as counterparties, equivalent to US$4.6 billion, which implied an associated credit risk of around US$147,000 million, given the possibility that the banks' counterparties might not have been able to fulfil their commitments under derivative contracts.[36] As we have seen, this possibility was not outrageous as the losses recorded by Procter & Gamble, Metallgesellschaft or the County of Orange revealed. Total off-balance-sheet commitments assumed by North American banks at year-end 2001, when the economic crisis made them even more relevant, amounted to US$2.4 billion, with US$732,000 million corresponding to the largest bank, Citigroup.

According to the Basle Committee on Banking Supervision, more than half of the banks carried out asset securitization operations, but less than one third provided information on the risks inherent in these operations. The risks inherent in private derivative transactions (over-the-counter transactions (OTCs)) carried out by the banks is still a 'black box' area that has yet to be clarified by the regulator, a factor that probably explains why banks tend to trade at a discount in relation to their profits compared with averages for other listed sectors. Moreover, banks often extend lines of credit to their clients, undertaking to make certain amounts of money available. Even if these lines are not drawn, the commitment remains in force. In the third quarter of 2001, it was estimated that commitments of this type amounted to US$340,000 million in Citigroup, US$268,000 in J.P. Morgan, or US$166,000 in Bank of America. Many of these commitments were offered as credit lines to be used if a customer were, for any reason, unable to use the bond market (credit commitments known as 'back-up loans'). Their importance can be vital at specific moments. Thus, when Enron and the distribution company Kmart started experiencing problems, they used these types of credit lines amounting to US$3,000 million and US$1,500 million, respectively, just before they went bankrupt. The conglomerate Tyco, immersed in financial problems, announced on 4 February 2002, that it would repurchase US$4,500 million of listed bonds using an available credit line of US$5,900 million. This announcement precipitated the fall of North American listed banks since this news caused off-balance-sheet commitments to appear suddenly on balance sheets, despite the fact that they were guaranteed by Tyco's accounts receivable and inventories.

Many banks act as leading banks in CDOs, which allows them, as we have seen in the case of securitization programmes, to remove assets from company balance sheets, finance them with debt, which they off-set with cash flows generated by the debt. The problem is that banks are sometimes exposed to first loss risks; in other words, if the asset in question (for example, a mortgage) cannot generate the unpaid cash (perhaps because bad debts have increased), the leading bank, and not the subscriber of the debt, might cover the initial debts, but this risk does not appear on many balance sheets. Many issues of CDOs do not offer debt securities on an equal basis. Instead, they establish multiple tranches of different quality debt, which means that securities range from those with maximum ratings (AAA) to others that are not sufficiently qualified for investment, and banks retain some minimum-quality instruments without reporting the inherent risk.

Banks also often use these CDOs to optimize their regulated capital, reducing their exposure to certain risks such as mortgage risks, and thus reducing the capital necessary to include those assets on their balance sheets. Reducing capital at a similar level of profit increases return on the actual value of equity. These transactions are used in many different scenarios, from simple securitization programmes (such as mortgages or credit card accounts receivable) to more complex transactions (such as synthetic leases to acquire real estate, and inventory investment programmes or natural resources exploration and production programmes).[37]

Sometimes, banks lead issues of guaranteed loan notes, which are based on the confidence inspired by the entity selling the debt securities, so that if the securities of the parent company are unpaid, the debt of the instrument is immediately included in the same category, normally giving rise to difficulties for the bank leading the issue. Moreover, to make part of these guaranteed loan notes more attractive, banks tend to capitalize these entities before placing debt, offering them lines of credit so that they can present more attractive balance sheets to investors in their debt. This risk forces North American banks to maintain 8 per cent of capital when they have similar risks open.

On other occasions, banks also subscribe 'surety bonds'. These are financing instruments that are based on the confidence that the counterparty of the company issuing the bond will fulfil its obligation. For example, Enron had opened derivative positions on energy markets that resulted in favourable movements for Enron, but which would not be paid for a number of years. In order to access the money immediately, Enron issued these surety bonds to J.P. Morgan, which expected to collect them once the derivative contracts had been concluded and Enron's counterparty fulfilled its commitment. In total, J.P. Morgan had Enron-related exposure in these types of bonds amounting to US$1,130 million.

Epilogue: credit crisis and creative accounting

In July and August 2007, several events triggered what was to be known as the 'credit crisis', which would soon evolve into a 'credit crunch'. The trigger behind the crisis was the increasing level of non-performing loans in US sub-prime mortgages. The deterioration of credit markets sent the global banking sector into one of the worst banking crises ever. In turn, losses in the financial system soon translated into a risk aversion, which resulted in reduced willingness to lend money. Almost immediately, this credit crunch would have an impact on the real economy, as consumers and corporations found difficulties in financing their consumption and investment projects. As a result, in February 2008 the financial markets were discounting a US recession and a serious global economic slow down.

Creative accounting had a role to play in the emergence of this crisis, as it was soon discovered that large financial institutions had kept very large sums of assets and liabilities off their balance sheets in SPE entities known as 'structured investment vehicles' (SIVs). In essence, these entities tried to generate returns by raising short term financing in the commercial paper market and then investing these sums in higher yielding longer-term assets, such as structured bonds, typically AAA paper backed by sub-prime mortgages.

The SIVs were sponsored by banks, and attracted third-party investors who wanted to profit from this opportunity. Banks would structure these entities so that the presence of these third parties would allow the bank to place the SIVs' assets and liabilities off its balance sheet. As the events in July and August 2007 resulted in increased risk aversion, the commercial paper markets' activity almost collapsed, as it was perceived that the assets backing such obligations, quite often mortgage-related paper, could result in much lower valuations than the stated ones. The SIVs, unable to roll over their short-term financing needs, also found no chance to dispose of portions of their AAA mortgage-related positions, as liquidity in these markets seriously dried up as a consequence of the crisis. Unable to dispose of their assets to face the maturity of short-term debts, the SIVs were doomed to failure. To avoid systemic and reputation risk, banks had no option but to take these assets and liabilities on their balance sheets. As SIVs operated with a very low capital base, the re-entering of these positions on the banks' balance sheets seriously undermined their already low level of capital base (which had suffered from having written off structured credit positions, mortgage-backed securities and loans to private equity institutions). As a consequence of this, the banks had to enter into important exercises of recapitalization, which often ended with the CEO abandoning his post (as was the case with Merrill Lynch and Citigroup).

Following the Enron scandal, the US accounting body, the FASB, changed the rules governing the consolidation of off-balance-sheet entities such as SPEs. The main change consisted in analyzing the residual interest concept or, in other words, which party is subject to the residual risks and benefits of the SPE, in order to determine its consolidation (FAS 140). If the sponsor is not subject to these risks, the sponsor entity becomes a qualified SPE and, hence, its assets and liabilities could be held off balance sheet, as it is understood that a bankruptcy of the sponsor should not have implications for the SPE. International accounting follows a similar approach in IAS 27. Yet, banks would structure these SIVs so that, from an accounting perspective, they would qualify to become off-balance-sheet, as they could show that the banks were not theoretically exposed to the majority of risks and rewards. Of course, the extraordinary circumstances experienced during the summer of 2007, with the collapse of some of the key markets in which these SIVs operated, would seriously challenge the existing assumptions (as traditional accounting and valuation techniques proved to be unfit to analyze these risks), and this challenge forced the reconsolidation, which aggravated the banking crisis. Hence, looking into the future, this issue will need to be addressed by much more concrete rules that elaborate on risk disclosure, so that investors can perform their own assumptions on the real value at risk which banks are incurring.

This case study illustrates a vital point when dealing with creative accounting. People tend to go back to accounting only when the scandal has erupted. Yet, a good investment professional or financier should enhance their forensic analysis skills during the good times, in order to screen for dangerous accounting practices and take wise investment decisions while it is still possible to do so.

Conclusion

The application of IAS in Europe meant that the recognized debt of Europe's top 28 listed firms increased 16 per cent with respect to the figure under previous accounting systems, displaying the greater depth of IAS when it comes to identifying off-balance-sheet debt. The recognition of pension fund deficits on balance sheets has been particularly crucial for adjusting debt figures. Thus, as a consequence of the application of IAS, the British chemical company Imperial Chemical was obliged to recognize £1,200 million in debt, the Dutch bank ING €2,900 million, and the French automobile company Peugeot €1,200 million.[38]

How can possible sources of off-balance-sheet financing be identified when examining company financial statements?

There are simple recommendations that companies can follow to protect themselves against these accounting techniques. We have seen how some companies 'cook' their balance sheet figures a few days before presenting their annual accounts. However, although they manage to alter debt figures, it is harder for them to alter the figure corresponding to financial expenses incurred throughout the year. So what is our recommendation? Calculate a company's debt figure by capitalizing financial expenses. The calculation is simple. Assume a company announces that it has debt of €150 million. We are sceptical and note that financial expenses amount to €10 million. According to the company's notes and our information, we know that the average cost of the company's debt is about 5 per cent. Simply divide €10 million by 0.05 to obtain a more realistic figure; that is, €200 million, which is €50 million more than the number initially reported.

Another simple and useful piece of advice is to not only to examine the figures that appear on a balance sheet, but also to analyze the notes to financial statements. Thus, if a company reports €600 million of debt, check whether there is a note on this debt in the notes to financial statements. If the company has offered debt guarantees to third parties, they must be included in these notes, thus giving us an idea of the company's real level of risk. The same thing applies to future payment commitments. If a company has agreed to pay €20 million per year over five years under an operating lease, these payment commitments, despite not appearing on the liability side of the balance sheet, must appear in the notes to financial statements. This information will indicate whether the cash flow generated by the company is partly committed.

It is also useful to read the audit report to determine whether auditors have issued a qualified opinion on the financial statements. Qualified reports are no longer permitted in the case of listed companies. Nevertheless, if a non-listed company carries out an operation to remove debt from a balance sheet using derivatives, it is normal for auditors to issue a qualified opinion. Finally, we would like to reflect on the asymmetric information that still exists in capital markets. The equity market considers that company information is limited to annual accounts, quarterly results and the information that listed companies decide to publish. However, rating agencies (such as Moody's) have access to considerably more detailed information on companies' financial positions. This asymmetry in information can cause the debt market to reflect information that is not reflected in the stock market. What better example than WorldCom, a company which the credit default swaps market considered to be close to suspension of payments when many analysts still actively recommended strong value-based purchases. For that reason, an information system that enables the integration of signals from all markets within our reach (stock market, equity derivatives, debt, and debt derivatives) would be a very useful factor for limiting our risk. On the other hand, when analyzing non-consolidated subsidiaries using the global integration method, such as off-balance-sheet SPVs, we should ask ourselves the following question: Is the parent company exposed to the operating risks of the non-consolidated company?

The following advice could be useful to recipients of financial information in order to scrutinize the possible presence of off-balance-sheet financing:[39]

- Read and understand the notes on contingencies.
- Look for information on operating lease commitments; not only the amount of commitments but also their maturity periods.
- Look for sudden changes in assets, especially fixed assets, inventories and accounts receivable, which could indicate transfers to off-balance-sheet entities.
- Check the asset rotation ratios to make sure that increases in asset values are consistent with growth in earnings.
- Check the notes on accounting policy to identify securitization operations or other asset transfers.
- Check the list of companies consolidated by the equity method, joint ventures and other enterprises not consolidated by global integration, and whose main purpose or activity is not obvious, to determine whether the lack of global consolidation is adequate.
- Consider the level of future financial commitments, as well as recognized obligations.
- Study the notes on operations with associated entities to find unusual references on SPV investment companies.
- Study the notes in the annual report to identify references to payment with recourse obligations.
- Study the company's accounts to identify indicators of accounting tricks used commonly in the industry, and determine the risk of the company in question.

- Look for information on other contractual commitments and the level of guarantees offered under these commitments.
- Identify guarantees offered for commitments to third parties or related companies.
- Look for derivatives contracts (including fowards, swaps, index-linked debt) of unusual size or nature in business hedging activities.
- Look for the use of shares (or equivalents) as collateral or consideration of an investment or exchanged for debt or other liabilities.[40]

In general, the liabilities on a balance sheet must inform us about the company's future payment obligations, thus offering us a measurement of risk. The problem of off-balance-sheet financing lies in the existence of an economic risk to comply with a commitment, yet this risk is not reflected on the balance sheet; hence, we can only refer to the deconsolidation of entities when the risks and rewards of the entity in question do not correspond to the parent company.[41]

4
Risk Management, Derivatives and Hybrid Instruments

In the beginning it is just a business problem. Then
people start playing with numbers to conceal the problem.
Christian Leuz, Professor of Accounting, Wharton

The valuation of derivative instruments has been a source of constant concern for accountants. We have seen how, in 1987, the FASB issued an order forcing North American companies to provide information on the market value of all off-balance-sheet financial instruments. Some instruments are referred to as 'hybrid' instruments because they combine the characteristics of variable income and fixed income securities. The advantage of these instruments is that the interest payable on them is tax deductible, yet they can be treated as equity by rating agencies, hence their popularity.[1]

In 1994, MG Refining and Marketing (MGRM), a North American subsidiary of Metallgesellschaft, reported losses of US$1,300 million as a result of derivative positions on energy products. The bail-out operation by 150 banks, totalling US$1,900 million, eventually saved the subsidiary from bankruptcy. Although the subsidiary was initially believed to have incurred such enormous losses due to speculation on energy prices, it was actually doing nothing more than covering its risk positions. MGRM sold oil products at fixed prices over periods of up to ten years. Under these contracts, it was exposed to hikes in oil prices because it was forced to buy petrol at higher prices than the fixed prices at which it had agreed to supply different customers. In order to cover this risk, MGRM purchased derivative instruments in the form of futures and swaps. Instead of rising, oil prices fell so, although MGRM benefited on long-term supply contracts, it lost money on derivative contracts, giving rise to very important margin calls. If it had applied International Accounting Standard (IAS) 39 instead of German accounting standards, these losses would not have caused that disastrous situation because they would have been offset by the higher value of the supply contracts.[2]

In the 1990s, North American accounting regulators began supporting the valuation of financial instruments at their market value. The multimillion-dollar losses incurred on speculative derivative positions by Procter & Gamble, the County of Orange and Gibson Greetings accelerated the need to promote accounting standards on derivatives capable of showing their market value. These reforms required companies to recognize financial instrument fluctuations in their profit and loss accounts, sometimes on a deferred basis through the 'other comprehensive income' account. If the financial instrument was created for hedging rather than speculative purposes, the higher or lower value of the derivative could be offset by the higher or lower value of the underlying asset. However, if hedging were imperfect, the differences would have to be charged to income.[3] This accounting reform brought an end to the use of derivatives as speculative instruments and made sure that companies used them to cover risks.

In terms of international accounting standards, in the initial wording, IAS 39 required derivatives and other financial instruments to be recognized in balance sheets at their market value, mainly in profit and loss accounts. The application of this standard could mean that the deterioration of a company's risk profile results in higher profits: bonds and debentures would be carried at market value, which would be lower after the deterioration of their risk profile, thus increasing company profits since the lower value of the debentures would be recorded as profit.[4] In a later amendment, dating from December 2003, IAS 39 restricted the market valuation of financial instruments:

• The item is a financial asset or financial liability that contains one or more embedded derivatives
• The item is a financial liability whose amount is contractually linked to the performance of the assets that are measured at fair value
• The exposure to changes in the fair value of the financial asset or financial liability is substantially offset by the exposure to the changes in the fair value of another financial asset or financial liability, including a derivative.

As a result of these changes, the debt issued by the company cannot be revalued. This situation would have been detected in the case of Freddie Mac, the entity sponsored by the North American government to promote mortgage loans, the accounting problems of which stemmed from valuing derivatives at market value and not using this market value for underlying assets. In January 2003, Freddie Mac announced it was reclassifying its accounts for the period 2000–2002. As a result, its book value increased by US$1,500 million. The root of the problem was that the company's directors tried to minimize the impact of FAS 133, the US equivalent to IAS 39. This standard required derivative contracts to be valued at market value, but FAS 115 did not require underlying assets to be valued at market. This could have caused an imbalance between underlying assets and derivatives, giving rise to a high degree of volatility in the firm's profits. Freddie Mac's directors opted to minimize this volatility in order to stabilize profit growth.[5]

Derivative instruments are often used to guarantee specific risks, and this hedging should increase the value of the derivative as money is lost in the risk in question and vice versa. In such circumstances, under IASs derivative instruments do not have to be valued at market value through the use of hedge accounting. In order for them to be classified as such, the relationship between the derivative and the risk must be proven; that is, the relationship between both must be clearly defined, quantifiable and effective. These standards limit the use of derivative instruments by firms for speculative purposes, restricting their use purely to the coverage of risks. This should avoid dramatic incidents in the future, such as the bankruptcy of the County of Orange in the US.[6]

Publicis

The French advertising agency Publicis issued a bond exchangeable for stock in Interpublic in the amount of €200 million. The structure also entitled Publicis to exchange debentures at their cash value and also granted Publicis a buy-back option on these bonds. With the application of IAS 39, the three derivatives had to be valued separately and at their market value, requirements which were not required by French accounting standards. The application of this standard would have resulted in an expense of €6 million in 2003, revenues of €11 million in 2002 and an expense of €5 million in 2001. In any event, standards[7] require a sensitivity analysis of the valuation of the financial instruments to be performed under different hypotheses of key variables in the valuation.[8]

Let us now go on to discuss hybrid instruments in their various forms.

Futures contracts: Deutsche Bank

Deutsche Bank signed futures contracts under which it agreed to purchase, in the future, a specific amount of stock from the bank itself in order to hedge its stock option programmes, where the number of shares was equivalent to the volume that the German bank estimated would be demanded by employees when exercising their stock options. Deutsche Bank, following standard market practice, sold put options on its own shares to finance the futures purchase contracts. FAS 150 requires options subscribed on company stock to be marked to market.[9] During the second quarter of 2003, Deutsche Bank had to reduce its treasury stock by €2,900 million and this stock was subsequently classified as external debt. This adjustment arose as a consequence of the application of the aforementioned North American FAS 150 standard, which requires certain financial instruments such as futures contracts on company shares to be recorded as debt.

Why do companies use hybrid instruments? Financial leverage is associated with greater stock volatility. Companies might use hybrid instruments to minimize share volatility or simply reclassify debt in other legal forms to present more attractive leverage ratios. These are simply financial assets that, without being debt, can neither be classified as shares; they are somewhere between the two. The key to identifying whether a hybrid instrument is closer to equity (stock) or borrowed funds (debt), lies in determining the following aspects:

- Whether the company is required to pay interest or a dividend to the holder of the hybrid instrument
- Whether the hybrid instrument has a fixed term with repayment conditions
- The order of priority for collecting hybrid instruments if the company goes bankrupt
- Whether the hybrid instrument entails profit sharing
- The degree to which returns on the hybrid instrument are associated with the volatility of the company's profits.

Although we will not study each of the main hybrid instruments, it is worthwhile observing how the ratings agency Standard & Poor's classifies hybrid instruments based on these criteria, from normal shares to common debt (see Figure 4.1).

Preferred stock: Balfour Beatty

Another financing instrument often used by companies is preferred stock. This type of stock pays specific dividends, which are normally very attractive and almost guaranteed, having priority over common stock in the event of liquidation of the company, which in return waives its political rights to those shares. This avoids companies having to approach the

1	Normal stock;
2	PERCS or PRIDES – preferred shares that must be converted into normal stock within three years;
3	DECS – equivalent to PERCs or PRIDEs, with the legal form of debt rather than preferred stock; this debt must be converted into shares within three years;
4	MIPS – preferred stock convertible into common stock (not obligatory) or perpetual preferred stock;
5	Perpetual preferred stock;
6	TRUST PFDs – preferred stock deferred over more than twenty-five years that generates dividends deferrable at the discretion of the issuing company if its situation makes this necessary;
7	MIDS – the same as TRUST PFDs, except that MIDS have the legal form of debt and not preferred stock (the range of the debt coupon might be determined by the company). They also have twenty-five-year maturity periods;
8	Convertible preferred stock with stated maturity of more than fifteen years;
9	Other preferred instruments with stated maturity of more than fifteen years;
10	Debt to be paid on a deferred basis with stated maturity of more than fifteen years;
11	HIGH TIDES – preferred stock with stated maturity of between five and seven years where one party independent of the issuer and the preferential shareholder determines the dividend in special circumstances, and they normally mature after between five and seven years;
12	Other preferred instruments with stated maturity of five to ten years;
13	Normal convertible instruments;
14	Accretive convertibles whose exercise price increases with time;
15	Bonds with maturity periods of more than seventy-five years;
16	Bonds that mature after between twenty-five and seventy-five years;
17	Auction preferred stock (frequent marketing) and mid-term debt;

Figure 4.1   Standard & Poor's classifications of hybrid instruments
Source: Dennis Jullens *et al.*, 'Does IAS39 Improve Financial Reporting for Derivatives?', 16 September 2005, p. 11.

debt market and increase capital, which could have a dilution effect for shareholders. The redeemable nature of this type of fixed-term stock, as well as the determinable portion of their dividend, makes these hybrid instruments (somewhere between debt and stock) the target of special scrutiny by the regulator. As with the IASB, North American Standard FAS 150 requires these instruments to be classified as debt and their 'dividends' as financial expenses, on the grounds that their economic nature is closer to debt than equity.

The British company Balfour Beatty recorded preferred stock of £150 million in its 2003 annual report, a substantial amount if we bear in mind that the company's book value was £230 million and its cash position £124 million. In accordance with UK Accounting Standards, this

preferred stock was treated as part of the company's equity. Nevertheless, under IASs, a substantial part of this preferred stock was reclassified
as debt, subsequently having an impact on the company's equity and
dividend payments, which were reclassified as financial cost.[10]

Convertible shares

The third type of hybrid financing instrument used most often by
companies comprises convertible shares, which are regulated by IAS
32. Before this standard was introduced, many European companies
used convertibles for financing purposes; since these convertible instruments are company bonds with a purchase option on the company's
own shares. Investors, in exchange for receiving this option, accepted
interest below that provided on similar bonds. This allowed companies to obtain self-financing at very attractive interest rates. Another
clear advantage of convertible bonds over capital increases was that
the dilution effect for existing shareholders resulting from new share
issues was deferred. This avoided their having to increase the number of
shares concurrently, since this would increase the P/E ratio of shares and
many analysts, for simplicity's sake, ignored convertible bonds when
considering future dilutions. The result was that shareholders suffered
dilution and a financial cost that was virtually undetectable on company annual accounts. The accounting solution adopted in IAS 32 is
simple: this hybrid instrument (the convertible bond) is divided into an
equity component and a debt or liability component, which is, in fact,
the composition of a convertible bond. Additionally, the debt component of the convertible bond must be reclassified as corporate equity
(stock) in the case of preferred perpetual stock, mandatory convertibles
(bonds are always converted to stock) or normal convertible bonds in
the money that mature within twelve months (the total probability of
conversion is therefore assumed).[11]

Reclassification of convertibles: ST Microelectronics

The semi-conductor manufacturer ST Microelectronics issued convertible bonds valued at US$1,200 million in 2003, at minus 0.5 per cent
interest. The negative interest rate was due to the fact that the bond did
not pay a coupon. However, if it was not converted, only 95 per cent
of the principal would be repaid and not 100 per cent. Why would
investors be interested in bonds that offer a negative interest rate?
Simply, because the value of the purchase option accompanying the

convertible bond compensates for the low or negative interest. Under IASs, the amount of US$1,200 million would have been divided between debt and equity. Assuming a 5 per cent debt cost, the debt component would have been US$667 million, and the conversion option would have been US$533 million. The company's balance sheets would therefore have contained US$667 million as financing debt and US$533 million in equity, thus diluting earnings per share, increasing the financial expenses component by US$34 million, instead of recognizing US$6 million in financial income. Overall, the company's estimated profits in 2004 would have been cut by 6 per cent.[12]

Mandatory convertibles: Adidas

Mandatory or contingent convertibles[13] are bond instruments that establish call options on shares. The difference with respect to other convertibles is that the buyers of these instruments cannot freely exercise them. Instead, the buyer must exercise the option if the share reaches a certain value. In practice, it is not very different to a deferred capital increase. Both international and North American accounting standards oblige companies to consider the impact that the conversion of these instruments could have on the number of shares when calculating the diluted number of company shares.[14] The particular characteristic of these instruments is that this calculation is not assumed at the time of conversion but in the present, without it mattering whether the shares reach the stipulated price to force conversion.[15] These standards are also applicable to preferred stock issues, which are mandatorily converted if the stock reaches a specific price.[16] North American listed leisure companies reduced their earnings per share by 7.4 per cent as a result of the application of this standard.[17] Major Western banks have also used mandatary convertible bonds in order to strengthen their balance sheets following the credit crisis that erupted in July 2007.

The German sports clothing company ADIDAS issued €400 million in convertible bonds in 2003 at a cost of 2.5 per cent with a mandatory conversion clause under certain conditions; for example, the obligation to convert the bond if the price of Adidas's shares exceeded 110 per cent of the total amount of conversion for 20 days during a 30-day period. In practice, the instrument allowed ADIDAS to obtain financing at very low rates (2.5 per cent) thanks to the terms and conditions governing conversion, which was mandatory and not optional in this case, and which compensated buyers of these bonds for the low interest paid on the bonds.[18]

Synthetic convertibles: Novartis

In 2001, Novartis issued purchase options on its own shares at an exercise price equal to zero, plus the same number of sale options to Deutsche Bank, which at the time had an exercise price above the price of Novartis shares. Deutsche Bank then issued a zero-coupon bond to investors, exchangeable for Novartis stock. The money obtained from the sale of this instrument among investors was paid to Novartis as compensation for the put and call options bought by Deutsche Bank from Novartis. In its 2001 annual accounts, Novartis increased its equity figure by €2,800 million (Swiss Francs 4,010 million); that is, this operation

Table 4.1   Recognition of assets

Type of asset	Balance sheet recognition	Recognition of variations in value
Derivatives	Market value	Profit and loss[1]
Globally consolidated financial investments, including associated goodwill	Market value	Profit and loss
Financial assets and liabilities kept until maturity – consolidated by the equity method	Historical cost[2]	Profit and loss
Financial assets and liabilities classified as speculative[3]	Market value	Profit and loss
Financial assets and liabilities available for sale[4]	Market value	Equity
Loans and accounts receivable generated	Historical cost	Profit and loss
Other financial liabilities	Historical cost	Profit and loss

Notes:
[1] If it is not a hedge derivative, *hedge accounting*.
[2] In the case of shares consolidated by the equity method, their book value will be increased by non-distributed income and decreased by dividends received. In the case of minority shareholder accounts, their book value will increase according to non-distributed profits, and will decrease according to dividends paid.
[3] Trading investments.
[4] The reasoning behind deferring the impact of recognizing these investments at market compared with the treatment of speculative investments consists in deferring the impact of the adjustment at the time of the sale. The SEC considers that any investment that can be forecast will be sold within a period of six to nine months if considered to be 'available for sale'. Cf. 'Heads Up on Current Accounting Issues & Trends', *Credit Suisse First Boston*, 18 March 2003.
Source: 'Hedging & NIC 39', *UBS*, September 2005.

was recorded as a capital increase. In economic terms, the transaction was equivalent to a convertible zero-coupon bond in Novartis shares. The transaction with Deutsche Bank had an accounting purpose but not an economic effect. In practice, Novartis had issued a convertible bond to itself. This gave rise to two possibilities. If the stock were converted, Deutsche Bank would exercise its call option. Therefore, Novartis would effectively be granting its treasury stock to investors that bought Deutsche Bank's instruments, followed by an issue of Novartis stock at a premium with respect to the listed price when the transaction took place. If this stock were not converted but the bond was repaid in cash, Deutsche Bank would have exercised its call and put options, thus receiving from Novartis the cash equivalent to the amount it had to pay investors. In economic terms, for Novartis the transaction was equivalent to having issued a convertible bond, but in accounting terms the amount of the issue was recorded as equity and not debt, since it should have been treated as a normal convertible bond in 2001. In practice, this accounting phenomenon increased equity without affecting debt because the options sold by Novartis to Deutsche Bank were not recognized as liabilities.[19]

Table 4.1 is a useful example of the way different kinds of assets can be recorded; always remember that if the market value resulting from the valuation of a balance item is lower than its book value, it must be determined whether it is the result of a monetary or non-monetary phenomenon. Otherwise, the value of the asset must be reduced by means of a loss.[20]

5
Recognition of Expenses, Balance Sheet Fluctuations, Cash Flow and Quality of Earnings

A game that, if not addressed soon, will have adverse consequences for America's financial reporting system. A game that runs counter to the very principles behind our market's strength and success.
Speech by **Arthur Levitt**, President of the SEC in 1998

Determining profit quality is crucial for recipients of financial information: US$100 in profit is not the same in two different companies, A and B, with the same potential growth, if the cash flow inherent in the earnings of company A is greater than that of company B. As a general rule, profit resulting from more conservative accounting policies accompanies greater cash flow; hence, profit resulting from aggressive policies and low cash flow is of better quality. Research has shown that companies with better quality earnings eventually perform better on stock markets than those with lower quality earnings.[1]

A recent study analyzing the answers given by 401 North American executives to questions on decisions relating to annual accounts concluded that these executives considered earnings-per-share to be the most important measurement of share performance.[2] The authors proposed four reasons to explain this hypothesis:

1. Earnings-per-share (EPS) is a simple metric that: summarizes corporate performance, is easy to understand, and is relatively comparable across companies;
2. The EPS metric gets huge media coverage;
3. By focusing on one variable, the analyst's task of predicting the future value is made somewhat easier; and
4. Analysts evaluate corporate progress by focusing on EPS.

Of the survey participants: 80 per cent reported that they would reduce spending on research and development, advertising and maintenance in order to meet the earnings target expected by EPS analysts; 55 per cent stated that they would delay starting a project with a positive current net value if that delay allowed them to meet an earnings target expected by the market. This means that projects that could add value to the firm might be sacrificed for the sake of reporting desired accounting numbers. Basically, it is a question of choosing between the short-term and long-term objectives of the firm. This decision can affect the quality of earnings.

It has been observed that pressure on many companies to meet quarterly earnings targets announced previously to the financial market has resulted in bad decisions – such as company acquisitions, asset sales or changes in accounting criteria to achieve the promised figure – resulting in greater mid-term share volatility, which has meant that large companies such as Motorola, Intel or Ford now only provide annual rather than quarterly forecasts.[3] Therefore, good financial analysts must be aware of areas of accounting where subjective interpretation could lead to the generation of higher or lower quality earnings.

In general, expense accounting is extremely subjective, and this subjectivity allows companies to alter their numbers to achieve higher or lower profits. The most common techniques consist of delaying the recognition of an expense, capitalizing expenses, and overestimating or undervaluing future expenses by recording provisions. However, each case is different, as we shall see.[4]

Stock and inventory variations

The North American technology company Cisco was forced to reduce the recognized value of its inventories by US$2,800 million in 2002.[5] Its inventories included items such as raw materials, auxiliary products, operating supplies, finished goods or work in progress. Inventories must be valued at the lower of cost or market, which means their book value can only be adjusted in one direction: downwards. The cost of inventories might vary depending on the valuation system used (FIFO, LIFO, mean weighted price, and so on[6]) and the market value of goods is calculated at replacement cost. This could be a very subjective criterion because the key lies in estimating the assumed selling price of the merchandise, which might vary according to market circumstances and the situation of the company selling the merchandise. In 2006, in a climate of rapidly increasing oil prices, the North American legislator examined the LIFO system applied by the oil company Exxon Mobil in the treatment of its inventories. This method allowed the company to reduce declared profits by US$5,600 million and report a profit of US$36,100 million instead of US$40,000 million, thus reducing its tax bill. This sparked off a debate among legislators on whether the LIFO system should be abolished to increase tax collection. Other North American oil companies, despite this being prohibited by the IASB, use the same method. This means that profits declared on either side of the Atlantic are not entirely comparable.[7]

The criteria for valuing these inventories are extremely important, since the appreciation of stock inventories can significantly boost trading profit and vice versa. One way to increase inventory value is through the excessive allocation of direct and indirect costs and general manufacturing expenses in the valuation of finished products or work in progress. In this way, by overvaluing final inventories, year-end inventories can be increased, gross costs can be reduced and profits can subsequently be increased.

In general, companies presenting sales inventories of more than six to twelve months are at risk of the value of these inventories being revised through accounting adjustments, since there might be a high risk of obsolescence, unless these inventories are raw materials. It is also useful to consider whether increases in inventories accompany increases in turnover, or whether the inventories/sales ratio is stable in time or similar to that of comparable companies.

Acerinox

Whenever analyzing the quality of profits, it is important to consider the proportion of profits attributed to stockpiling in periods of increasing raw material prices because the recurrence of such gains is questionable. The Spanish stainless steel company Acerinox reported large profits in the period 2004–2005 due to sharp increases in the price of nickel, a key raw material in stainless steel production. Acerinox accumulated inventories and rising nickel prices were reflected in the corresponding increase in the price of stainless steel, causing the company's profit margins to burgeon. However, a change in the price cycle had the opposite impact on the company's accounts. In the fourth quarter of 2005, Acerinox announced a €45.7 million provision to adjust the value of its inventories to fair market value; as a result, Acerinox reported EBITDA of €26.1 million, compared with €72.7 million in the previous quarter.

Capitalization of expenses

Imagine a fruit store. The owner uses €100 to purchase plastic bags to deliver fruit to customers. Is the €100 outlay an expense or an investment? Something suggests that the plastic bags should be classified as an expense. If the €100 had been used to purchase a calculator, would the €100 be an expense or an investment? In this case, the calculator would be considered an investment (although it is not clear why 'something' suggests the plastic bags are an expense and the calculator an investment). Let us consider a third scenario: an intermediary brings one hundred customers to the fruit store, and we know that each customer shops at the store on average for about two years. We pay the intermediary €100 in commission, but is that an expense or an investment? Here, our sixth sense begins to fail us and we begin to doubt whether it is one thing or the other.

The golden rule for discerning whether cash outflows must be recorded as an expense or as an investment is to determine whether we expect to obtain the anticipated profit from the use of that cash before or after twelve months, where twelve months represents the accounting year. If we expect to obtain the profit within that period, the cash outflow will normally be recorded as an expense, otherwise it will be recognized as an investment. In any event, it is important to understand that the money leaves the company, but whether it is recorded as an expense or an investment could have a very important influence on the apparent progress of the company. This means that cash outflows that appear in 'grey areas', where it is initially difficult to determine whether they are expenses or investments, might be forcibly interpreted and the cash outflow could be assigned to one account or another, accordingly.

In general, cost capitalization can be detected by determining whether or not the company adopts a policy similar to that of other companies in the sector (in WorldCom it was clearly more aggressive). It is also useful to determine the market value of capitalized costs – such as direct publicity expenses. Remember to consider whether there are general accounts such as deferred assets, where these types of capitalized expenses might be hidden.

The question that we must always consider is: When is an asset an asset? Once again, the answer is that an asset is the consequence of cash outflows that expect to generate a profit beyond the applicable accounting period. WorldCom capitalized US$38,000 million as assets by breaching the standard described, since those US$38,000 million corresponded to expense items, not investments. This money was not immediately recognized on the company's profit and loss account, but appeared plurianually in the form of write-offs. Moreover, since the activated expenses were taken to income as write-offs, the EBITDA was never exposed. As a result, WorldCom improved its short-term net income and also substantially increased its EBITDA. Since market attention focused on this accounting parameter, the mass capitalization of expenses allowed WorldCom to maintain very high EBITDA although, paradoxically, it was building up negative operating cash flows. The best protection against this risk is to focus the analysis on the cash flow statement, which presents cash outflows regardless of whether these are recognized as expenses or investments. At one stage, there was so much confusion in the telecommunications industry, when it came to distinguishing expenses or investments according to the accounting system applied, that the market, in order to value telecommunications companies, decided to abandon EBITDA as a metric of company evolution and focus on operating cash flow, defined as EBITDA minus recurrent investments and variations in working capital.[8]

Amortization/depreciation policy

The subjective treatment of asset amortization, despite not representing cash outflow for the company, has meant that similar items have been written off in different periods or at different values in different countries, or even within the same country (in the US, buildings can be depreciated over 7 to 40 years). The variable used most to alter amortization is the estimated residual value of an item, since the redeemable amount is the result of the acquisition value less the residual value, the residual value being clearly subjective. Due to the laxity of accounting and tax legislation, the length of asset amortization periods can also vary enormously. In general, lengthening the useful life of assets or increasing their residual value can imply a lower amortization burden, resulting in greater profits and more recognized assets. This might entail the risk of having to adjust the value of the assets downwards in the future if auditors consider that the book value exceeds the actual value of the asset in question. The most effective way to detect abusive use of amortization is to divide the amortization expense by total amortizable assets and compare the resulting percentage with percentages of other companies in the sector.

Provisions in accounting

> During the first half of 2003, our company [Sarah Lee] completed certain restructuring activities for amounts that were less than previously reflected in the financial statements, and the recognition of these completed transactions increased pre-tax income and net income by US$ 30 million and US$ 21 million, respectively.[9]

Provisions recorded in the balance sheet are liabilities that reflect possible future cash disbursements. A provision is recorded in the profit and loss account – it is an expense that does not imply a cash outflow – and the variations in the account on the liabilities side of the balance sheet reflect disbursements. If the company ever estimates that the provisions recorded in the balance sheet exceed those that are really necessary, these provisions can be reduced, thus generating profit and vice versa. The complexity of this accounting item is that if a company records provisions valued at €4 million in one year and reduces provisions valued at €3 million in the following year, the year-to-year change in profits will be €7 million. The subjective recognition and reduction of provisions is therefore a key factor to take into account, since it will determine part of the growth in corporate profits. Provisions have normally been used to adjust the market value of inventories and accounts receivable. In the first instance, accounting standards make it obligatory to record provisions if the book value of the inventories exceeds their market value; in the latter case, provisions must be recorded if the value recorded in accounts receivable is higher than the value the company expects to recover, taking into account expected debts. In both cases, there is much room for subjectivity. As a result, companies are often guilty of over-provisioning.

Provisions have been used abusively on many occasions:[10]

1. Some companies, under strong market pressure to meet analysts' forecasts, decrease provisions more than they should in order to meet the promised earnings figure;
2. As indicated in 1998 by the then President of the SEC, Arthur Levitt, in his speech 'The Numbers Game', companies sometimes record excessive provisions in good years to create 'reserves' that they can use in bad years to mitigate fluctuations in profits.
3. Companies have often recorded large provisions just before an acquisition. In this way, the book value of the acquired company is reduced, increasing goodwill, which is amortized over a longer period than the acquired assets.[11]
4. Provisioning of expenses as 'non-recurring' and associated profits as 'recurring'. Thus, regular employee restructuring is carried out through the payment of indemnities that are treated as non-recurring, or directly charged to reserves, as Spanish banks used to do. Associated benefits – that is, a smaller personnel expenses account – are recurring. In other words, the 'bad' is non-recurring, the 'good' recurring.

There is probably no better exponent of these practices than the Canadian telecommunications company Nortel which, in October 2003, after an accounting review by an independent audit committee when it announced it was examining US$900 million of the liabilities recorded in its balance sheets as at 30 June 2003, also took advantage of this opportunity to revise net income and equity in 2000, 2001 and 2002. These variations were the result of the company's previous provision policy, aimed at concealing future payments and creating reserves for use so that the reported level of operating profit – in turn influenced by the amount of provisioned and reduced provisions – met certain pre-defined targets and also allowed its senior executives to obtain US$ multimillion bonus packages. In 2002, a very difficult year for industry since operating profit was far below the figure directors needed in order to receive their huge bonuses, the company decided to eliminate the small profit the company planned to report by recording excess provisions. In 2003, these excess provisions were reduced, thus artificially bloating profits in order to achieve the established target required to entitle directors to receive the maximum variable remuneration. Such practice was prohibited under North American accounting standards – those used by Nortel. As a consequence of this revision, the firm's managing director and chief financial officer were fired. In May 2006, the North American automobile company General Motors announced that it was changing its results for the first quarter of 2006 from a loss to a profit of US$445 million. The reason was none other than its commitment to pay US$1,000 million to its employees in the period 2006–2011 for medical benefits. The company had initially recognized this amount as a provision that quarter and deferred it over period of seven years.[12]

These practices are prohibited by international accounting standards, specifically IAS 37, which establishes very serious measures for reforming provisions accounting. A provision is defined as a 'liability of uncertain timing or amount'. Provisions should be recognized when an entity has a present obligation as a result of a past event, and they can be recorded if a future cost arises independently of the company's future shares. Therefore, if a company sells a given asset to avoid the future cost that the asset in question might generate, no provision can be initially recorded. The measures established under IAS 37 are as follows:

1. Provisions can only be recorded for past events and never for future events, if the event enabling the obligation to be met is probable – that is, more than 50 per cent probability of it occurring – and if the provisions are quantifiable and determinable;
2. The standard prohibits provisions to cover most future restructuring operations, and restricts these to highly evaluated cases;
3. The standard prohibits 'big bath' provisions, which are generic provisions for future events treated as exceptional results;

4. Provisions recorded immediately before acquisitions are prohibited; they must be recorded when the event requiring them arises;
5. The provisions for environmental risks must be recorded linearly, not gradually;
6. The standard increases provisions that must be recorded before foreseeable future losses;
7. Provisions before future repairs are prohibited.

Recognition of provisions: BMW

In 2001, the German automobile company BMW switched from the German accounting system to IFRS. As with many German companies, BMW tended to overprovision for deferred expenses in order to have a cushion for difficult years. As a consequence of the transition to IAS, BMW reduced its balance sheet provisions by €574 million or 16 per cent. In its profit and loss account, the impact of reclassifying the year 2000 from German accounting standards (HGB) to IAS produced a reduction in earnings of €485 million because BMW decreased year 2000 provisions to improve its net earnings, a practice that is prohibited by IAS.

Excessive provisioning: Nortel

In January 2005, the Canadian telecommunications company Nortel recognized that it had made mistakes in its provisions policy. During that year, Nortel identified a total of US$303 million in provisions that were not longer deemed necessary. North American accounting standards, which were used by Nortel used in its financial reporting, establish that if excessive provisions are identified, they must be reduced by increasing profits. However, Nortel's accountants decided not to perform this operation and instead maintained these provisions in the company's balance sheet as a reserve for a quarter in which the company would have difficulty in meeting analysts' forecasts.[13]

Restructuring provisions: Crédit Agricole

IAS 3 prohibits the recognition of provisions recorded for restructuring purposes during acquisition processes in order to improve profits after acquisition. By recognizing acquisition provisions, the net value of assets acquired can be reduced and the value of goodwill subsequently increased. This provision did not have an immediate impact on the profit and loss account, but its recognition was accompanied by amortizing goodwill, which in the past was amortized over twenty years. IAS 3 stipulates that expected costs of the restructuring of an acquired entity must be treated as costs after acquisition unless the acquired entity had a pre-existing liability for restructuring, as established in IAS 37 'Provisions, Contingent Liabilities and Contingent Assets'.

In 2003, Crédit Agricole applied French accounting regulations governing acquisitions when it took over Crédit Lyonnais. In its 2003 annual report, Crédit Agricole reported that it had recorded a €836 million restructuring provision for the acquisition of Crédit Lyonnais. Of this amount, €304 million had been recorded as a provision in Crédit Agricole's profit and loss account and €532 million as a liability for restructuring in Crédit Lyonnais as part of the transaction. Thus, Crédit Agricole was able to incur expenses after the acquisition of up to €532 million without this affecting its profit and loss account; hence, the comparison of figures before and after the acquisition would presumably be highly favourable. If it had applied IAS 3, it would not have been able to record this figure of €532 million as a provision before the acquisition was completed.[14]

Expenses taken to equity: the case of Spanish banks

For many years, Spanish banks were characterized by having much better efficiency ratios (costs divided by revenues) than other European banks. In 2003, the Bank of Spain allowed banks to offer certain employees the opportunity to take retirement earlier than established in the applicable collective labour agreement. The net effect of this accounting treatment consisted of withdrawing all costs associated with these employees in the profit and loss account from the moment the employees accepted early retirement, even if they continued to work in the interim. These expenses were transferred to a provision equivalent to the expenses that this future employment would generate, and this provision was in turn adjusted to equity. By reducing corporate equity, banks were able to increase their ROE. In 2004, the Bank of Spain prohibited this accounting treatment. From 1999 to 2004, Banco de Santander recorded provisions for this item equivalent to €6,300 million, BBVA €4,400 million, Banco Popular €641 million and Banco Sabadell €116 million.[15]

Recognizing amortization/depreciation

From an accounting perspective, amortization must be calculated systematically according to the useful life of the assets in question. Although various accounting systems provide amortization tables for calculating the useful life of goods according to their nature, these tables normally establish maximum and minimum percentages, leaving room for certain variations in the recognition of amortization expenses. The accelerated depreciation of goods is sometimes permitted, and this is a new source of potential variation in recognized earnings.

IAS 16 stipulates that residual values used to estimate amortization rates must be reviewed regularly. In spite of the fact that amortization is a non-accountable charge, its importance is enormous, since higher amortization rates reduces earnings, increasing the P/E ratio multiple. The redeemable amount of a good is equivalent to the value of the asset (historical cost or revaluation value, where appropriate), less the residual value. In the case of buildings, the residual value is crucial for determining the annual depreciation charge. The residual value must be equivalent to the estimated amount, and would be obtained from the sale of the building at the end of its useful life. The new rule introduced by IAS 16 stems from the fact that, under European national accounting systems, the residual value is normally determined according to the value of the asset at the time of acquisition or valuation, rather than being reviewed periodically as established in IAS 16.[16]

Amortization of licences: Vodafone

Another important component of amortization accounting is intangible assets. If we look at the methods used to amortize mobile telecommunications operating licences, the adoption of IAS has brought about important changes. Vodafone has second- and third-generation licenses for developing its activities. The company paid £15,000 million sterling to purchase third-generation licences and recorded this amount in its balance sheets as intangible assets. The adoption of IAS forced Vodafone to amortize these licenses on a straight-line basis, whereas previously it had amortized them in accordance with UK accounting standards; that is, according to network usage, which meant that the slower adoption of technology also resulted in slower amortization rates. As a result of this accounting change, Vodafone's amortization expense increased in 2005 by £244 million pounds.[17]

Extraordinary items

Only a plant hit by a meteorite is considered extraordinary.[18]

In the December 2003 revision of IAS 1, the IASB[19] withdrew the concept of 'extraordinary' items. Until then, extraordinary items referred to earnings or expenses originating from events or operations that were clearly different to the company's ordinary purpose and, therefore, were not expected to re-occur in the future. The IASB prohibited references to 'extraordinary' items due to the abusive use of this term by many companies that, in practice, tended to present anything positive in their profit and loss accounts as 'ordinary', in spite of the fact that their recurrence was questionable, and anything negative as 'extraordinary', even though these items were often recurrent expenses such as severance pay. In spite of everything, IAS 1 allows certain items to be separated from the profit and loss account without referring to them as 'extraordinary'. It is up to companies and their auditors whether these items are recognized if they believe that they could be useful to the financial community. Although they do not have a defined name, terms such as 'exceptional', 'one-offs', 'non-recurring' or 'abnormal' are employed, and they are used frequently when reporting on unusual amortizations of assets, restructuring charges, asset disposals, important legal indemnities and withdrawal of provisions.[20] Many companies have also often not treated extraordinary sales as such, recognizing earnings as non-recurrent income, but charged all sales to the 'other income' account, with the subsequent positive impact on operating accounts.

In line with international accounting standards, North American accounting regulations, by means of FAS 146, limit much abuse committed in relation to the classification of ordinary and extraordinary income. In general, it stipulates that extraordinary items can only be recognized near the time when the payment in question is expected to be made, thus limiting abuse consisting of recording large extraordinary items much earlier than the expected disbursements. For example, if a staff-restructuring provision is recorded, there must be a clear commitment to restructure the workforce and, if the firm engages regularly in this practice (recognizing lay-off provisions as non-recurrent and savings of lay-off expenses as recurrent), the provisions will be reclassified as recurrent. Moreover, if the company expects to incur costs relating to the physical transfer of assets or personnel, these will only be recognized when the income associated with that decision is obtained, and never before.[21] In general, the best recommendation for determining whether a series of expense or income items are recurrent or non-recurrent is to perform a historical review. If a company systematically records extraordinary losses in similar amounts, the best option is to reclassify them as ordinary losses.

'Pro forma' accounts and dilution of earnings-per-share: Procter & Gamble

'Pro forma' accounts are accounts in which a company extracts items it considers to be 'non-recurrent' to facilitate inter-annual comparisons. The danger is that this practice is very subjective, and 'pro forma' accounts are normally used exclusively to remove losses and never income. Such was the abuse of this technique that the SEC was forced to issue the 'Q' regulation in 2002, which made it obligatory for companies always to inform the market profit number per 'pro forma' share earnings using the format, including the size of font of the letters used in the communication, which had to be the same as the one used to indicate book earnings-per-share. Companies were also required to reconcile both earnings per share in detail so that the market could determine whether or not these items had been correctly excluded.

'Pro forma' accounts are also known (sarcastically) as 'earnings without bad stuff', in reference to the subjectivity inherent in the inclusion and exclusion of certain items in 'pro forma' accounts. For example, when Telepizza offered 'pro forma' figures for the evolution of its business in 2000, it excluded the restaurants it had opened in France (which were a complete failure); the Spanish media company Recoletos, in its 2001 figures, presented 'pro forma' accounts excluding its Argentine activities, which were immersed in a fiasco that affected all Argentina that year.

Forecasts are normally presented to the market in the form of estimated earnings-per-share, which the company expects to obtain in a specific quarter or year. It is important to specify here that earnings per share can be calculated in a 'basic' or 'diluted' manner. The basic form is very simple and consists of dividing earnings by the number of shares issued. However, it has no economic relevance: if company A controls 95 per cent of company B and the latter owns 5 per cent of treasury stock, in practical terms company A owns 100 per cent of company B. However, if company B has issued convertible bonds, stock options and/or warrants on company B's stock, company A's real stake in company B could actually be smaller. Therefore, the calculation of diluted earnings consists of increasing the number of shares issued by the expected conversion of the convertible bond and by possible share issues resulting from the conversion of options and/or warrants, and reducing the number of shares by the number of own shares. The first three adjustments (convertible bonds, options and/or warrants) are difficult to calculate, and it is normal for companies to present the number of shares in diluted form.

The North American consumer goods company Procter & Gamble came up with the concept of 'diluted net earnings'. It excluded the firm's restructuring costs, personnel lay-off expenses and reductions in the value of assets subject to restructuring, under its so-called 'Organization 2005' plan. In 1998, the company's earnings per share were US$2.07 per share, but the earnings announcement was important for the information on core earnings per share, according to Procter & Gamble's definition, which stood at US$3.12. Procter & Gamble used the described techniques to overestimate restructuring provisions and thus create a 'cushion' to increase future earnings. Furthermore, the accelerated depreciation of assets subject to restructuring offered the necessary media coverage to justify the massive labour force restructuring, which affected 6,000 jobs. Thus, in 1998 the company's net profit, taking into consideration these amortizations, was reduced year-against-year by 6 per cent, while its operating cash flow increased by 24 per cent.

Capitalization of expenses

In general, when dealing with the problem of the capitalization of expenses, consideration must be given to two conflicting accounting principles: the principle of prudence, and the principle of matching income and expenses. According to the former, costs should be charged to income as they are incurred, while the latter considers that these costs must be capitalized while they are able to generate income. Let us look at the problems associated with this dilemma.

Indirect asset production costs could be allocated as assets under certain accounting systems if the production cost components include the part reasonably corresponding to the costs indirectly attributable to the goods in question. Thus, if we want to increase profits, more indirect costs will be allocated to assets and vice versa.

In many accounting systems, interest on loans taken out to finance fixed asset production costs can be capitalized. This permissiveness is justified on the grounds that the cost of loans obtained to finance the production of assets is no different to other production costs. On the one hand, according to the principle of matching income and expenses, interest costs must correspond to future income that is only generated when the asset in production starts to be used. However, there are powerful arguments against the capitalization of financial expenses. It is pointless for the cost of an asset to vary according to whether its production has been financed with equity or debt. On the other hand, when expenses have been fully amortized, the information contained in the financial expense account will be distorted. Critical variables, such as interest coverage, might also be seriously affected if the capitalization of financial expenses is permitted.

Areas where capitalization of expenses can be identified

Self-manufactured assets. These are intangible assets, such as software, or tangible assets, such as real estate assets. When a company manufactures an asset internally, it must take decisions on which expenses to capitalize. These costs would normally be incremental costs that would not have been incurred if the assets had not been manufactured, but the incremental cost concept differs from country to country.

Start-up expenses. In certain countries these expenses can be capitalized, even though they are not strictly assets. With the introduction of international accounting standards, this problem has been reduced substantially by prohibiting the capitalization of start-up expenses. The Spanish cable company ONO was authorized to capitalize costs such as organization, consultancy, contracting, training or publicity expenses, which were defined as 'pre-maturity' expenses to be amortized in five years after the start-up of business. In 2002, the company changed this criterion and began to apply the accrual principle, giving rise to an extraordinary item of €140 million.

Real estate investment vehicles. These companies have capitalized asset acquisition costs, sometimes including losses incurred immediately after the transaction.

Assets that can be divided into different components (multi-element assets). There is the risk that expenses incurred in relation to multi-element assets could be amortized over longer periods than is natural. For example, if a building is depreciated over 50 years and its elevator over 10 years, the cost of the elevator could be capitalized by adding its value to that of the building, and amortized in 50 years.

Incident acquisition costs: legal costs, counselling expenses, and so on. Maintenance expenses. These must only be capitalized if they create value for the associated asset; if they are simply incurred to maintain the asset in good condition, they must be treated as an expense.

Questions to consider in relation to the capitalization of expenses:

- Does the company have a clear policy regarding the assets that should be capitalized in acquisitions and in self-manufactured assets manufactured assets?
- What criterion should be used with respect to the capitalization period?
- What is the annual figure for investment in maintenance?
- Has the company recently changed its accounting policy on the capitalization of acquisition expenses?
- Are short-term assets capitalized?
- Are costs broken down by components? If so, are they amortized differently? If not, what happens when the component is replaced?
- Is in-house work assigned as a general cost allocatable to a capitalized asset?[22]

Research and development costs: EADS

One of the interesting differences between the UK and different European accounting systems and the US system is the way in which research and development expenses are treated. In the US, all such expenses must be written off when they are incurred, whereas in Spain and in the United Kingdom they can sometimes be capitalized and consequently amortized.

IAS 38, 'Intangible Assets', prescribes the treatment of the capitalization of research and development expenses. It requires companies to consider all research-related disbursements as expenses and only allows development costs to be capitalized as intangible assets. The difference lies in the moment when it is economically feasible for a company to expect to recover such costs – for example, the registration of a patent – and also the cost of the asset can be adequately measured. The aeronautical company EADS incurs €2,000 million in R&D expenses every year. The switch to IAS benefited EADS because it was able to treat a larger volume as assets than it would have been able to under the old accounting standards. As a consequence of this accounting change, in 2004 the company's forecast for operating income increased by €100 million.

Deferred tax assets and liabilities

Deferred tax assets and liabilities arise as a consequence of timing differences between when taxes are paid and when they are recognized. These differences are due to a disparity between financial accounting and tax accounting. For example, if a company records a restructuring provision to cover expected future severance payments such a provision might represent an expense for financial accounting purposes. For tax accounting purposes, it will only become an expense once the payments are made. The problem is therefore temporary and not permanent. Once a transaction has been recognized in financial and tax accounting, these assets or liabilities should disappear.[23]

Sometimes these assets arise as a consequence of losses generated by a company, and these losses could create a tax shield if it is expected that they can be offset against future income. In these cases, the loss is reduced by the amount of the tax shield, thus generating 'tax income', which is actually not a cash inflow. The accounting benefit of the tax shield simply has to be recognized currently. The inflow produces a tax asset, which must be written off as income generated in the future, and which will gradually reduce the value of the asset until the negative tax base has been fully utilized. The problem with these assets is that their quantification is very subjective; in order to recognize them, there must be a strong likelihood that sufficient income will be generated to use the tax shield before these negative tax bases expire, and this period will depend on local tax regulations. Sometimes, these assets can never be used and the amount of these assets must be reduced by means of an extraordinary loss. For example, the North American technology company Sun Microsystems recorded debt in this respect in 2003, thus diminishing its deferred tax assets by US$1 billion and reducing its corporate equity by a similar amount. The problem, as always, is that taxable income, when recognized, is ordinary; when companies acknowledge that they cannot use this income, it becomes extraordinary. In general, both the IAS and North American accounting standards, specifically FAS 109, recognize these tax bases as assets if there is more than a 50 per cent chance that sufficient income can be generated in the future to take advantage of these assets.

In summary, although the 'tax' balance in a profit and loss account is normally negative, thus reducing pre-tax income, some companies present positive 'tax' balances, as if the Inland Revenue had paid them money. In these cases, the companies do not actually receive any money, but companies reporting losses reduce their volume by anticipating the tax shield which concedes having lost money, because when the company receives this money, it can normally offset past losses and thus not pay tax until the accumulated losses have been written off. For example, if a company's pre-tax loss is €100 million and it expects to obtain income in the future to offset tax shields recognized currently, it could declare 'tax income' of €33 million, and hence its net income would be a loss of €64 million. The counter item on the asset side of the balance sheet of the €33 million in 'income' is an account that entitles the company to tax receivables equivalent to the total amount of tax income recognized by the company. Once the company earns money, it will not pay anything to the Inland Revenue until the negative tax bases have been used up. However, if these are recognized on the balance sheet, it will simulate an accounting payment, thus reducing the 'negative tax base' asset until it disappears. Thereafter, normal accounting treatment will be applied.

In such cases, it should be borne in mind that the accounting principle of prudence requires these 'assets' to be recognized if we are uncertain that the company will obtain future earnings that can offset these on-balance-sheet tax bases, since the Inland Revenue only allows such losses to be used as tax shields for a finite number of years. International accounting standards only allow these tax bases to be capitalized if the likelihood of obtaining sufficient income for all the tax bases to be used before they expire is greater than 50 per cent. However, the temptation for companies experiencing difficulties to reduce the declared volume of losses using this technique is overwhelming because, by reducing losses, they also reduce the impact these have by reducing equity, which could avoid painful measures such as capital increases.

Overcapitalization of tax shields: Spanair

At the beginning of this book we described how the airline company Spanair used this technique to record €97 million as tax assets based on future forecasts. After an audit by its parent company, of the €97 million €44 million were considered to have been recognized incorrectly. The corresponding adjustment was applied, consisting in their elimination with a resulting reduction in corporate equity in the same amount.[24]

It is sometimes crucial to examine the amount of unpaid tax credits on the asset side of a company's balance sheet because these might even exceed equity. Therefore, if the auditor determines that the current operating income does not coincide with the forecasts on which the tax shields were recognized, this could lead to the partial or total amortization of these tax bases and the subsequent bankruptcy of the company unless the shareholders agree to increase capital. For example, the telecommunications network construction company Avánzit recognized €62 million in unpaid tax credits in 2001, equivalent to 28 per cent of its equity of €228 million, while the company was immersed in a serious crisis that prevented it from meeting its business targets, thus putting into doubt the value of its tax shields. Eventually, the company was forced to implement an important restructuring plan.

In certain cases, a deferred tax liability is created, the result of recognizing benefits in financial accounting that have not yet been reported to the tax authorities. For example, if company A owns 1,000 shares in another listed company that have been acquired at €100 each, and in one year the price of the shares increases to €150, company A will have obtained a profit of €50,000 under IFRS regulations. However, no tax will be payable on these shares until they are sold, thus giving rise to a deferred tax liability.

Companies sometimes record large provisions for expected future tax liabilities. These tax provisions are treated as extraordinary items. They grow in size in order to be reduced in the future and thus generate stronger earnings increases. On other occasions, firms decide that they will not be able to use tax assets and instead record extraordinary provisions to write them off completely. However, this amortization could be exaggerated, as revealed in subsequent years when the inherent impact of improving net earnings by reducing tax liabilities becomes evident. Of course, in this case the profit achieved in this way is treated as 'ordinary'.

Pernod Ricard

The French beverages company Pernod Ricard reported a 20 per cent decrease in equity of €384 million in its 2004 first quarter results as a consequence of a deferred tax liability, resulting from the acquisition of certain brands of beverages. The capitalization of their market value had produced income that revealed the existence of a tax liability corresponding to the tax payable if the brands were ever sold. However, Pernod Ricard claimed that this situation was unfair, and argued that since these brands were part of its main corporate purpose and were not available for sale, it had provisioned the tax liability despite the fact that these brands would perhaps never be sold and, therefore, the taxes never paid.[25]

Alteration of short-term assets

Since creditors often ask companies to whom they lend money to have short-term[26] debt ratios that never exceed a maximum of 1.5, companies that are close to this limit, in order to avoid the penalty clauses applicable if they fail to comply with this requirement, reclassify long-term assets – such as financial investments which, theoretically, cannot be sold in less than twelve months – as short-term assets and thus avoid infringing the imposed limit. The lesson to be drawn from this practice is the importance of performing detailed examinations of companies with very high short-term debt ratios in order to determine the extent to which many assets declared as 'short-term' are, in fact, short-term.[27]

Recognition of reserves: Royal Dutch Shell and Repsol

A key element for valuing companies in the raw materials sector is the level of reserves. This concept is particularly relevant in the oil industry. On 9 February 2004, the Anglo-Dutch company Royal Dutch Shell reclassified 3.9 million barrels, 20 per cent of its total reserves, from 'proven' to 'probable'. Although this may seem to be a semantic issue, the difference is crucial; in order for a barrel from reserves to be classified as 'proven', the field to which it belongs must currently be in production and the reserve must be shown to be economically and legally producible under existing conditions. If these requirements are not fulfilled, the reserves will be considered 'probable'. Oil investors keep a close eye on 'proven' reserves because they allow them to calculate reserve replacement; that is, the volume of reserves required to maintain current production levels, and thus reliably estimate future production volume. Therefore, Royal Dutch Shell was severely punished by the stock market on the date of their announcement, and received notice of a fine of US$150 million from the SEC.

Repsol accounted for reserves in a different way, as revealed publicly in 2006. In January that year, Repsol announced that it would reduce its proven oil reserves 25 per cent by 1,254 million barrels, thus reducing its total reserves to 3,330 million barrels. The year before it had recognized 4,925 million barrels and two years previously 5,433 million barrels. The announcement caused its shares to plummet 8 per cent that same day. Of the reduced barrels, 509 million corresponded to its Argentine subsidiary, YPF, since it had recognized as own reserves barrels that actually belonged to the Argentine state in wells that were exploited by Repsol, while the remainder corresponded to its Bolivian assets, following the decree nationalizing hydrocarbon assets promoted by the Evo Morales government.[28] The SEC investigated this reduction in reserves – since Repsol owned securities listed on the New York stock market – and the case is now settled.

Pension funds

There have been many cases of the manipulation in pension fund accounting, especially in countries where pension fund commitments have traditionally not be externalized; namely, the US, UK and Germany. To simplify, internal pension funds, or promises made by companies to their employees on future pensions, can be divided into two categories:

- Contribution systems, in which contributions are made to the fund each year and the result of this investment is the amount received by the employee upon retirement.
- Benefit systems, where the company guarantees the amount received at retirement.

The benefit system is the most problematic because companies must assume various hypotheses in order to account for this promise. On the one hand, they must discount the future commitment currently, and the rate at which they discount that future income is crucial for determining current liabilities. Furthermore, the amount of money the company provisions currently to cover future pension commitments is normally accounted for in accordance with actuarial and not market criteria. For example, if a company has invested €100,000 in variable income securities to cover an amount payable in the future at the beginning of 2002, and during that year the stock market falls 20 per cent, accounting logic suggests that the recognized assets will be €80,000. However, actuarial logic imposes itself and at year-end assets valued at €108,000 are recognized because actuarial principles dictate that the long-term variable income can generate an annual return of 8 per cent. The opposite is also plausible. If the company has invested in shares or bonds and stock market or bond market prices increase above estimated returns, then only the actuarial return is recognized in order to isolate a long-term component from variations in short-term returns. As the long-term returns expected by actuaries are larger in variable-income than in fixed-income instruments, companies were encouraged to assign very high percentages of funds to variable-income securities. With the 2001–2002 stock market crisis, this questionable accounting practice revealed that recognized assets were far higher than the actual value of the provisioned pension funds, prompting accounting regulators to react. Since then, both international and North American accounting standards make it obligatory for companies to present, even in footnote form, information on the market value of assets so that investors can compare differentials with book values. The problem had been so flagrant that during 2001, a year of significant stock market crashes, 237 companies listed on the S&P 500 assumed returns on internal pension fund assets above 9 per cent with, on average, two thirds invested in variable-income instruments and one third invested in fixed-income instruments.[29]

The second problem concerns the discount rate applied to future pension commitments. Companies normally apply very high discount rates to reduce the current value of pension liabilities. However, the accounting legislator considered that it was not very reasonable for a company financed at, for example, 5 per cent on the bond market to deduct employee pension contributions at, say, 9 per cent. The difference could mean that companies would recognize currently less money than they actually owed. The reform of UK accounting standards first, and then North American and international accounting standards, forced companies to discount these future flows at a discount rate equivalent to the highest quality bonds they had issued. This substantially increased the current recognized values of liabilities. The difference between that amount and the actual value of pension fund assets gives the value of the corresponding deficit (or surplus), which companies have been required to disclose since 2003. Financial authorities monitor the size of this value very closely. For example, a company with €3,000 million in debts and an unrecognized internal pension fund deficit of €1,000 million is valued as if its real debts were €4,000 million because the deficit of this fund is basically nothing other than a debt payable to employees. It would be frightening to think what would happen to government debt securities if the same criterion applicable to companies were applied to the social security system.

Cash flow

Cash flow statements are considered to be a useful source for validating the quality of earnings or assets declared by companies. For example, if a firm reports low profits, it can always renegotiate the terms of payment with its suppliers, reducing payment periods in exchange for discounts on the prices paid for raw materials. Although it is able to declare better profits, its working capital worsens, as would be revealed from a simple examination of its balance sheet. If the company is burdened by high debt, it could renegotiate the payment terms with its suppliers, extending these payment periods in exchange for higher prices on supplies. Once again, the balance sheet would show that the improvement in working capital is reflected in the profit and loss account by a deterioration of earnings. Cash flow statements are useful because they show us these alterations as cash inflows and outflows, organized according to their nature; that is, operating, investment or financing cash flows.

In different accounting systems, it was not obligatory for companies to present statements of changes in financial position or cash flow statements, and certain companies took advantage of this to avoid providing information on a key financial statement in modern business. However, with the introduction of international accounting standards, cash flow statements have become obligatory. A cash flow statement explains the cash inflows and outflows of a company and reconciles these with the final cash recorded in the company's balance sheet. In other words, it is a mathematical reconciliation that, in principle, cannot be altered using creative accounting techniques. However, these financial statements must be examined meticulously because many companies, aware that investors focus on operating cash flow (cash inflows and outflows resulting from normal corporate activity before investments), reclassify operating cash outflows as if they were investments.[30] This boosts operating cash flow, which in turn increases cash outflows from the investment cash flow account. Thus, if a company obtains an operating cash flow of €100,000 with a factory, the factory requires machinery repairs valued at €20,000 and the company also builds a second factory for a total sum of €75,000, then the operating cash flow will be €80,000, the investment cash flow – €75,000 and the sum of both, or free cash flow, €5,000. However, the company can reclassify the €20,000 corresponding to maintenance repairs as investment cash flow, thus increasing operating cash flow to €100,000. This practice is incorrect and unethical but is frequently used by companies. Hence, the most useful variable to monitor in a statement of changes in financial position is operating free cash flow, equivalent to free cash flow less non-recurrent investments. In the previous example, the free cash flow of €5,000 would have to be added to the €75,000 invested in the construction of the second factory, since this is a non-recurrent process. Therefore, free operating cash flow would be €80,000 and this variable would be a good starting point for examining the cash generating potential of the company in question. Another common technique consists of classifying sales of operating assets as operating cash flow when this is, in fact, investment cash flow.

Statements of changes in financial position are crucial for studying the evolution of corporate business. The obligation for companies to present these statements following the adoption of the IFRS is very welcome. Nevertheless, the quality of cash flow statements can be improved. 'Indirect' systems for presenting cash flow statements are permitted in the US and in Europe. Under these systems, the differences between net profit and cash flow must be presented. However, they do not require companies to specify each non-cash item that is not cash and changes in liabilities are not considered. Thus, the acquisition of a screen company with high debt does not necessarily have to appear on a cash flow statement. However, under a direct system, which starts with EBITDA and gradually lists each item that affects cash flow from taxes actually paid to variations in net debt, the information provided is much more valuable and harder to manipulate.

Delphi

The chief financial officer of the automobile components company Delphi was accused of manipulating the company's cash flow account. The SEC considered that Delphi had received a loan in December 2000 for US$200 million from Bank One as if it were for a sale of precious metals. This loan was recorded by Delphi in its operating cash flow account, which totalled US$268 million in 2000 – far better than the rest of the sector, which was experimenting strong losses: real operating cash flow was only US$68 million, but the loan, instead of being recognized as a liability, was recorded as a sale contract that increased cash flow. Obviously, the sale was subject to a repurchase agreement, pursuant to which Delphi had to repurchase the metals from Bank One in January. By altering its accounts, the company was able to alter its cash flow in 2000 by US$200 million, and its net profit by 60 million in 1999 and 16 million in 2000.[31]

Case study: accounting in the film industry

The film industry in the 1980s and early 1990s was perceived as a cauldron of accounting abuse, largely due to the specific accounting system applicable to this industry because film production and post-production processes tended to be completed in different accounting years. Different types of abuse were committed. On the one hand, the capitalization of advertising expenses was legal, unlike in most industries. Production companies also had a tendency to inflate the value of assets, giving rise to extraordinary items when it was discovered that these items had not been recognized. These abusive accounting practices forced many production companies into bankruptcy or close to bankruptcy, notable cases being Cannon, Orion Pictures or Carolco. The applicable regulation was FAS 53, which attempted to develop an amortization system for films based not on movies as a whole but, rather, on each individual film. The future revenues and expenses of each film had to be estimated assuming constant income, and the film would be amortized in proportion to the ratio of annual earnings divided by expected total earnings. Publicity could be capitalized and amortized using the same criterion. The problem was that around 60 per cent of film industry costs were amortizations, while in other industries this expense ranged between 5 per cent and 10 per cent. Also, if 75 per cent of a film's earnings were obtained in year 1, profits were concentrated in the short term and could give rise to extraordinary liabilities in the mid-term. Since the estimation of long-term earnings was very subjective, the future worth of movies was sometimes overvalued, and this gave rise to great insecurity from an accounting standpoint. In order to remedy this situation, the North American accounting authorities proposed modifications to the system for estimating income by prohibiting the inclusion of sales estimates in new markets or through new technologies. Costs would also be adjusted by prohibiting the capitalization of distribution expenses and by promoting information on the criteria for allocating the indirect costs of each film. Finally, the maximum period for amortizing films was limited to ten years.[32]

Case study: the American International Group (AIG) accounting scandal

In February 2006, the North American insurance company AIG announced that it would pay a fine of US$1,500 million to conclude litigation instigated by the North American Accounting Standards Board and the New York District Attorney's Office in relation to the accounting scandal involving the company in the period 2000–2001. AIG had concluded finite reinsurance transactions with General Re in the fourth quarter of 2000 and the first quarter of 2001 in order to simulate improvements in its reserve position amounting to US$500 million, in spite of the fact that these could not be classified as insurance transactions because they were accounting operations, since the risk was not transferred. The company carried out this operation, which increased reserves through a €500 million increase in premiums, because analysts had criticized AIG's weak reserves position in the third quarter of 2000. AIG transformed operating losses in the form of deficits amounting to US$200 million, which it transferred to Capco, an insurer based in Barbados, and transferred life insurance policies to 'different items' in order to reduce the profitability ratio of this 'different items' account, known as combined ratio.[33] The scandal cost AIG the loss of US$58,000 million in stock market value.

Accounting scandals involving insurers are not new. In fact, accounting in this sector is especially subjective, which might explain why investors tend to apply discounts to insurance valuation multiples. This subjectivity is particular rife in the case of embedded value figures or the volume of earnings companies expect to obtain in the future with life insurance policies; future profits might be spread out over decades and therefore easily susceptible to manipulation.[34]

Conclusion

This chapter has presented various recommendations on the improvement of financial reporting in different areas. Recurrent and non-recurrent aspects must be clearly separated from operating and non-operating aspects. Non-recurrent adjustments to pension funds should be identified separately. These tend to reflect the performance of pension funds and not the operative performance of the company. Profits and losses resulting from sales of non-recurrent assets must be identified separately. Earnings from sales of real estate assets are often included in the operating section of income statements despite not actually being operating profits. Companies that incur losses from asset sales try to sell other assets to compensate for these losses and only report the net income. Companies are therefore advised to report the results of all significant asset sale transactions. Detailed information on operating income, operating capital used and operating cash flows broken down by business unit is critical for making reliable forecasts on the evolution of each component, particularly nowadays when companies are characterized by their complexity. Companies in the US have been obliged to present this information annually since 1977. This became obligatory for European companies following the application of IFRS in 2005. Nevertheless, it is important to highlight that divisional information is normally not audited.[35] Companies must also report on changes resulting from acquisitions and currency variations in order to identify organic growth and provide more reliable information on their future growth potential. Claims that reporting this information would be too costly to companies is unconvincing because companies are required to keep virtually all this information for internal accounting purposes.[36]

It is also important to consider the pitfalls of the concept of EBITDA highlighted in this book. Director remuneration has sometimes been linked to the evolution of EBITDA, as in the case of the French company Universal Vivendi when Jean Marie Messier was Chairman and CEO. The accounting subjectivity of EBITDA is such that it is extremely dangerous to treat it as an acceptable variable for the creation of value, and exaggerated references to its evolution by executives raise eyebrows. In general, the best way to gauge the quality of EBITDA is to compare it with operating cash flow. For example, according to results reported by the Spanish utility company Endesa, 2005 was a record year. The company's EBITDA climbed to €6,020 million. However, operating cash flow was only €3,362 million because Endesa included tariff deficit income in EBITDA, which it will have to obtain from the government in the future. As a result, this was not calculated for 2005 cash flow purposes. In any event, it should not be forgotten that companies with larger volumes of debt tend to use more aggressive accounting methods. For example, the financial leverage of the Spanish telecommunications operator Jazztel reached 74 per cent in 2001. However, the company had off-balance-sheet commitments totalling €34.6 million, debt guaranties of €93.1 million and capitalized tax bases of €35.9 million; if these three items had been adjusted, they would have increased recognized leverage substantially. In any event, in particularly dramatic circumstances adjustment becomes inevitable. Jazztel was forced to exchange a substantial amount of debt for shares in 2002 in order to recapitalize the company.

With regard to asset valuation adjustments, which might be performed if the accounting value of an asset is greater than its actual value according to the discounted cash flows the asset in question is expected to generate, we should always be very sceptical. The market value of assets is a very subjective question, and this subjectivity eventually means that directors of struggling companies take advantage of this subjectivity to avoid having to reduce the value of assets through losses. In contrast, directors who have recently joined struggling companies use this subjectivity differently, by maximizing immediate losses to reduce assets to a possible minimum, since this reduction also entails a reduction in equity. Even if the company's new directors do not improve a small fraction of corporate earnings, by reducing the volume of equity, the actual value of return-on-equity ratio will increase simply as a consequence of this new accounting entry.

Another extremely important variable is earnings quality because companies reporting quality profits benefits normally display better mid-term performance on the stock market than firms with lower quality earnings, where quality is the differential between pro forma and book income. If we were to group the 50 securities with the best quality earnings and the 50 securities with the lowest quality earnings in the period 1998–2003, the first group would have grown annually by 12.3 per cent, compared with zero per cent in the case of the second group. The main factor explaining this effect is the fact that extraordinary losses, which are excluded from pro forma earnings, are often actually ordinary losses, thus reducing future earnings contrary to expectations, resulting in disappointing stock market reactions.[37]

In general, earnings quality must be determined taking into account aspects such as the underlying cash flows inherent to the earnings, amount of off-balance-sheet finance which could be understating financial costs or earnings apparently generated by questionable pension fund accounting. In 2001, 20 per cent of the profits of S&P 500 companies originated from the wild actuarial hypothesis that returns theretically obtained on pension fund assets exceeded the cost associated with pension commitments promised to employees (9.5 per cent compared with 7.25 per cent, respectively), which is paradoxical in a year when the stock market was sinking but, 'actuarially' speaking, investments in shares continued to yield profits.[38]

6

Subjectivity in the Consolidation of Companies

Beware of false prophets who suggest that you can appraise mergers just on the basis of their immediate impact on earnings per share.
Richard A. Brealey and Stewart C. Myers, *Capital Investment and Valuation*, Brattle Group, 2002, p. 462

Mergers and acquisitions dominated business in the period 1998–2001, and are very much back in the limelight again today. These operations give rise to an accounting problem that should be analyzed in detail if scandals such as those that appeared after the first wave of mergers and acquisitions are to be avoided, and which were due to excessive prices paid by many companies and the perverse accounting of such acquisitions. Before analyzing the causes, we must look at the facts. In a study of 3,688 North American firms involved in acquisitions in the period 1973–1998, it was deduced that the returns obtained on the shares of acquired companies averaged 16 per cent. The average higher-than-market return offered by acquiring companies was only 0.7 per cent. In Europe, a study was performed with a sample of 228 companies in the period 1993–2000. The acquired companies' returns averaged 9 per cent. The acquiring firms reported average returns of 0.7 per cent, as in the sample of North American companies. In other words, acquisitions do not normally create value. Attempts are often made to create value not as the result of integration in itself, but as the result of accounting trickery. Corporate transactions are almost always presented as having a positive or negative impact on earnings-per-share (EPS). If the impact is positive, firms tend to report the beneficial aspects of the operation. However, these are nothing more than optical illusions. If company A has a P/E ratio of 20 and acquires company B, which has a P/E ratio of 10, the acquisition will enhance earnings-per-share. But does that mean that it creates value? Not at all. Company B has a P/E ratio of 10 because it is a worse company than company A or because the market in which it operates is less attractive. The new group must not have an earnings-per-share ratio of 20 but a multiple between 10 and 20. Therefore, economically speaking the positive or negative impact these operations have on EPS, and which the market is so obsessed about, is completely irrelevant. Telefónica places much emphasis on EPS enhancement in acquisitions, yet this does not make sense. If Telefónica, trading at 13 times price earning, acquires a mining company trading at six times, the deal would be accretive, but would it add value?

Part of the accounting problem associated with company acquisitions is the flexibility that has characterized the way in which the market value of acquired assets is determined. When a company acquires another company, using the acquisition method, the acquiring company updates the book value of the acquired company by adjusting the market value of its assets. The difference between the price paid and the adjusted book value is referred to as 'goodwill'. However, the concept of the market value of acquired assets is immediately subjective: many companies exploit this subjectivity skilfully to alter their accounts. For example, the Finnish paper group UPM Kymmene revalued its forests after applying IFRS standards and thus boosted its earnings.[1] The problem is that the useful life of a tree is 70 years; therefore, the cash flow discounts expected to be obtained from that tree would have been very subjective. UPM's own chief financial officer, Kari Toikka, criticized this accounting measure of valuing forests on the basis of cash flows discounts over 70 years, instead of recognizing the value paid and invested in these trees: 'An old accountant like me sometimes asks: does it all make sense? What does the balance sheet now show?'[2]

Until very recently, goodwill was amortized on a straight-line basis and it was realized over a more or less long timespan (normally 20–40 years); companies were encouraged to reduce the values of acquired assets as much as possible. This allowed them to reduce the future depreciation of fixed assets, typically redeemable in shorter periods of time than goodwill, thus boosting profits. Companies also recorded large restructuring provisions as cover for future payments potentially arising from the integration of companies, such as severance payments. Since these provisions were treated as 'extraordinary' items, analysts tended to exclude them when calculating earnings-per-share. Of course, the cost savings generated by lay-offs were treated as 'ordinary' items. Companies also tended to over-provision for these expenses in order to create 'cushions'; this allowed them to recognize these over-provisions in difficult years and release the excess to increase profits. Once again, released provisions were treated as 'ordinary' items even though these provisions were 'extraordinary'.

One company known to engage in such practices was the North American technology company CISCO. When it acquired a technology company, it minimized the market value of this company's intangible assets (usually technological investments capitalized due to their capacity to generate future earnings) and then increased goodwill. This substantially reduced amortization because capitalized investments are normally amortized in five years, whereas goodwill was amortized over 40 years.[3] The interesting point is that CISCO reduced the value of technology it purchased, even though it was paying for this technology. As a result, the accounts did not reflect the company's decisions.

We will now look at other cases in which the interpretation of accounting was critical for communicating the soundness of an acquisition.

Proportional or full consolidation: AHOLD

Under full consolidation, 100 per cent of the consolidated company's assets and liabilities are included with those of the parent company in the consolidated accounts, less the income allocated to external shareholders in the minority shareholders account. Under proportional consolidation, the percentage shareholding in the subsidiary is included. If the stake is 50 per cent, this percentage could be multiplied by each magnitude and included in the asset and liability accounts of the parent company. With the equity method, only the percentage of pre-tax earnings in the subsidiary net of dividends is added to the 'income or losses of companies consolidated by the equity method' account. Although the impact on net income is the same as when the full consolidation or equity methods are applied, since the equity market focuses much more on operating magnitudes – such as operating earnings or EBITDA – the full consolidation of a subsidiary has an important impact when it comes to increasing these items.

Table 6.1 Impact of the consolidation of JMR on the earnings of Ahold and Jeronimo Martins (million €)

	1997	1998	1999	2000	2001
Ahold consolidated	22.593	28.864	32.824	21.542	66.593
JMR	1.004	1.209	1.307	1.471	1.531
JMR in % of total	4.600	4.700	4.000	2.900	2.300
JM	2,117	2.991	3.280	3.915	4.200
JMR	1,044	1.209	1.307	1.471	1.531
JMR in % of total	49.300	40.400	39.800	37.600	36.500

Source: 'Footnotes', *UBS*, 28 April 2003.

The Dutch distribution company Ahold had a 49 per cent stake in the company Jeronimo Martins Retail (JMR), and Jeronimo Martins (JM) owned the remaining 51 per cent. Paradoxically, both Ahold and JM had been consolidating JMR using the full consolidation method since 1992. JM did so because it considered that its stake was over 50 per cent, and Ahold affirmed that it had substantial control in the company due to a series of agreements that it claimed gave it control over the company. The auditors of both companies were convinced to accept this full consolidation in both companies, defying all logic and infringing accounting principles, which should prevent the same company from being consolidated by the full integration method into two different full companies.

On February 24, 2003, Ahold announced that, in the future, it would switch to the proportional consolidation method, claiming that it had decided to implement this change following the disclosure of information previously not accessible to its auditors. According to IAS standards, the key aspect to be considered is control, but this can be achieved either through political control of more than half the shares or through control of the company's operating and financial activities, which can be achieved with less than half the shares. This means that the problem will continue in the future.[4] In any event, the numerous accounting infringements committed by Ahold did not save it from litigation. Some statements were published in different media, inviting Ahold shareholders prejudiced by the alteration of the company's financial statements to recover part of their losses.

The statements revealed that Ahold's shareholders were entitled to claim compensation for the accounting scandals involving the Dutch firm between 30 July 1999 and 24 February 2003. In total, Ahold had to pay €1,100 million in compensation three years after the accounting scandal and its auditors, Deloitte, went to court over the same scandal, with claims ranging from €2,000 million to €3,000 million.[5] Ahold's managing director and chief financial officer were forced to resign in March 2003 as a consequence of the scandal.

Goodwill: Vivendi Universal

After 2001, there were many famous cases of extraordinary losses acknowledged to amortize recognized goodwill. For example, AOL Time Warner reduced the value of its goodwill by US$54,000 million.[6]

IFRS 3 on business combinations replaced IAS 3 and established a series of standards that could be described as revolutionary if compared with national accounting standards, and that are very similar to the

FAS 141, 142 and 144 standards in North America. This standard pro-hibited 'pooling' to recognize acquisitions. Companies used 'pooling' to simulate mergers between equals in order to combine the balance sheets of acquiring and acquired companies. The differential between the price paid for the acquired company and its book value was recorded in a 'consolidation reserve', which could have a positive or negative balance, and which was not subject to amortization. In this way, the assets of the acquired company were recognized at book and not market value, thus restricting the capital used and increasing the returns on the capital invested. The abuse of this method was so flagrant – particularly in the US, where companies continued to use pooling despite the establishment of twelve criteria to restrict its use – that it was prohibited in 1998.[7] In Europe, it was prohibited on 31 March 2004. Companies were, instead, required to use more traditional accounting methods to recognize acquisitions; hence, the differentials between prices paid for certain assets and their updated book value had to be recognized as goodwill on the asset side of their balance sheets.[8] It is important to emphasize the importance of goodwill in corporate assets. At year-end 2002, the goodwill of companies with stocks invested on the S&P 500 totalled US$1 billion, equivalent to one third of corporate equity or 15 per cent of market capitalization.[9] Just imagine the overall effect that a reduction in the recognized value of goodwill could have.

Before we can identify companies with overvalued goodwill, we must first identify companies whose goodwill represents a high percentage of their total of assets. Of these companies, those with goodwill exceeding their stock market capitalization must be identified. These firms are most susceptible to reductions in the valuation of goodwill. Companies whose goodwill exceeds equity are also at risk.[10] The best example is probably the French conglomerate Vivendi Universal, which reduced the value of its goodwill by €12,400 million in 2002. The company's CEO at the time, Jean Marie Messier, took importance away from these value reductions by stating that they did not affect the company's cash flow. This was questionable. A reduction in the value of goodwill normally reveals the ineptitude of directors in business combination operations; reductions in goodwill simply confirm that too much money has been paid for the acquired company and that overpayment affects cash flow. For example, in fourth quarter of 2000 Vivendi Universal bought the Internet company iFrance.com for €149 million, with net assets worth €3 million (thus giving rise to €146 million in goodwill), sales of €1.8 million and losses during 2001 of €4.4 million. With acquisitions like that, it is not surprising that the company ended up adjusting the value of goodwill. It should also be considered that goodwill is recognized as an asset because it is perceived to have an ability to generate cash flow.

Once it is written off, it means that the management no longer perceives this to be the case; hence, there is a close link to valuation.

Furthermore, IFRS 3 prohibited general provisions recorded before acquisitions and limited abusive practices when concluding business combination deals, assigning zero value to intangible assets such as patents, in order to increase the value of goodwill, a practice developed by European and North American companies without distinction. This allowed them amortize goodwill in 20 years, instead of four or five years as in the case of intangible assets. In general, intangible assets have to be recognized if they are likely to generate economic income in the future. The application of this principle becomes especially relevant in the case of capitalizable research and development expenses, which must be amortized in five years.

IFRS 3 revolutionized the accounting treatment of goodwill by establishing that goodwill resulting from business combinations concluded after 1 April 2004, could not be amortized on a straight-line basis, as established in the majority of European accounting systems. Instead, acquired assets had to be valued on an annual basis and, if the resulting value was lower than the value initially paid for them, a loss had to be provisioned to reduce the value of goodwill by the amount resulting from the destruction of value.[11]

Pooling: Astra Zeneca

The British pharmaceutical company Astra Zeneca used the pooling method in 2002 in its UK accounts, but its North American accounts were prepared using acquisition accounting standards because pooling had already been prohibited in this accounting system. We have already explained how pooling was used by companies to reduce capital investments, since the acquired assets were recognized at book and not market value. The result of these differences was that Astra Zeneca reported an ROE of 25 per cent in 2002 under UK accounting standards and only 8 per cent under North American accounting standards.

Accelerated amortization of goodwill: Gamesa and Richemont

On 30 June 2000, the Spanish aeronautical firm Gamesa announced that it was writing off consolidated goodwill obtained from the acquisition of 30 per cent of the dependent company Gamesa Energía S.A. The total sum amortized was €107.8 million[12] and it was charged to goodwill-paid-in surplus. The company normally amortized goodwill over 10 to 20 years depending on when it expected to recover its investment and according to results. In this respect, there are no reasons to justify its decision to amortize this goodwill fully. This accelerated amortization of goodwill should have been recognized in the consolidated profit and loss account and not directly used to reduce corporate equity. As a result, the company's ROE increased when the denominator decreased and allowed it to report better results than those it could have initially expected to obtain if it had amortized goodwill as envisaged from the outset; that is, over 10 years. It might have done so to improve results after it was floated on the stock exchange and to make the takeover operation more attractive than it was in the first place, since the earnings-per-share after the company was floated on the stock market increased as amortization corresponding to goodwill was excluded.

In the second quarter of 2003, the Swiss luxury goods company Richemont announced that, in line with Swiss bookkeeping regulations, it was amortizing €3,400 million of goodwill directly against reserves, against IAS 22 principles establishing that goodwill must be amortized as an expense in the profit and loss account. The advantages for Richemont were evident since reducing goodwill allowed it to reduce invested capital, if defined as the sum of net fixed assets, gross goodwill and working capital. Thus, when comparing the company's reported returns on capital based on an examination of this simple accounting entry to reduce goodwill against reserves, Richemont discovered a company with huge returns, which made it more attractive to investors.

The equity method: L'Oréal

In 2004 the French cosmetics firm L'Oréal had a 19.5 per cent stake (and 27 per cent of voting rights) in the French pharmaceutical company Sanofi. As a result of the merger between Aventis and Sanofi that took place that year, L'Oréal's stake in the new enterprise decreased to 10.2 per cent (17 per cent of voting rights). L'Oréal consolidated its stake in Sanofi using the equity method of accounting, on the grounds of its important influence in the pharmaceutical company. The contribution of these profits recognized using the equity method of accounting represented almost 30 per cent of L'Oréal's total profits. When its stake was diluted following the merger, consolidation by the equity method was less justified (the reference percentage according to IAS is 20 per cent, far from L'Oreal's 10.2 per cent). The deconsolidation of its shareholding meant that the only income L'Oréal was able to recognize were the dividends paid by Sanofi-Aventis. This measure resulted in a 20 per cent reduction in earnings-per-share in 2004.[13]

Provisions recorded during acquisition: ATOS

Companies have used many accounting tricks to improve their ratios in acquisition operations. We have seen how some companies used acquisition provisions to reduce the book value of the acquired company and increase the goodwill resulting from acquisition, until this practice was eventually prohibited. Firms have also used 'earn-outs', which are similar to provisions for payments to directors of acquired companies if they are able to meet certain targets. 'Earn-out' provisions are revised from year to year but their accounting effect is also a reduction in the book value of the acquired company, an increase in the value of goodwill, amortizable over a long time, and is never recognized as a personnel expense, when it is really no more than variable remuneration expensed currently and not an expense inherent in the acquisition process.

In 2001, Atos, a French systems integration company, acquired KPMG's consulting branches in the United Kingdom and Holland for €657 million and promised 1.4 million new Atos shares to their directors as variable remuneration if they achieved certain sales objectives and operating profits in 2002 and 2003. The problem was that when these objectives were achieved, the company was obliged to pay the corresponding compensation, thus diminishing its net profits, which could in turn affect estimated future earnings. The North American advertising company Omnicom considered that these payments had to be capitalized and not recognized as expenses. In general, the risk of such commitments is that they are potential obligations that do not appear on balance sheets.[14]

Conclusion

In theory, it would be easier for investors to interpret consolidation methods if they were provided with lists of parent company holdings in each subsidiary, as well as the financial results and figures of each subsidiary. This would allow investors to evaluate the income/loss and debt of each company and the risks or benefits of the acquisition for the parent company.[15] Nowadays, information is available on the percentages of holding companies, but this is normally limited to equity figures and their contribution to group profit or loss.

Transparency must also be improved in intra-group operations. Particularly complex are so-called 'transfer prices' at which assets are bought and sold between different companies from the same group, and depending on whether the transfers are recognized at real cost or at an altered price, they might have important tax, accounting and even corporate effects.[16] For example, in 2005 the Spanish company Puleva Biotech sold 6.7 of a total of €7 million to group companies, revealing the importance of transfer prices for calculating profit.

Minority shareholders have also been abused by the actions of certain companies. This occurred with the sale of minority shareholders' 4 per cent holding in the virtual mobile telephony operator Xfera. This 4 per cent stake was owned through Inversión Corporativa, wholly owned by the Benjumea family, and the sale was to Abengoa, 55 per cent owned by the Benjumea family and 45 per cent owned by minority shareholders. Inversión Corporativa was valued at €670 million, when many analysts gave Xfera a zero or even negative value; in fact, Xfera was sold for €1 in May 2006.[17] This operation was investigated by a Spanish Court.

7
Creative Accounting in Public and Private Entities

...across-the-board, political parties do not include all the contributions they receive in their annual accounts.
Spanish National Audit Office, *Expansión*, 7 June 2006

Public entities

In June 2006, the Spanish National Audit Office published a report accusing political parties of lack of transparency in their financial reporting. Among other accusations, the Audit Office highlighted that political parties do not consolidate their local delegations and therefore avoid having to recognize the subsidies received by the latter. For example, most parties 'forgot' to consolidate their delegations in Strasbourg, prompting the Audit Office to issue the following statement: 'It is important to highlight that these omissions undermine the concept of a political party as a single economic-financial reality in which its entire territorial and institutional organization must be integrated'. The report also drew attention to important differences between loans to political parties reported by Spanish financial entities and loans actually recognized by political parties in their accounts, since the latter did not recognize interest accrued on past-due debts, amounting to €14.4 million, on a principal of €21.8 million. In total, political party debt amounted to €192.2 million. It is therefore not surprising that these parties 'forgot' to consolidate interest on past-due debt, which unfortunately is so often 'pardoned' at a later date by financial entities in a deplorable exercise of systemic disease.

Joaquín Almunia, former Secretary-General of the Spanish Socialist Party (*Partido Socialista Obrero Español* (PSOE)) and European Commissioner for Economic Affairs in 2005, accused various governments of contracting the services of investment banks to practice creative accounting in public finances, thus hindering supervision by the European Union. This might be explained by the fact that 12 of the 25 member states presented tax deficits equivalent to more than 3 per cent of gross domestic product (GDP), the limit recommended by the EU. The most disgraceful case involved Greece, which, unable to fulfil the requirements established at Maastricht, forged the public accounts it presented to the Union for years after 1998.[1]

This book would lack something if it did not devote a few pages to comment on some of the creative accounting techniques used most often by public entities, usually governments. The private sector, driven by the desire to maximize value for shareholders, has evolved towards never-before-seen levels of efficiency. This fact should not be obfuscated by studied examples of creative accounting, designed specifically to create value not through operating or financial improvements introduced by firms but through accounting manipulation. Governments have introduced legislation to limit creative accounting practices and to improve corporate good governance. The paradox is that governments have made hardly any progress in applying this same legislation to themselves; once again, revealing the historical constant of double standards in governance, and constant inefficiency at all levels of the public sector. For example, one cannot help but be overwhelmed by a sense of real and regretful sarcasm when looking at the efforts of legislators to force all directors of listed companies to publish details of their salaries, and yet there is still no way of knowing the remuneration received by the Governor of the Bank of Spain,[2] whose salary is financed with Spaniards' taxes.

In the spring of 2006, a Spanish court ordered the judicial intervention of two stamp investment companies that fed off small savers, guaranteeing them high returns on stamp-backed investments, and accused them of accounting fraud. The mechanism consisted in 'investing' captured savings in stamps with a repurchase commitment and guaranteed interest of 8 per cent upon retirement. Obviously, the commitment depended on the financial soundness of the counterparty, in this case the stamp investment firm, whose main assets were stamps. These were overvalued because these two companies controlled the market; hence the value of the stamps was extremely subjective. According to accusations presented by the Spanish Prosecutor's Office, they were valued at ten times their real market value.[3] Meanwhile, cash payments were made using existing captured savings, a mechanism referred to as the 'Ponzi method', or pyramid fraud, making it very difficult for future commitments to be met with existing assets.[4] It is believed that many of the 343,000 savers affected will never be able to recover their money, amounting to around €4,500 million. One radio commentator described how the conspiracy resembled a pyramid fraud, based on enticing slogans such as 'If you invest your money with our company today, we promise to pay you back much more when you retire', and the system was kept afloat because the new savings captured were used to pay people who had already retired. The commentator encouraged listeners to analyze these details: is this not the same situation as the public pension system, which almost all economists predicted would go bankrupt in a matter of years unless it was reformed in time? Why do politicians throw up their hands in horror at this scandal involving stamp investment businesses if it is exactly the same as the one they are responsible for promoting in the guise of the pension system?

In January 2006, the French government announced that it had finally managed to meet the public deficit limit imposed in Maastricht; that is, 3 per cent of GDP. For a number of years, France had exceeded this limit, together with other countries in the Euro Zone (the deficit in 2005 had been 3.7 per cent). The government made this announcement on the back of forecasts of a decrease in the tax deficit in 2006, at €43,700 million, €3,300 million less than previously estimated. However, the French economic press showed that the deficit reduction was no more than an illusion produced by creative accounting. The French tax system had changed that year, and now companies with turnovers of more than €1,000 million were required to pay their taxes in advance: this is how the deficit was reduced by €2,300 million. Without this 'adjustment', France would have exceeded the 3 per cent deficit limit. That must have weighed heavy on the conscience of the Minister of Finance when he euphorically announced the deficit forecast of 2.9 per cent, since, using the Latin principle of *excusatio non petita, accusatio manifesta* ('He who excuses himself, accuses himself'), he commented that the improved deficit was 'not due to an accounting issue'.[5]

In any event, the obligation imposed by Maastricht for public debt not to exceed 60 per cent of GDP, or at least be diminishing, prompted different governments in the mid-1990s into frantic use of a range of techniques in order to reduce debt instead of curtailing public expenditure. One oft-used system was the so-called 'German system', introduced in Spain in 1996 by the *Partido Popular* in operations amounting to as much as €16,000 million. Using this technique, payments corresponding to infrastructure construction work were not made until such work had been finished, and costs and debt were deferred; this goes against the principle of accrual. The Spanish National Audit Office has stated that this system might have increased the price of construction work by

30 per cent,[6] but anything goes to convey a statistical lie! Nevertheless, this system can no longer achieve its perfidious objectives because new European regulations, referred to as SEC-95, force governments to use the accrual system regardless of the moment of payment.

'It's not surprising that the British drive on the other side of the road and do not have the metric system', commented Dalia Grybauskaite, European Budget Commissioner, an ironic remark concerning the creative accounting techniques used by the Blair government to value the United Kingdom's contributions to the European Union. For over 20 years, the United Kingdom had accepted the principle that customs income was the direct income of the European Union and was therefore not treated as payments by the United Kingdom to Brussels. However, in autumn 2005, prior to the negotiation of the European budget for the period 2007–2013, the United Kingdom reclassified these figures as the UK's contribution to the European Union, in order to strengthen its bargaining position.[7]

Another example of clearly hypocritical conduct on the part of the legislator is the pressure on companies to present non-externalized pension fund deficits on their balance sheets. This obligation, which is nevertheless very sound, should be also be applied consistently with the obligation for governments also to publish their deficits in respect of the commitments undertaken with social security contributors, which could also cause certain countries to go bankrupt if they were treated according to their true nature as additional debt.[8] In 2005 the British government, which does disclose its pension commitments, used creative accounting to reduce these by deducting very long-term future commitments at a real rate of 3.5 per cent, equivalent to AA-rated bonds,[9] when it should really use the 1 per cent closer to AAA-rated bonds, government-risk bonds, which is how these commitments should really be classified. If this adjustment were made, the pension deficit would increase by £960,000 million, according to the actuarial consultants Watson Wyatt.[10]

We have seen how sale and lease back operations are used by *many* companies for off-balance-sheet financing purposes, since money obtained from asset sales, usually at prices higher than book value, are recognized immediately on balance sheets, whereas commitments to occupy property for a given number of years do not appear as liabilities. Governments use similar mechanisms to reduce their debt. In December 2005, the Italian government created a fund with assets amounting to €800 million to launch a sale and lease back programme that had to reach the target of €3,000 million before 2007, and the French and Belgian governments are carrying out similar projects.[11]

Another favourite technique of public administrations to conceal debt consists of accumulating debt in public enterprises. We have already studied the case of debt guarantees awarded by the State to public enterprises such as *Radio Televisión Española* or RENFE, but the autonomous regions also use this system aggressively, to the extent that regional debt recognized in this way by 2006 stands at €7,080 million, 1 per cent of Spanish GDP. By parking this debt in mixed enterprises, huge investments are made in infrastructures, so the European Union did not classify these commitments as public debt in 2007. This technique has been used aggressively in Catalonia, where debt amounts to €3,502 million, Valencia with €1,538 million and Madrid with €488 million.[12] The Community of Madrid, with Ruiz Gallardón's government, used this system aggressively through Mintra, the public enterprise responsible for extension work on the Madrid Metro. The debt accumulated by Mintra rose to €3,000 million, but it was never consolidated in the Community's accounts until the European Union forced it to do so, causing a tremendous headache for the new President of the Government of Madrid, Esperanza Aguirre. The Ruiz Gallardón government used a similar technique in the case of work to enlarge Madrid's ring road, known as the M-30. The firm Madrid Calle 30 was declared a 'mixed enterprise' and its debt was not consolidated. This was also criticized by Brussels. Catalonia has also used this technique aggressively to undertake infrastructure projects through GISA and IFERCAT, mixed enterprises that accumulate non-consolidated debt (getting round European Regulation SEC-95) to carry out works.[13] The Community of Valencia has an accumulated debt of nearly 11 per cent of regional GDP, the highest in Spain. What is pathetic about this matter is that it does not matter which political group is governing each Community. It is all about spending tomorrow's resources today and, if possible, concealing the debt while you are at it.

Agencies inspired by the example set by public administrations have also used creative accounting profusely. Fannie Mae, the Federal National Mortgage Association (FNMA), an enterprise sponsored by the US government after the great recession to facilitate access to mortgages, was involved in an accounting scandal in 2005. The Office of Federal Housing Enterprise Oversight (OFHEO) published a 340-page report accusing the enterprise of manipulating its financial statements during the period 1998–2003 for a total of US$10,800 million, and failing to adjust its derivative positions to market value in order to maximize variable remuneration payable to its directors, who were, in turn, closely related to the public administration. Jamie Gorelick was named Vice-chairman after leaving the Clinton administration. James Johnson, the firm's Managing Director in the 1990s, was an adviser to John Kerry in the 2004 elections. And the Director, Ann McLaughlin Korologos, was Labour Secretary in the Reagan administration.[14] These appointments show that Fannie Mae was not only a corporate scandal, but also a political scandal. In total, Fannie Mae will spend US$800 million revising its accounts.[15]

Following the publication of this special examination report, Fannie Mae was ordered to pay US$400 million in compensation and return the bonuses illegally received by its directors, amounting to US$90 million in the case of Franklin Raines, Managing Director during that period, and US$30 million in the case of Timothy Howard, the firm's former Chief Financial Officer.[16] Fannie Mae even manipulated its profit and equity figures after 2002, when the Sarbanes–Oxley Act was already in force.

The most striking example of Fannie Mae's rotten corporate culture was that even its in-house auditors, whose interests and objectives must be geared towards providing a true and fair view of financial statements rather than by numbers, were remunerated on a profit basis, in a flagrant conflict of interest. When Franklin Raines, Fannie Mae's Managing Director, announced in 1998 that the company had to double its earnings-per-share of US$3.23 to US$6.46 by 2003, Sampath Rajappa, Fannie Mae's former internal watchdog and head of its internal audit office, rallied his team:

> By now every one of you must have 6.46 branded in your brains. You must be able to say it in your sleep, you must be able to recite it forwards and backwards, you must have a raging fire in your belly that burns away all doubts, you must live, breath and dream 6.46 ... Remember, Frank has given us an opportunity to earn not just our salaries, benefits, raises ... but substantially over and above if we make 6.46. So it is our moral obligation to give well above our 100 per cent.[17]

In conclusion, it is pathetically amusing to see how legislators, appointed by political parties voted in by the people, are guilty of such blatant hypocrisy by establishing reporting standards that they themselves are unable to respect. The revival of accounting preached by so many, and of which this book is a modest exponent, will not be achieved until public administrations comply with the first principle, which the private sector is so hypocritically required to comply with. For example, the European Union, despite requiring all listed companies to adopt IFRS, issues annual accounts that have not been audited for decades.

Parmalat

Parmalat's accounting problems were evident.
Enrico Bondi, Judicial Administrator of Parmalat after the
suspension of payments, *Financial Times*, 1 March 2006

Introduction

Parmalat was created in 1961 in the city of Parma, Italy. The privatization of many municipal dairy companies in Italy during the 1960s provided an important opportunity for Parmalat to grow, and it eventually acquired many of these local companies. Parmalat's innovative approach was revealed with the introduction of 'Tetra Pack' cartons – it was the first dairy company to use these cartons.

In 1970, the company began diversifying its business: part of this diversification process included the acquisition of Parma football club, as well as international expansion, notably in Brazil. In 1990, the Tanzi family floated 49 per cent of Parmalat on the stock market and, in 1993, after the introduction of legislation forcing companies to rotate auditors, Parmalat appointed Deloitte & Touche as its auditors, breaking a long association with Grant Thorton. In April 2003, Fausto Tonna, Parmalat's Chief Financial Officer for many years, surprised the markets by presenting his resignation and, in December that year, Parmalat was unable to pay a bond valued at €150 million, even though its balance sheet showed liquid assets of €6,000 million. In these circumstances, at the end of November the company admitted to having almost €600 million classified as cash in a venture capital fund called 'Epicuruum', based in the Cayman Islands, but it was unable to recover the liquid value of its participation. On 9 December 2003 Parmalat's Chairman, Calisto Tanzi, presented his resignation[18] and, on 14 December, Bank of America declared that an alleged current account, in which Parmalat, through its subsidiary Bonlat in Bermuda, claimed to have US$4,900 million, was false. On 11 December Parmalat's shares lost 47 per cent of their value, 15 per cent the next day, and 20 per cent the day after. This prompted the ratings agency Standard & Poor's to reduce the Italian company's debt from a B+ rating (investment grade) to a CC rating (junk bond), and then dropped this rating again on 15 December to D (bankrupt), after which the bonds traded at 20 per cent of their nominal value. On 23 December 2003 Parmalat requested bankruptcy protection and, on 29 December, Tanzi was arrested. At the time of his arrest, he declared 'I understand nothing about accounting.'

On 17 December 2003, Citigroup's analysts stated that, aside from the qualifications expressed by Deloitte & Touche, stating that the company's EBITA and financial expenses had been altered in the sums of €40 million and €80 million respectively, 'We cannot find any other evidence to indicate that the accounts have been manipulated.'[19]

Causes behind Parmalat's accounting risk

What happened to make a great multinational such as Parmalat transform into a bankrupt enterprise with completely manipulated accounts? There were various factors that gave rise to the accounting risk:

- International expansion in high-risk areas such as Latin America, and particularly Brazil, which resulted in huge operating and currency losses
- Diversification strategy frustrated as a consequence of the losses that integrated companies (such as Montevideo Football Club) contributed to the group, and with which there were also no evident synergies (soccer and milk)
- Intra-group transfers of assets at doubtful prices that were not eliminated from the scope of consolidation, through contracts with 'third parties' that were really front companies based in tax havens, in which financial derivatives were used, and in which Del Soldato, Bonlat's Chief Financial Officer, was the 'expert'
- Strong presence of subsidiaries in tax havens (offshore), through which most financial operations were performed, such as debt issues and bond buy-backs; they were used not because of the tax advantages but because it was impossible to verify whether these companies' accounts were real or not
- Laxity on the part of the auditor Grant Thorton; even though it had ceased to be the group's auditor in 1993, it continued to audit the latter's main subsidiary (Bonlat) in a tax haven, with evident incompetence (unless the courts determine it has greater responsibility)
- Dissipation of the responsibility of the parent company's auditors through the technique of only taking responsibility for companies they had audited and not audits performed by other firms. Deloitte & Touche was responsible for auditing the Parmalat Group, but it washed its hands of all responsibility in the auditing of the accounts of the Group's subsidiaries such as Bonlat, which was audited by Grant Thorton, as well as other subsidiaries in tax havens (one of Parmalat's telephone operators was later identified as the managing director of 25 of these subsidiaries)

- Inefficiency of the capital, stock and bond markets, which were unable to anticipate the scandal until the company defaulted on its first debt repayment
- Incompetence of the Italian regulator, Consob; despite examining Parmalat's accounts, it was unable to prevent the fraud until this finally erupted in all its fury
- Bad management of the company, which was really used by Calisto Tanzi as a private instrument to satisfy his recreational interests (acquisition of football teams) or imperial desires (geographic expansion without the means to achieve it) using the money of minority shareholders (who owned almost half the company)
- *Omertá*, or family and business networks that are sometimes created in Italy, in which many businesses are created with no protection for shareholders since only the interests of the *omertá* matter, often through pacts of silence.

Analysis of the accounting scandal

Off-balance-sheet debt

In its audited accounts for the first quarter of 2003, Parmalat reported a net debt position (gross debt minus cash) of €1,800 million, despite a net financial debt figure of €3,800 million. Why this difference?

Parmalat made very intense use of securitization before closing its accounts and presenting them to markets. It used securitization to 'sell' collection rights to financial entities in return for small discounts. This practice was not, in itself, abusive (it was able to optimize the management of working capital), but its use might be considered fraudulent if it were used to capture liquid assets and thus present a lower net debt balance. It is interesting to note that securitization, if used as a normal part of business activity, should generally vary with sales revenues or turnover. However, in June 2003 Parmalat's revenues fell 11 per cent but the company still securitized €611 million.

Parmalat also concealed €111 million in debt in a special vehicle investment company, Bucconero (a 'black hole'). Parmalat also used debt guarantees to pay €88 million: €65 million guaranteed to Parmalat's associated companies; and €23 million to third parties. Parmalat also had to pay €57 million in obligations deriving from operating lease transactions, as well as another €464 million in preferred stock issued with predetermined principal maturity dates. Finally, Parmalat owed €361 million in 'other debt payable' not classified as 'financial debt'.

One final and important factor prompted the company to manipulate its debt figures. Parmalat had minority shareholders with an

18.18 per cent stake in its Brazilian subsidiary, Parmalat Participaçoes. Parmalat had promised these shareholders that the subsidiary would be floated on the stock market before 31 December 2003, but financial upheavals in Brazil in the period 2002–2003, as well as the election of Lula da Silva as President of Brazil, meant that the flotation operation never got off the ground. However, these circumstances were not responsible for the accounting problem but, rather, the fact that Parmalat had offered a sale option to these minority shareholders on its stake in the subsidiary, which they could exercise against Parmalat if the subsidiary were not floated on the stock market. The crisis facing Parmalat in December 2003, when it was unable to pay the €150 million bond, was daunting. The Brazilian subsidiary would not be floated and, therefore, the minority shareholders would exercise their sale option on Parmalat's stake: in order to respond to this obligation, Parmalat had to find €333 million in financing, an amount that did not appear on its balance sheet.

In any case, when examining the real debt position of a company it is also important to look at the maturity periods of issued debt payments. Firms might not have very large debts but, if a high proportion of this debt matures short term, this could lead the company to suspension of payments if it lacks financing to meet its obligations. This is what happened to Vivendi Universal in 2002.

Although the rating agencies rated Parmalat's debt incorrectly (remember, rating agencies have access to much more information than stock market analysts), they did reduce the company's debt rating after it defaulted on the payment of the first bond, albeit to a level at which the company was still considered 'investment grade' quality investment. Such a rating reduction could have increased financial costs by 400 base points.[20] Rating reductions carried out by rating agencies might also force debt 'hidden' in non-consolidated entities (such as vehicle investment companies) to 'appear' again on the parent company's balance sheet as a result of the reduced rating, a condition normally imposed by creditors of non-consolidated companies. The inept performance of the rating agencies in the Parmalat, Enron, WorldCom, Credit crisis and other scandals has prompted many people to call for a reform of a market, which behaves, in practical terms, like a duopoly between Standard & Poor's and Moody's.

Finally, we can highlight three other unusual features of Parmalat's debt. Although Parmalat theoretically had abundant liquid assets, it continued to issue new bonds, and this is puzzling. Parmalat also issued bond structures at lower-than-EURIBOR rates of interest, suggesting that the traded bonds also offered a derivative 'sold' by Parmalat to the bond buyer, who in return accepted this low nominal interest rate.

These derivatives clearly worsened the company's risk profile. The third element, Parmalat's net debt, stood at €1,800 million at year-end 2002, and the same amount was reported as net debt at the end of the third quarter of 2003. In other words, despite reporting profits, Parmalat was not generating free cash flow. This would have come to light, had it presented a statement of changes in financial position or cash flow statement.

False cash position

According to Parmalat's third quarter accounts, it had liquid assets of more than €8,000 million, consisting of €4,200 million in cash, €2,200 million in short-term assets, €1,500 million in bonds, €500 million in an investment fund, €600 million in exchange bills, and €500 million in 'other financial assets'. However, it soon became apparent that this seemingly sound position was nothing more than a smokescreen.

Bonlat was a subsidiary company based in the Cayman Islands. Most of the Group's liquid assets were placed with this company: €6,900 million, to be precise. Since its head office was based in a tax haven, this figure could not be checked by anyone except the auditors, Grant Thorton. The auditors requested a document proving the existence of this money. Tonna's friends at Bonlat scanned a Bank of America logo, passed it through the fax machine several times and then drafted a letter under the Bank of America logo, confirming the existence of a current account in Bonlat's name in that amount. Crucially, Grant Thorton considered this letter to be sufficient confirmation of the company's cash position. It was also striking that Parmalat was unable to pay a measly €150 million bond when it claimed it had €4,900 million in its current account. As we have seen, in December the Bank of America denied the existence of a current account containing these funds. This episode triggered Parmalat's stock market collapse.

Parmalat stated that it had repurchased billions of euros in corporate bonds through Bonlat, thus reducing its net consolidated equity figure. This repurchase operation was also hard to fathom, since the repurchase price was equivalent to 60 per cent of the value of all the bonds issued by the company, or 150 per cent of its stock market capitalization value at the time. Of course, these bonds were repurchased through a subsidiary based in a tax haven, which meant that they could not be verified, except by Grant Thorton, the subsidiary's auditor.

In November, after investigations by the Italian stock market regulator Consob, Parmalat admitted that €600 million classified as liquid assets in its third quarter accounts (closed in September) were actually invested in a venture capital fund called Epicuruum, based in the

Bermuda Islands. This fund could invest in non-listed firms in America. Parmalat undertook to recover this investment to improve its solvency position. The disclosure of this information prompted other Epicuruum investors to ask the fund to return their investments, but because these Epicuruum funds had been invested in non-listed companies they could not be recovered.

Another important aspect of Parmalat's financial position was its profitability: calculated as financial income divided by financial assets, this was 5.85 per cent. This was much higher than the profitability figure for government bonds, suggesting that very high risk with investments had been made with liquid assets. However, Parmalat declared that its liquid assets were invested in minimum-risk assets, such as government or very high-quality bonds (BBB-rated bonds or better). Parmalat is more likely to have been guilty of so-called 'currency mismatching', which consists of investing in high-interest-rate currencies such as Brazilian or Australian bonds, even on a leveraged basis (requesting money lent in low-interest-rate currencies, such as Japanese Yen or Swiss Francs). This technique allows companies to obtain higher-than-market profitability but at the expense of assuming important risks, since high-interest-rate currencies tend to be exposed to higher inflation rates and could, therefore, lose value.

Finally, from a tax standpoint it made little sense for the company to have a high volume of financial debt accompanied by a high volume of liquid assets because financial income generated by these assets is taxable.

Other accounting abuses

Parmalat also used its subsidiary Bonlat to conceal losses incurred in the Group's unsuccessful process of expansion. Bonlat concluded transactions with struggling companies using derivative instruments in order to conceal losses. Non-consolidated companies were used to perform these operations in order to record favourable accounting entries in companies making losses; otherwise, these would be eliminated in consolidation. To support the financial 'machinery' behind these operations, Parmalat granted loans to Bonlat in exchange for injecting liquidity in its subsidiary and Bonlat, in turn, injected liquidity in the front companies in exchange for loan receivables payable to these non-consolidated companies. In turn, these front companies used the liquidity to conceal the losses of struggling subsidiaries. They thus became creditors through derivatives or similar instruments, although responsibility for payment of these instruments rested with the subsidiaries, which had very little financial solidity. This meant that, when the time came, they were unable to fulfil their payment obligations with the front companies. In turn, the front companies could not repay the loans to Bonlat, and Bonlat could not pay the loans it had received from Parmalat. The correct accounting treatment would have been to record a provision for possible losses to adjust these accounts receivable. However, in practice, this was not done because it would have forced the company to recognize that these loans had been granted on operations designed to conceal losses. This shows that accounting scandals are usually never isolated incidents.

Another one of Parmalat's most deviant reporting methods involved currency derivatives. In 2002, Parmalat signed a contract to invest €496.5 million in the Epicuruum fund based in the Cayman Islands. This contract also included a currency swap for a notional sum of €850 million,[21] with the first instalment payable in 2007, as a means of hedging variations in the dollar/euro exchange rate, since the aforementioned fund's investments were made in dollars. The agreed swap exchange rate was US$1.05. Since the investment in the Epicuruum fund was in dollars, and Parmalat presented its financial information in euros, if the dollar depreciated with regard to the euro, Parmalat received money (offsetting the loss in value of the fund); if the dollar increased in value against the euro, Parmalat paid money (this payment was offset by the higher value obtained from the dollar participation in Epicuruum). There would have been nothing abusive about this non-financial contract from an accounting standpoint had it been recorded in the correct section of the profit and loss account. Basically, the bad evolution of Parmalat's business during the first quarter of 2003 prompted it to commit one of its accounting sins: it cancelled the contract prematurely and recognized the payments received as the consequence of the depreciation of the dollar (US$40.7 million) not as 'financial income' to compensate 'exchange loss' (for a total of −US$28.9 million), but as 'other operating income'; namely, through the 'sales' entry. In the past, Parmalat had used this account to reflect sales generated by other lines of business, such as ice creams or juices. Since the payment of US$40.7 million was not accompanied by any inherent material or personnel costs, it distorted the operating profits reported to market. As a result, the reported EBITDA margin was 12.4 per cent, when the real margin (excluding this non-operating income) would have been 11.6 per cent.

It was especially shocking to discover that the company had also incorrectly recorded exchange losses incurred in its Brazilian activities. In the third quarter of 2003, the company had to reclassify €33 million in 'exchange losses' that had previously been classified (first quarter, 2003) as 'extraordinary losses'. Claiming that the weakness of the Brazilian real was a passing phenomenon triggered by the Brazilian election process, the company had declared this exchange difference as extraordinary to prevent it being taken into account by the stock market, which tends to focus more on the 'recurrent' (rather than extraordinary) aspects of business. After seeing that the real did not recover with regard to the euro during the third quarter, the company was forced to reclassify the amount as a financial loss.

Finally, as the owner of Parma Football Club, Parmalat amortized the intangible value resulting from the payment made to sign new football players (€215 million) over a ten-year period, but this period was longer than the terms of these players' contracts. This practice, which is legal in Italy, was prohibited by the European Union because it did not link the amortization of the asset to its useful life, and thus gave Italian clubs an advantage over other European clubs. If it had applied the mandatory EU standard, Parmalat would have been forced to reduce its corporate equity by €173 million through an extraordinary loss.

Impact of the accounting scandal on the company's value

As mentioned previously, Parmalat's market capitalization value plummeted 65 per cent in December 2003 following its admission that a US$6,900 million account was false. Nevertheless, it is worth examining in closer detail certain valuation aspects of the financial reporting techniques described.

Many investors often apply discounts to multiples required to purchase shares if more than 50 per cent of the company's capital stock belongs to a family or an individual. This is because the risk assumed by minority shareholders is relatively high if good governance standards are underguaranteed: Tanzi's use of Parmalat's capital stock to satisfy his football obsessions (Parma and Montevideo football clubs), for example.

It is common for agency conflicts to arise between shareholders and bondholders in companies with high levels of real debt. The priority for bondholders is to sell enough company shares to guarantee repayment of the bond principal. In contrast, shareholders want to wait for the best moment to disinvest their shares so that they can pick up the residual amount when the debenture has been paid. This happened to the German company Deutsche Telekom, which became heavily indebted as a consequence of the payment of third-generation licences undertaken in 2000. When expected profits from such investments were not obtained, the stock market value of many telecommunications operators decreased rapidly in 2001, giving rise to serious misgivings about their capacity to repay bonds. In the case of Deutsche Telekom, which also owned the US mobile telephony operator USA Voicetream, the bond market pressured as much as it could in 2002 in order to force the sale of this subsidiary and thus guarantee repayment of its bonds. Meanwhile, the equity markets opted to postpone this type of sale due to the depressed value of telecommunications assets in 2002. Agency conflicts can also arise between banks (which could have granted loans to companies) and the bondholders themselves, since they might have conflicting interests according to the conditions applicable in different types of financing (banks are normally in a better position to bargain than bondholders, who tend to be much more dispersed).

Another relevant factor is risk premium. If the regulatory authorities in a given country are generally considered not to be strict because accounting standards offer companies a greater margin for abuse, or due to a recurrent structure of bad management, investors can apply higher risk premia to invest in the assets of that country. This could be a competitive disadvantage for companies in that country, since they are forced to compete with higher financing costs.

Information asymmetry is also important. While stock markets usually have limited information on which to formulate opinions (their decisions are based on audited annual accounts, which are assumed to be reliable), rating agencies have access to much more detailed information. This gives rise to asymmetry between those responsible for issuing opinions in the different markets. Corporate financing might also be subject to certain conditions (covenants) known to the lender but not to the stock market. This also produces greater information asymmetry. This asymmetry could mean that the bond market of a company or the credit default swaps market anticipates a financial crisis before the stock market does. This highlights the importance of obtaining all available information on an investment (including information on the stock market, bonds and derivatives).

Consequences

It is interesting that Parmalat's accounting irregularities were committed over a period of 13 years, during which time the company was listed on the Milan stock exchange. In fact, the capital market, directors, regulators, auditors, rating agencies, investment banks, analysts and lawyers all failed to protect investors despite the alarm signals. They failed in this because of numerous conflicts of interests, perverse incentives, poor internal controls, corruption and immorality.[22]

The Parmalat scandal was in many ways similar to Enron or WorldCom. The forged letter, recognizing the existence of a current account containing US$6,900 million, showed that Parmalat had stooped even lower on the fraud ladder if compared with the fraud abuse committed by the two North American companies. However, the ultimate purpose of most of Parmalat's operations was not to make the Tanzi family wealthier but to conceal the multimillion losses incurred in Latin America. That is what made Parmalat different to Enron or WorldCom, where the managers of these companies became millionaires at the expense of accounting scandals. However, in 2004 certain embezzlement cases came to light, such as the diversion of US$620 million from Parmalat to the family's travel business; and Tetra Pak, Parmalat's packaging systems supplier in Sweden, had paid commissions to the Tanzi family,[23] The President of the Italian bank Capitalia, Cesari Gedronzi, was suspended by a court for helping the Tanzi family divert €50 million from Parmalat to the family's travel company Parmatour and for forcing Parmalat's directors to buy the Ciappazzi mineral water bottling plant at a price above its fair market price.[24]

The accounting 'hole' swelled to €11,000 million. But it was not just the EUR 4,900 million current account that was false. Parmalat had also concealed off-balance-sheet debts of €1,700 million, and had fraudulently reported bonds and loans in its favour amounting to €3,600 million. In total, final debt came to €14,000 million, eight times that recognized by Calisto Tanzi's team, and operating profits recognized between 1998 and 2003 had been inflated to €200 million.[25] They drove a company with 36,000 employees in 29 countries to the edge of the abyss.

It has yet to be determined whether the auditors' were responsible, accomplices or victims of the abuse committed by Parmalat. The police investigated Grant Thorton's offices in Milan in order to clarify the audit firm's responsibility. In any event, Grant Thorton had been associated with Parmalat for more than 20 years, so it seems clear that they were liable, due to abuse or neglect. As regards the parent company's auditors, Deloitte & Touche, in the summer of 2005 a New York judge determined that despite the company's 'umbrella' structure, where the partners in each country owned the respective national companies in compliance with regulations governing the national ownership of audit firms, the parent company would be responsible for any liability originating from its responsibility in the Parmalat case.[26] This decision was taken because one Deloitte & Touche auditor in Brazil, Wanderley Olivetti, sent emails with questions to his Italian colleagues about the financial solidity of Parmalat's subsidiary, Bonlat, in March 2001 and 2002. On 5 April 2002, Parmalat's Chief Financial Officer, Fausto Tonna, threatened to 'replace the auditor immediately' because of these questions. After this, Adolfo

Mamoli, a member of Deloitte & Touche's Italian division, asked the company's global CEO to arbitrate in the matter. In May, Olivetti toned down his expressions of concern about Bonlat and in December, when it was discovered that Bonlat was the key piece in the accounting scandal, he considered Deloitte & Touche's potential international liability in the matter.[27]

We cannot end this section without mentioning the impact of similar crises in financial entities. In the words of Parmalat's founder, 'Parmalat never had any trouble getting loans'; 'banks ran after us to make sure we had all the financial resources we needed despite our accounts not being entirely transparent'.[28] Bank of America was forced to record provisions of US$114 million for loans granted to Parmalat, and another US$92 million for credit default swaps purchased from Parmalat, which were worthless after the company went into suspension of payments. It was also exposed to claims amounting to US$2,000 million presented by Parmalat's current directors for (allegedly fraudulently) assisting Calisto Tanzi and the previous directors to structure operations resulting in the falsification of the company's annual accounts. Citigroup, the world's largest bank, recorded provisions valued at US$4,950 million as cover for similar claims presented by Parmalat. The concentration of loans granted by Italian banks to Parmalat put the country's financial system at risk (the government approved an emergency decree to protect Parmalat from creditors for a period of 120 days), and it is calculated that the damage to the Italian economy might have been equivalent to as much as 1 per cent of Italy's GDP (which totalled around €1,200,000 million). Morgan Stanley signed an agreement in the third quarter of 2005 to pay €155 million as a global settlement for claims in the Parmalat case after it was accused of helping the firm issue billions of euros in Parmalat bonds and sold before the scandal to Nextra, the fund management unit of Banca Intesa, knowing full well that the company was going into bankruptcy. Nevertheless, Morgan Stanley never admitted that it had acted wrongfully. Parmalat was ordered to pay Nextra €160 million in compensation. Parmalat's former shareholders and bondholders are still in litigation with UBS, Deutsche Bank, Morgan Stanley, Citigroup, J.P. Morgan, Deloitte & Touche and Bank of America. Parmalat itself settled claims with Crédit Suizze and UBS for €172 m and €283 m relatively, northern bank admitting doing anything wrong.[29]

In terms of Parmalat's senior executives, Calisto Tanzi, known for his austerity and strong religious character, is currently on trial and faces up to 15 years' imprisonment. The North American regulator (SEC) has also filed litigation against Tanzi for US$1,500 million to compensate ruined investors. Tanzi's partners in crime Tonna (Parmalat's Chief Financial

Officer) and Del Soldato (Bonlat's Chief Accounting Officer) have been sentenced to prison terms of more than one year for minor crimes (violations of securities market regulations, with maximum sentences of five years' imprisonment), and now face much more severe charges of manipulating accounts and fraud. Giovanni and Stefano Tanzi, Carlisto Tanzi's brother and son, have been sentenced to prison terms of one year and eleven months, respectively.[30] The judiciary is expected to prosecute 64 people in all in this case, including former employees and auditors.[31] The trial, which started in May 2006, took place simultaneously with the Enron and WorldCom trials. The Chief Financial Officers of these two companies declared themselves guilty and accepted shorter prison sentences in return for accusing senior executives responsible for fraud. In the case of Parmalat, Fausto Tonna declared that Calisto Tanzi was the person with the real power to authorize fraudulent accounting practices in the firm.[32]

After recapitalizing the company – by exchanging €20,000 million in debt for shares – banks such as Intesa and Capitalia were converted into shareholders in Parmalat, each with a 7.5 per cent stake. The Italian dairy firm was refloated in October 2005, with a capitalization value of around €3,500 million; of this amount, it is calculated that €1,400 million corresponded to the value of its dairy assets (seven times the EBITDA that these activities generate), while the rest corresponds to the estimated value of compensation that Parmalat will receive in the numerous lawsuits it has with different investment banks (for a total of €13,100 million; this means it expects to receive 15 per cent of this figure, compared with the 30 per cent that Enron received in similar litigation).[33] Nevertheless, by year-end 2005 the company's shares had fallen from €3.2, when it was floated in October that year, to €2 at the end of December.

WorldCom

> *WorldCom put extraordinary pressure on itself*
> *to meet the expectations of securities analysts.*
> Report ordered by the **Court hearing the WorldCom**
> **bankruptcy case**, November 2002

Introduction

On 22 June 2002, WorldCom announced to the New York stock market that it had committed an accounting fraud valued at US$3,800 million over five quarters, specifically all four quarters in 2001 and the first

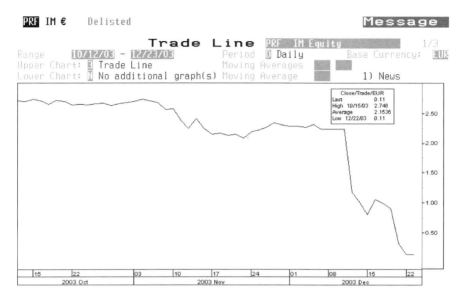

Figure 7.1 Parmalat stock price from 12 October 2003 to 23 December 2003
Source: Bloomberg.

quarter of 2002. One month later, the company declared suspension of payments.

In August 2002, WorldCom owned up to another accounting fraud of US$3,300 million involving the manipulation of its EBITDA during the period 1999–2001 and the first quarter of 2002. By the end of the year, the company's accounting hole had swollen to more than US$9,000 million. With assets valued at US$107,000 million during its stock market boom years, in June 1999 WorldCom reported a market capitalization value of US$180,000 million and debts of US$41,000 million, making it the biggest bankruptcy in history. It was also the biggest accounting scandal. By then – summer 2002 – WorldCom, in addition to its 80,000 employees (17,000 would soon lose their jobs), had the second largest long-distance telecommunications network in the US, the largest local network, the largest international network, and the largest Internet data traffic network.[34]

WorldCom was founded in 1983 by Bill Fields in Mississippi under the name 'Long Distance Discount Services' (LDDS) to provide long-distance telecommunications services. In 1985, Bernie Ebbers was appointed Managing Director and transformed the company into an aggressive takeover machine that culminated in 1989 with the company's flotation on the North American stock exchange. In the 1990s, when Scott Sullivan was the company's Chief Executive Officer, the firm continued its programme of acquisitions and, in 1995, it changed its name to World-Com, more in line with the new global ambition of a company that only ten years previously had been a modest enterprise from the south of the US. In 1998, WorldCom carried out its most famous takeover, that of the telecommunications giant Microwave Communication Inc. (MCI), which it bought for US$40,000 million. Soon, the company's turned its strategic sights on providing Internet-based data access and trans-fer (WorldCom's fibre optic network came to be the most important in the US, transporting half of North American traffic on Internet), a market that at the time had a promising future and was enjoying expo-nential growth. WorldCom also tried to increase its exposure in the mobile telephony business by acquiring Sprint for US$120,000 million, but opposition from North American and European regulators pre-vented what would have been the most important takeover in history. Nevertheless, by 2001 WorldCom had acquired almost 75 companies, mostly using own shares and, to a lesser extent through debt, which by that time stood at around US$30,000 million. By 2002, the com-pany was operating operated in over 65 countries, with over 20 million customers.[35] However, there was one sign that indicated that World-Com's accounts were not as well as they should have been: although it reported an EBITDA of US$3,700 million in 2001, its operating cash flow was in the red at −US$1,600 million.

Circumstances that caused the accounting scandal

Analysts' forecasts

Listed companies usually provide investors and analysts with forecasts for the following year or specific quarters. These forecasts are typically presented as the earnings-per-share the company expects to obtain in a specific period. If companies do not present these forecasts, they closely track the estimates of investment banks tracking their shares, and these estimates are referred to as 'consensus estimates'. In order to avoid sur-prises or very broad-ranging consensus estimates, which can both cause unwanted share volatility, companies often informally 'guide' analysts on the accuracy of their forecasts. In this way, both officially and unoffi-cially, companies play a very important role in the development of these forecasts. Whenever a company is unable to meet these estimates, it issues a 'warning' (profit warning) to notify the market, which normally reacts by severely punishing the shares *and* the company's directors, who have been unable to fulfil these forecasts. The alternative to admitting the truth is to manipulate numbers to achieve the promised targets. This is how accounting scandals start.

In the case of WorldCom, despite the slowdown in Internet traffic, the company continued sending out messages to the market that Internet traffic was doubling every 100 days, which was very far from the truth. But, at the time, the market bought the message and analysts consequently modified their forecasts according to these growth announcements. The question is why does a company feel the need to exaggerate its numbers when reporting to the market? There are various answers, but the main reason is usually the desire and need for shares to rise (or not fall), either because directors' remuneration is linked to share performance or because shares are used like 'stickers' to pay for acquisitions.

Once over-the-top forecasts have been sold to the market, if the market believes the company the latter's shares will respond positively in the short term, but if the market discovers that the forecast was misleading then future corrections to stock value will be much more severe. So, despite being aware of this, why might directors be inclined to exaggerate numbers? Directors are often remunerated through stock options, which can be exercised on a specific date. It might be in the director's interest to 'heat up' stock options in the short term, without much concern about the mid-term impact. On other occasions, exaggerated stock prices are simply a reflection of human nature, but anything overblown paves the way for disappointment in the future. This disappointment can be postponed (but never avoided) by creative accounting.

Mergers and acquisitions

Companies that make very intense use of mergers and acquisitions are the most likely to use creative accounting techniques. This does not mean that all companies engaging in takeovers are guilty of manipulating their accounts, far from it. We are only saying that an intense acquisitions policy is usually a factor that induces the use of creative accounting techniques. This is because acquisitions are typically financed with equity or own shares, through capital increases, or bank or syndicated debt. In the first instance, good share performance is essential for a company to maintain its acquisitions policy because, if shares lose too much value, the dilution impact of new operations on original shareholders would be enormous and these might block future operations. In the second instance, financing by banks, bank syndicates or investors in debentures or similar securities issued by the company is normally conditioned by a series of criteria or conditions (covenants) that limit the financing granted to the achievement of a series of financial ratios. If the company fails to meet any of these conditions, the bank or investor that has bought the company's debt securities can demand reimbursement of the principal, and this can give rise to a serious financial crisis. To avoid this happening, companies sometimes 'cook' the books to make it seem as if they are complying with the conditions imposed on them. In their corporate mergers and acquisitions policies, companies must integrate firms with more or less similar cultures so that they can extract synergies. Although WorldCom managed to integrate with the companies it acquired until 1998, after taking over MCI – a company that was much larger than WorldCom – fighting between different units, lack of coordination and anarchy were rife.[36] In fact, at one point the company had several different head offices at the same time, all distributed around America, and each run by its own managing director.

'Good governance', personalized leadership, culture and auditing

WorldCom's Board of Directors had 13 members. Of these, nine were independent directors. However, investigations after the company went into suspension of payments revealed that decisions were taken by the tandem of Ebbers and Sullivan, and then simply submitted to the board for formal approval. Major acquisitions were negotiated directly by Ebbers and, once agreed, passed to the Board for approval during very short meetings, sometimes even by telephone. How could a company with so many 'independent' directors be guilty of such bad governance? The Aldama and Olivencia reports codes of good corporate government, even though they recommended the inclusion of independent directors on boards of directors, warned that it was not enough to merely classify directors as 'independent'; if a director's remuneration was over-the-top, his or her independence would be clearly questioned. Moreover, if independent directors, despite not having any business relationship with the company where they are directors, work for other firms that do render services to the company where they are directors, their independence would be seriously undermined. In the case of WorldCom, almost all the 'independent' directors were directors or executives in companies previously acquired by WorldCom, except for shareholders with important stakes in WorldCom through shares or stock options. The style of leadership promoted by Ebbers and Sullivan also seriously increased the risk of scandal. Ebbers played the role of 'charismatic leader' but, while selling his shares and stock options to pay for his million-dollar ranches, he would also make daily telephone calls to WorldCom employees who wanted to sell their stock options on shares, asking them for explanations.

Sullivan established an accounting control system bordering on the Dantesque: the company's internal auditors reported directly to him, the audit department's prestige was undermined within the organization, it had virtually no resources and was often refused information. Sullivan's meetings with the Board of Directors' Audit Committee, of which he was paradoxically a member, were a joke, lasting only a few minutes, with accounts being approved by 'rounds of applause'. On repeated occasions, the Board also approved million-dollar loans to Ebbers, which he used to buy mansions or plantations or to make million-dollar donations to his university. The Board only dared to ask Ebbers for guarantees when it was too late, accepting his shares in the company as a guarantee on loans. When the company's shares divebombed, the damage they had caused to the company was enormous since these guarantees could not be enforced.

The overriding culture at WorldCom was a breeding ground for accounting abuse. The subsequent trial revealed that Ebbers had instructed his employees to 'hit the numbers!' By paying million-dollar compensation to his closest employees, the 'boss' bought their loyalty in the commission of these crimes. Arthur Andersen, WorldCom's auditor until almost the very end, invoiced three times more in consultancy fees (US$50 million from 1999 to 2001) than for auditing services (US$14 million).[37] Although Andersen considered WorldCom to be a 'high risk' client, it did not follow up these concerns, and suspicions expressed by certain Andersen employees fell on deaf ears. When Andersen changed the partner responsible for auditing WorldCom, the latter decided to change auditor and switched to Ernst & Young, which just happened to be the company the former Andersen partner responsible for auditing WorldCom had moved to. The most Dantesque thing was that this partner was made the new partner responsible for auditing WorldCom's accounts at Ernst & Young!

Capital markets

There were clear conflicts of interest in many of the investment banks that advised or did business with WorldCom. The clearest example was the bank Salomon Smith Barney (SSB), whose corporate finance division had invoiced WorldCom over US$125 million in advisory services on mergers and acquisitions. The Chairman of Citigroup, SSB's owner, was a WorldCom director. SSB's star telecommunications analyst, Jack Grubman, gave a 'strong buy' recommendation on WorldCom with a target share price of US$125 when this was already falling, at around US$75. Grubman also sat on different Boards of Directors where decisions were taken on mergers and acquisitions. This meant that he was able to acquire privileged information that he could not share with the rest of the market. Later enquiries revealed that Grubman lost confidence in WorldCom but, when he started having second thoughts, he came under pressure from Citigroup's Chairman not to change his recommendation. Also, Salomon Smith Barney gave preferential treatment to Ebbers, offering him shares in technology companies that were going to be floated on the stock market. At the time, shares in such companies increased in value in a matter of hours, generating huge profits for those fortunate enough to be granted shares based on completely corrupt criteria. In exchange for these shares, Ebbers chose SSB for his corporate finance operations, which basically means he was being bribed with these shares, thus undermining WorldCom's interests by not choosing the best prepared or most economical bank for the company's business. Another investment bank that wanted to participate in a WorldCom bond issue received a complaint from the company that the bank's bond analyst 'was giving WorldCom a very bad time with his negative recommendation on the company's bonds', and the investment bank's manager said that 'he would speak with him to sort it out'. These examples show how the separation of information that should have existed between the various departments of the investment banks in the form of barriers (known as 'Chinese walls') was nothing more than play-acting.

Sunk costs

The expression 'sunk costs' is used to refer to costs that have already been incurred. In the future, we can only estimate the cash flows expected from the present to the moment when decisions are taken on a project. Historical costs must be excluded because they might cause wrong decisions to be taken. Although economists commonly accept this thesis, in daily management many executives attach great importance to past investments, and this makes it difficult to conclude unprofitable sales or deals. Problems could arise if the personal decision of a company CEO to invest in an asset or company yields much lower-than-expected profits. The CEO can admit the error before the Shareholders' Meeting, but there are times when, instead of admitting the error, accounting tricks are used to conceal the failure of an investment or asset. This is what happened with the huge investments undertaken by WorldCom in fibre optics in the late 1990s. With its sights firmly set on the future of the Internet, at one point Ebbers had accumulated half the fibre optics lines in the US. However, the multiplication of data transmission capacity in 2000 caused fibre optics prices to tumble. While other operators recognized this fact in their accounts (from 2000 they reported that the profitability of their fibre optics segments had suddenly worsened), WorldCom deceived the market by reporting profit figures that were simply false, fraudulently tying amortization rates to income.

Analysis of the accounting scandal

This section explains very succinctly how WorldCom used different creative accounting techniques to abuse accounting regulations and manipulate its accounts:

Revenue recognition

Pressure to meet forecasts presented to the market prompted WorldCom to cook its revenue figures in two ways. It 'over-invoiced' many of its clients, thus increasing turnover and operating income. When a client protested and reported the 'error', WorldCom did not cancel the sale and illicitly obtained revenues, but instead recorded an extraordinary provision as 'miscellaneous expenses'. It also had numerous contracts with customers that forced the latter to accept minimum consumption conditions and, if they did not fulfil these minimum consumption requirements, WorldCom was entitled to impose the corresponding penalty. However, in practice it was almost impossible to collect these penalties because customers simply changed operator. Although World-Com knew that it could not collect these amounts, it continued to record income from this item in order to maintain 'acceptable' rates of growth in sales. In total, WorldCom manipulated US$1,800 million in revenues. North American and International Accounting Standards now prohibit companies from recognizing revenues whose collection is not 'reasonably assured', not even through bad debt provisions. A sale for which you do not expect to obtain any income is not a sale.

Capitalization of costs

One of the fraudulent accounting techniques that made WorldCom famous was its method of capitalizing costs. The company entered deals in which it leased its fibre optic networks for data transmission purposes. As available market capacity multiplied (a phenomenon that was especially intense after 2000), the price of fibre optic lines fell. However, WorldCom continued to capitalize as 'unused cost' part of the expense in fibre optic lines incurred as 'construction in progress' and amortized these lines according to the income received and not according to the useful life of these lines. This practice was prohibited under American accounting standards, yet Sullivan gave instructions for this to be done anyway. When the Board of Directors' Audit Committee discovered what was going on, Sullivan continued to defend his decision, claiming that the recognition of income had to be tied to recognized costs, even though this was illegal. And this is the reason he was fired.

Acquisitions accounting

Since WorldCom was continually acquiring new companies, the accounting techniques used to reflect these acquisitions were key in determining whether this strategy would benefit or prejudice the company. WorldCom managed to pretend its results were not as bad as real results in different ways. When it acquired technology intensive companies, WorldCom chose not to recognize the intangible research and development assets of the acquired firm (this was the reason it overpaid for companies). Instead, the excess price with regard to the book value of the acquired company was recognized on the asset side of WorldCom's balance sheet as goodwill. What was the purpose of doing this? Intangible assets were normally amortized in five years. However, by treating these assets as goodwill instead of as intangible assets, the impact on the financial accounts was diluted over a period eight times longer.

In addition, when the acquisition was about to be completed, World-Com used a technique known as called 'pre-acquisition provisioning', which consisted of recording huge provisions for expenses that would have to be paid once the acquired company had been integrated. These expenses were normally just severance payments to employees laid off as a result of synergies. The accounting fraud in this case was that this provision was treated by WorldCom as an 'extraordinary' item so that stock market analysts would exclude it when calculating the company's earnings-per-share ratio (Wall Street tends to focus on 'recurrent' aspects), while the inherent gains from the operation (lower personnel expense resulting from severances) were treated as 'ordinary'. Finally, another problem arose as a result of amortizing goodwill over this long 40-year period; namely, that the falling value of technology and telecommunications companies after March 2000 revealed that the values that appeared on the balance sheets of the acquiring companies did not give a 'true and fair view' of the company's financial position. WorldCom's goodwill was huge (US$50,537 million in 2001, compared with total assets of US$103,914 million); if it had been adjusted to actual values, the reduction would have been massive and would have placed the company in a financially unsustainable position. As a result of different acquisitions accounting episodes, including the 'WorldCom scandal', the North American and International Accounting Standards Boards have introduced serious measures: companies are now obliged to value their goodwill at its actual value, pre-acquisition provisions are prohibited and intangible assets of acquired companies cannot be taken to goodwill.

Earnings-per-share

WorldCom had promised the market earnings-per-share of 46 cents in the second quarter of 2000. When it could not achieve this figure, Sullivan gave instructions for part of the 'minimum differences reserves' to be released (generated as a result of the unforeseen non-payment by clients of the penalties for not achieving minimum consumption levels) so that earnings-per-share would increase from of US$0.4532 to US$0.4552, and, if rounded, US$0.46, the promised figure.

Stock tracker

These are shares that try to replicate part of a listed company's activity, thus offering investors limited exposure to an area of interest. WorldCom issued these types of shares replicating the most stable business with the lowest growth (residential telephony resulting from the acquisition of MCI), leaving the activity of supposedly strongest growth (fibre optics) tied to WorldCom's shares. The problem with these instruments (popular in around 2000) is that if the company has a single structure, the criteria for allocating costs to a subsidiary or other company could be very arbitrary (in fact, Sullivan unashamedly favoured WorldCom on MCI's stock tracker). Market logic also establishes that if an economic exposure is to be isolated, the simplest thing is to float that subsidiary on the stock market.

Synergies

To justify the exorbitant amount of money that WorldCom offered for MCI (US$40,000 million), the company announced that it would extract synergies valued at US$5,500 million. When one company acquires another, it typically announces a number of synergies it expects to obtain in the operation. Any overpayment on the correct price of the company (the famous 'control premium') is only justified if it is equivalent to the synergies that the company expects to obtain from its integration with the acquired firm; anything else means it is overpaying. There are two types of synergies: income synergies and cost synergies. Income synergies refer to the potential capacity of the new combined company to sell more on a combined basis. For example, one sales force distributes medical drug A, another medical drug B, and the new united team distributes medical drugs A and B to all customers, thus achieving additional earnings.

Income synergies are usually very difficult to achieve, and they can sometimes generate losses. For example, when the French bank Crédit Agricole announced it was buying Crédit Lyonnais, it promised the market that it would obtain income synergies (the theory was that wholesale banking would now be able to sell products of both entities to the customers of both banks, thus generating more business). However, in practice, they failed and the new entity lost wholesale business. Why? Many companies that had loans or deposits with both entities decided not to keep all their eggs in the same basket and transferred their products to third parties as the merger was completed. In the case of cost synergies, these are more tangible because they usually consist of severance payments and income obtained from joint purchases from suppliers. The important feature of cost synergies is that they must be quantified as a percentage of the combined cost base, and this percentage must be compared with other percentages obtained in similar mergers and acquisitions. In any event, companies tend to exaggerate synergy figures when they announce merger or acquisition operations, seeking to limit the poor stock market reception to overpaid mergers. It is therefore prudent to apply a discount to synergy forecasts 'promised' by acquiring companies.

Release of deferred expenses provisions

A key indicator of the industry in which WorldCom operated was its ratio of line cost expense to revenues (which was called the 'E/R' ratio). In spite of greater competition, WorldCom reported that its E/R ratio was stable at about 42 per cent in the period 2000–2002, while its competitor Sprint, for example, reported a worse ratio of 49 per cent in the same period. WorldCom's real ratio was actually 51 per cent. It manipulated its accounts by releasing deferred expenses provisions recorded in excess previously to have a 'cushion' to absorb variations in revenues, a practice prohibited under American accounting standards. In total, Sullivan ordered US$3,300 million to be released, an exorbitant amount that was greater than the 'excess' deferred expenses, and even affected real deferred expenses. Some of the company's employees opposed this abuse and its British subsidiary brought this matter to the attention of Arthur Andersen UK.[38]

The impact of the accounting scandals on the company's stock market value: the EV/EBITDA multiple

The accounting metric manipulated most by WorldCom was EBITDA. This was because between 1999 and 2002 EV/EBITDA (Enterprise Value/Earnings before Interest, Taxes, Depreciation and Amortization) was the metric used most by telecommunications analysts to determine whether the shares of like-for-like companies were cheap or expensive. If WorldCom could inflate EBITDA growth, since this item is included in the denominator of metric, the latter would decrease and the company would appear to be 'cheaper' than other companies in the sector. This guaranteed that shares performed well, since this was crucial to increase the value of stock options distributed to WorldCom's executives, to make sure shares granted to financed acquisitions yielded profits to acquired shareholders, and to keep share prices attractive in order to accomplish further acquisitions. The EV/EBITDA metric was used to value companies from the sector because it was a pre-amortization item that could be isolated from the potential effects of different national accounting systems on the amortization account, an accounting effect that apparently had no significant effect on cash flow. By capitalizing many expenses, WorldCom was able to give the impression that many of the company's cash outflows were investments, which created balance sheet assets. In turn, the assets were reflected in the profit and loss account in the form of an amortization item, which was below EBITDA; hence, EBITDA never included the money that left the company as capitalized costs. In contrast, other more conservative companies from the sector treated the same items as costs, presented above EBITDA, which was therefore lower. However, the message that the market missed was that the most capital-intensive firms, those that invested more, tended to trade at lower multiples, because less cash flow reached the pockets of shareholders. For example, car companies normally trade at almost two times EBITDA, since a high percentage of their earnings goes towards investments. In contrast, companies from, let us say, the systems integration sector tend to have multiples that are more than 10 times their EBITDA, since their investments are much smaller. Therefore, WorldCom had to be 'penalized' because its level of investments, concocted using accounting tricks, was extremely high, but the market failed to value this crucial fact. Today, the stock market uses this multiple much less to value the telecommunications sector, focusing on the 'Enterprise Value'metric on operating cash flow, thereby deducting investments in fixed assets or working capital from EBITDA. In this way, whether a company is more or less aggressive in its expense capitalization policy is no longer relevant because this is recorded as an expense (less EBITDA) or as an investment (less operating cash flow).

Consequences

By 2002 WorldCom was the greatest bankruptcy in history. It left 17,000 people jobless and an accounting hole of US$9,000 million, and its market capitalization value of US$180,000 million went up in smoke. Its relevance was such that it aggravated lack of confidence in the financial market, and fuelled the economic crisis that was brewing in 2002.

In August 2005, Ebbers was sentenced to 25 years' imprisonment (his defence focused on his apparent ignorance of accounting),[39] which is practically equivalent to a life sentence because he was already 63 at the time of the trial. The sentenced imposed on Ebbers, together with the two founders of the cable company Adelphia, John Rigas (15 years) and his son Timothy (20 years), marked a 'before' and an 'after' in executive accounting fraud. Sullivan collaborated with justice and confessed to all the plotting; his testimony was crucial to him receiving a light sentence of only five years, compared with a maximum of 165 years, to which he would have been exposed if he had declared himself 'not guilty', and 25 year if he had declared himself 'guilty'.[40] It was also crucial in the charges brought against his former boss, whom Sullivan blamed for starting the scandal by giving instructions to 'hit the numbers'. The agreement also included the sale of Sullivan's mansion and his pension fund to compensate victims. Apart from Ebbers and Sullivan, David Myers, WorldCom's former controller was sentenced to one year and one day, and Buford Yates, the company's former Accounting Manager, was also handed a one year and one day prison sentence.[41] Although the Sarbanes–Oxley Act (North American legislation introduced to fight against accounting scandals) was conceived after Enron, its approval by Congress was only possible after WorldCom. Although the cost of its application has been criticized – around US$35,000 million according to the Institute of Business Accountants – particularly in relation to internal financial controls,[42] Sarbanes–Oxley represents cornerstone legislation that has gone a long way to making the quality of business earnings better than it has ever been, at least at the time of writing.

The healthy, refloated company, now named MCI, paid a US$750 million fine to the SEC in 2003 for accounting fraud.[43] MCI was acquired by Verizon in 2005 for close to US$6,000 million. It is also important to highlight that although accounting fraud is usually used – specifically used, in the case of WorldCom – to manipulate short-term share prices, in the medium and long terms it is much more harmful in stock market, ethical and criminal terms. Moreover, companies that have bad accounting reputations on the market typically trade at substantial discounts, and therefore lose any advantage they tried to achieve by manipulating their financial statements.

Enron

> *When corporate fraud happens, it is often attributed to driverless car syndrome: the persons responsible for the company in times of scandal will deny they were even driving at the time of the accident.*
> **Harvey Pitt**, President of the SEC from 2001 to 2003

Figure 7.2 Enron's stock price from 1993 to 2000
Source: Bloomberg.

Introduction: chronology of events

The gas pipeline business in the US had been subject to deregulation since 1978, giving gas companies greater freedom to choose their preferred means of gas transport and allowing the market to take decisions on gas and gas transport prices. As a result, the volatility of both assets increased dramatically. A former Exxon executive, Kenneth Lay, estimated, from his new post as CEO of InterNorth, that this deregulation process would generate important business opportunities and, in 1985, he founded the Texan company Enron, the result of the merger of two natural gas companies: InterNorth and Houston Natural Gas. At one point, Enron owned 60,000 km of gas pipelines in the US, the biggest network in the country, making it a very asset-intensive firm. However, the deregulation imposed on the energy transport business was a difficult period in the late 1980s. After this period, in 1989 one of Lay's former partners at McKinsey's, Jeffrey Skilling, joined the company as Managing Director of Enron's financial subsidiary. Deregulation had caused sharp hikes in energy prices, and many companies needed to protect themselves against such increases. Taking advantage of these conditions, Skilling imposed a change of strategy: from being a traditional gas and oil transport company, in 1995 Enron would become a firm specializing in providing sophisticated services for the management of energy-associated risks. In Kenneth Lay's words:

> We don't necessarily mean to be the largest or most profitable – at least not now. We just aim to be the leader in all the businesses we're in worldwide.[44]

Taking advantage of its vast gas pipeline network, the Texas firm decided to serve as the counterparty to numerous companies anxious to protect themselves against rising or falling gas prices. By combining national demand in both directions, Enron was able to offer these financial services at attractive prices, pocketing substantial brokerage revenues in the process. This business model was developed and soon Enron traded a wide variety of products, including electricity, bandwidth, pulp and paper, and derivatives for weather-related risks.[45] Many of these hedge agreements were offered by Enron's Internet platform, Enron Online. On 13 December 2000, Skilling was named Managing Director of the Group, while Lay stayed on as Chairman. That year, Enron reported US$100,800 million in revenues and had assets worth US$65,500 million.

Enron, and its Chairman, Kenneth Lay, were important contributors to Republican Party campaigns. Kenneth Lay had a very close relationship with George W. Bush Jr, and the former member of the National Energy Board, Wendy Gramm, was an independent director at Enron and member of its audit committee. Between 1989 and 2001, Enron and its employees donated almost US$6 million to political parties; 74 per cent of this money went to the Republican Party, the rest to the Democrats. Enron was also the main donor in George W. Bush's election campaign in 2000.[46] By that time, its political clout was such that when energy prices tripled in California before the blackouts, Lay managed to avoid price caps being by arguing that this regulation would have a negative effect on the North American economy in the long term.

But the year 2000 was Enron's last year of glory. Its shares performed brilliantly, rocketing from US$40 in January to US$83 in December, thus guaranteeing its directors massive bonuses. But, in 2001, its shares began falling sharply. On 14 August, in the midst of this downturn, Skilling stood down as Managing Director, stating personal reasons. Kenneth Lay took over as Managing Director. That day, Lay sent an email to the company's employees, in which he stated:

> All of you know that our stock price has suffered substantially over the last few months. One of my priorities will be to restore a significant

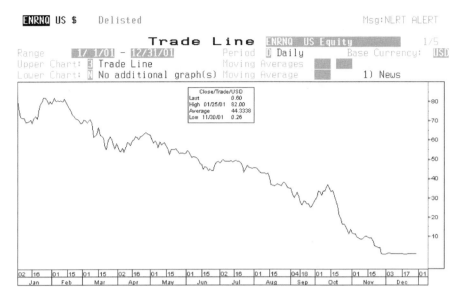

Figure 7.3   Enron's stock price in 2001
Source: Bloomberg.

amount of the stock value we have lost as soon as possible ... I want to assure you that I have never felt better about prospects for our company ... Our performance has never been stronger, our business model has never been stronger, our growth has never been more certain ... We have the finest organization in American business today.[47]

The day after Skilling's resignation, Lay received an anonymous letter that read:

I am incredibly nervous that we will implode in a wave of accounting scandals ... Skilling is resigning now for 'personal reasons', but I think he wasn't having much fun, looked down the road and knew this stuff was unfixable and would rather abandon ship now than resign in shame in 2 years ... The business world will consider the past successes as nothing but an elaborate accounting hoax.[48]

Soon, the accountant Sherron Watkins identified herself as the author of this letter. On September 21, 2001, Enron's lawyers carried out an accounting audit and reassured Kenneth Lay that there was no reason for alarm.

On 16 October, at a conference with stock market analysts to present third quarter results, Enron announced an equity reduction of US$1,200 million as a consequence of accounting adjustments.[49] On 1 November, it announced another correction, reducing the value of its assets by a further US$590 million, after which Standard & Poor's put Enron on negative credit watch. Paradoxically, Lay had sold US$300 million in Enron stock before these announcements were made to the market, but he transferred the entire amount to NGOs.[50] On 22 November, the firm admitted that its accounts were being investigated by the SEC. Two days later, Enron's Chief Financial Officer, Andrew Fastow, was fired; he had been appointed Chief Financial Officer in 1998 at the age of 36.[51] On 28 November, Enron performed another adjustment; this time increasing recognized debt by US$4,000 million because the rating agencies had lowered its debt rating to 'junk' category.

Enron's shares peaked in August 2000 at US$90.75. On 30 November 2001, they were trading at US$0.26. Enron filed for bankruptcy on 2 December 2001. It was the biggest bankruptcy in US history. On 23 January 2002, Kenneth Lay resigned as Chairman and Managing Director.

Risk factors

Although it is difficult to trace the genesis of the Enron accounting scandal, there are several risk factors that clearly contributed to the scandal:

- Enron had declared that its main strategic objective was to achieve an 'asset light' balance sheet in order to optimize returns obtained on invested capital. Analysts rated the quality of the company based on its capacity to obtain returns on capital above the cost of that capital. Returns on capital were, in turn, calculated as operating income after tax divided by invested capital. Invested capital was equal to the sum of net fixed assets, goodwill and working capital. By releasing consolidated assets, it managed to reduce the level of net fixed assets, thus obtaining higher returns with a smaller denominator. To develop this asset-light strategy, Enron performed numerous transactions to deconsolidate these assets, as well as the debt used to finance them.
- Enron was constantly concluding derivatives contracts and therefore preserving its good rating from agencies was crucial because no one would participate in derivative transactions with a company whose

compliance with obligations under derivative contracts was questionable. This forced Enron not to present debt levels that might seem 'dangerous' to agencies and counterparties in derivatives contracts.

- Enron owned the main gas pipeline in the US, but deregulation in the North American energy transport market caused a structural reduction of growth generated by this business. If growth of basic business declined, it could either be recognized or 'force the accounts' to maintain past growth rates. Enron plumped for the second option.

- The diversification carried out by Enron to overcome the decline in its main business segment was also a source of risk. Participation in many different businesses fostered the appearance of losses in some of them, and the temptation to 'hide' these loses with the profitable units was very high.

- Enron's auditors, Arthur Andersen, which had been auditing the Texan company for 15 years, invoiced US$25 million in auditing services and US$27 million in consultancy services in 2000.[52] The temptation to lower auditing standards to maintain the high-margin consultancy business was also very great.

- Enron's relations with the capital market were subject to many conflicts of interest. As with the case of WorldCom, the recommendations that stock and bond market analysts gave on Enron might have been corrupted by the very succulent commissions that Enron paid on corporate finance operations. A good example of this conflict of interests was the dismissal of BNP's analyst for recommending shareholders to 'sell' securities in August 2001, five months before Enron went bankrupt.

- The valuation of derivative contracts subscribed by Enron at market value proved to be extremely problematic because many of them were not derivatives traded in organized markets (exchange traded derivatives or ETDs), whose value could be easily calculated; they were very specific unlisted derivatives known as 'over-the-counter' derivatives (OTCs). The values of these instruments might be very subjective according to certain hypotheses that are introduced in the model, particularly expected future volatility.

- Enron's corporate culture encourages entrepreneurship, but also leadership. As we have seen, Enron hoped to become a leader in all its areas of business. This culture is not, in itself, negative. For example, General Electric practices this culture very successfully. However, if there are no adequate control mechanisms, the accounting department might be forced to feign leadership that does not actually exist.

- Decision-taking in Enron, as in WorldCom, was highly personalized in the figures of Kenneth Lay, Jeffrey Skilling and Andrew Fastow.

Table 7.1 Analysts' recommendations on Enron shares

Date (2001) and event	Number of analysts covering Enron	Recommendation 'Strong buy'	Recommendation 'Buy'	Recommendation 'Hold'	Recommendation 'Sell'
18 October (a)	15	12	3	0	0
8 November (b)	15	11		3	1
28 November (c)	14	3	3	7	1
29 November (d)	12	2	1	7	2

Notes:
(a) Two days after, Enron announced US$618 million losses, a US$1,200 million reduction in equity and changes in its accounting statements for the first quarter 2001.

(b) Enron announced a formal investigation by the SEC into its accounting practices; this lead to a review of all its accounts since 1997; Enron also announced that it was in merger talks with Dynergy.

(c) The recommendation agencies reduced the recommendation on Enron bonds to 'junk', scuppering its merger talks with Dynergy.

(d) This is the penultimate day that Enron was listed before announcing bankruptcy. Enron shares trade at US$0.36 dollars.

Source: Bong (2003: p. 17).

The Board of Directors, which was in theory formed entirely by 'independent' directors, did not question the company's strategy or accounting until the final moment.

- The bonuses received by Enron's directors encouraged account manipulation, since the company's bonus programme of US$230 million was payable according to whether share price targets were reached in 2000. With so much money at stake, once again the temptation to cook the books, and thus maintain the good corporate performance and get rich, was extremely high. In April 2000, Enron's shares were worth US$70 and rose to US$83 in December, thus reaching the established targets. Under this remuneration programme, the company's directors were paid the US$230 million 10 months before Enron filed for bankruptcy: the Chairman received US$11 million, the Managing Director, US$7.5 million, and the Chief Financial Officer US$3 million.
- Enron had very weak cash flow. This, in itself, is not sufficient to produce an accounting scandal, but it is common in companies that 'cook' their numbers.
- Enron manipulated its accounts according to the EPS expected by analysts. Jeff Skilling was accused of manipulating accounts to achieve the promised EPS, which was one cent higher than real EPS. During the trial, Skilling's and Lay's defence claimed that these changes to refine initial estimates were a routine measure carried out by accountants, who revised them regularly to find legitimate earnings. Declarations by Enron's former investor relations manager, Mark Koenig, are very illuminating: on 17 January 2000, the day before Enron was due to announce fourth quarter results, he informed Skilling and others that the consensus recommendation on Wall Street had been raised one cent to 31. Enron planned to announce 30. 'I tried to see what could be done to ensure earnings met expectations.' The earnings reported to the market the next morning were 31 cents, although Koenig stated that he was not sure how that figure had been reached, although he believed they had 'cooked' the number to achieve the desired consensus recommendation from analysts.[53]

Analysis of the accounting scandal

We have previously seen how debt can be removed from balance sheets through non-consolidated entities, and particularly through special vehicle investment companies. These entities are not bad as such but they can be used to isolate risks arising from specific activities and to find investors willing to finance an activity with a known and recognized risk, allowing financial costs to be reduced. The problem is that Enron made abusive use of this mechanism. During the 1990s, Enron used its subsidiary Enron Global Power & Pipelines to concentrate the presence of capital-intensive assets and the corresponding debt used to finance these assets. By doing so, Enron was simply copying the strategy employed by Coca-Cola, which concentrated the most capital-intensive assets of its business, its bottling plants, in a subsidiary, Coca-Cola Bottling, in order to float most of the capital of this business and thus deconsolidate its balance sheet. In this way, Coca-Cola improved its asset profitability ratios and eliminated much of its debt, guaranteeing effective control of the bottling plant with a smaller stake that was still almost 50 per cent.[54] But Enron's Chief Financial Officer, Andrew Fastow, ceased to find this method attractive because of the amount of information that the company had to present because its subsidiary was a listed company exposed to regulatory pressure from the SEC. In order to limit these 'disadvantages', Enron repurchased all this company's capital stock and then used special purpose vehicles (SPVs) to remove assets and debts from its balance sheet. For Fastow, SPVs had the advantage of being more agile and manageable instruments for carrying out transactions.

The North American accounting system prioritized legal substance over economic substance when determining whether or not SPVs had to be consolidated.[55] This meant that non-consolidation was achieved if a third party owned at least 3 per cent of the capital of the SPV (the requirement is now 10 per cent), if the governing body of the entity, deemed to be more than half of voting shares, was controlled by 'independent' directors of the parent company to be deconsolidated, and finally if the assets transferred to the SPV so that it could develop its business activities had to be sold at market prices, without the seller of the assets being able to obtain any returns under a guarantee and with full freedom for the SPV to establish pledges on same. In contrast, UK accounting standards only emphasize economic substance when determining consolidation. Thus, the SPVs were consolidated in the company most exposed to profits or losses resulting from the fluctuation of the values of the SPVs' assets. For this reason, it has been stated that the Enron scandal would not have happened if it had been subject to UK accounting standards.

Enron carried out a massive deconsolidation of subsidiaries using SPVs, and that deconsolidation was approved by the Board of Directors, the auditors and the accounting supervisors, because, on paper at least, deconsolidation was legal. By and large, Enron continued to create SPVs to which it transferred specific assets. The SPV, in turn, issued 'collateralized debt obligations' (CDOs) guaranteed with these transferred assets, and interest payments were performed using the cash flow generated by these assets. Transactions structured in this way were legal, as was the deconsolidation of the SPV if 3 per cent genuinely belonged to a third party and most of the directors were 'independent'. Enron included investment bankers among the 'third parties' that owned the 3 per cent necessary for deconsolidation, notably Merrill Lynch, who were really not independent at all because they received million-dollar commissions from Enron to give advice on corporate finance operations. However, since these assets were often strategic for Enron, control was guaranteed using questionable or genuinely illegal techniques. Also legal, but questionable, was Enron's decision to include its own employees as 'independent' directors, such as its Chief Financial Officer, Andrew Fastow, and the Chief Accountant, David Myers. Illegal activities included secret contracts between the SPVs and Enron that allowed the latter to take important decisions on the use of assets. Sometimes the SPV issued debt was not only guaranteed by the SVP's assets, it was also accompanied by additional guarantees from Enron. Therefore, in practice, the risk to which the Texas firm was exposed was greater than the declared risk. Finally, debt issues by several of these SPVs were subject to conditions, or covenants, that established that Enron's debt rating could not fall below a certain level. If it did, the debt, under these conditions, would be reconsolidated in Enron's balance sheet. As already explained, on 28 November 2001, after the decrease in Enron's junk debt rating, the company was forced to adjust its reconsolidated balance sheet by US$4,000 million. Arthur Andersen stated that it was unaware of most of these clauses that had forced the consolidation of these SPVs on Enron's balance sheet.

The best example to explain these ideas is the SPV Whiteline, which was deconsolidated from Enron's balance sheet with its assets and a total debt of US$2,400 million (of course, by transferring the assets through their sale at a price higher than book value, Enron obtained a profit that was recognized in its books, in the same amount as the disappeared debt). However, one clause established that this deconsolidation would be declared null and void (that is, it would be reconsolidated) if one of the three rating agencies (Standard & Poor's, Moody 's or Fitch IBCA) gave Enron's debt a junk rating; as we have seen, this happened on 28 November, prompting the reconsolidation of Whiteline and another SPV with a total of US$4,000 million in debt. The partner controlling Whiteline was an Enron employee.

In one of the most famous transactions involving an SPV, Enron created a company – LJM1 – in which Fastow had a US$1 million stake, and another US$15 million were contributed by two Merrill Lynch bankers of whom Fastow was a customer. Enron's problem was that it had shares in a tech company whose stock market value increased dramatically in 1999. Enron's Board of Directors decided to hedge this participation, but failed to find effective methods in the market due to the existence of listed options that could neutralize the value of these participations for Enron. To get round this problem, it used LJM1, which hedged the value by granting Enron a stock option on the Internet shares. In return, LJM1 received a share package from Enron worth US$50 million. The problem was that Enron's counterpart to guarantee the value of its technological subsidiary was a company – LJM1 – whose main asset for covering this insurance was Enron's shares. Therefore, if Enron's share price fell substantially, LJM1 would not have sufficient capital to pay the insurance, which is what eventually happened. That is why this type of hedging was referred to as 'incestuous'.

Enron used three companies deconsolidated from the balance sheet and with head offices in the Cayman Islands to acquire Enron assets through bank loans guaranteed by Enron itself. The transfer prices were higher than market and yielded profits of US$591 million in a four-year period, and also reduced the real level of debt.

Consequences

Enron's employee pension fund invested 62 per cent in Enron shares. However, due to the internal regulations of the fund, Enron could not sell the stock when it went in free-fall, particularly from 29 October to 12 November. Meanwhile, by selling his stock options Kenneth Lay pocketed US$119 million, Skilling obtained US$113 million and Andrew Fastow US$19 million. Andrew Fastow also became wealthy as an 'employee' of the SPEs that concluded transactions with Enron, and received more than US$30 million in different bonuses. These payments seriously biased Fastow's independence, since he could have taken decisions that damaged Enron's interests in favour of the SPVs in which he participated as an employee and shareholder. From a total workforce of 20,000 employees, 5,000 lost their jobs. The prosecution focused on the fact that the company in which Fastow was a general partner (LJM), although in theory it was responsible for the sale–purchase of assets for Enron as an independent entity, actually acted as a company designed specifically to manipulate financial results. In his 240-page confession, Fastow recognized having pocketed US$240 million. Skilling declared to *The Wall Street Journal* in the summer of 2001 that, 'The fact that Fastow was CFO and general partner of LJM was not a conflict of interests, but in the best interests of shareholders' and, two months later, he told employees that 'Enron had very strict corporate governance and control systems in its agreements with LJM'.[56] The day after his declaration, Fastow admitted having collected US$45 million from the SPV, for which he was fired by the Board of Directors.

Noteworthy accounting changes have been introduced in the wake of the scandal of Enron's SPVs. The overriding criteria now are economic rather than legal. Thus, both North American and International Accounting Standards focus on companies that are more exposed to the highest losses or gains that SPVs can generate, and that company is the one that will have to consolidate the SPV.[57] Moreover, the board of directors of the company attempting to consolidate an SPV cannot interfere in the control of its assets and, for deconsolidation purposes: the SPV must have sufficient capital to perform its activity; 'third parties' participating in the SPV must have a vote; the guarantee of specific returns by the deconsolidated company to the investor of the SPV is prohibited; and a minimum requirement is established that special purpose enterprises (SPEs), in order to deconsolidate fully, may receive surplus returns after interest on the debt has been paid (and these returns do not correspond to any other company, in which case this company must integrate the SPV).

On 14 March 2002, the Department of Justice declared Arthur Andersen guilty of obstruction of justice in the Enron case. This charge led to the disappearance of the audit firm. Arthur Andersen, an emblematic auditing and accounting firm for 100 years, suffered irreparable damage to its image as a result of the Enron scandal in a business in which image is essential for attracting and holding onto clients. The North American Justice Department withdrew the company's license for 'destroying documents' relating to the Enron case and Michael Kopper, Managing Director of Arthur Andersen's Finance Division, was found guilty of obstructing the US Justice Department. Although the Supreme Court of the United States declared this sentence null and void in 2005 – due to defects in the handling of the case, and the lack of evidence that the firm was 'aware it was doing wrong' – Arthur Andersen is already a corpse and it will never recover (most of its partners moved to Deloitte & Touche).[58] Nevertheless, it is worth considering whether the media image of this famous audit firm was really accurate, presented as a rotten organization and not as healthy organization with the odd rotten apple. On the face of it, perhaps we should be fair and say that the second definition is probably more accurate.[59]

On 23 August 2001, a BNP analyst advised shareholders to sell their stock and was fired for his troubles. This reveals the strong conflicts of interests existing between different divisions of investment banks. In 2005, J.P. Morgan agreed to settle the claims presented against it in the

Enron case and paid compensation amounting to US$2,200 million to the victims, represented by the Board of Trustees of the University of California. In the case of J.P. Morgan, the recommendation on Enron was to 'buy', while it hedged the issue of US$1,000 million in Enron stock and syndicated more than US$4,000 million in loans to the Texan company. When the agreement was announced, J.P. Morgan also recorded a further US$2,000 million as an additional provision for other litigation, open in relation to its liability in the Enron case. At the beginning of 2005, Citigroup paid US$2,000 million to settle part of the claims at the beginning of 2005, and Lehman Brothers paid a total of US$491.5 million. Lawsuits against Merrill Lynch, Crédit Suisse First Boston, Barclays Bank, Toronto Dominion Bank, Royal Bank of Canada, Royal Bank of Scotland and Goldman Sachs are still open. In total, the University of California's lawyers are claiming damages amounting to US$40,000 million in stock market value lost by Enron's shareholders, and US$2,500 million by bondholders. The prosecution's case against the banks claims that these helped Enron to structure deals that allowed it to reduce balance-sheet debt, while stock market analysts maintained positive opinions on its value. Many banks were unable to collect their insurance policies, which covered them against losses resulting from accounting frauds, because insurers argued that these clauses were not applicable if the banks themselves participated in the fraud by virtue of abuse or neglect. Thus, Swiss Re refused to pay its policy to Bank of America because of the Enron case, alleging this fact, which means the trial is still open. Crédit Suisse First Boston was forced to pay US$100 million for illegally allocating primary shares using arbitrary criteria. When trying to recover this amount from its insurer, it presented a lawsuit against Chubb Insurance Co. Judge Karla Muskovwitz ruled in favour of the insurer, stating that 'the reason for my decision was that Crédit Suisse First Boston could not enjoy the money it earned illicitly to prevent such conduct in the future'.[60]

On 21 August 2001, Michael Kopper, a former Enron executive, was declared guilty for his participation in entities deconsolidated from Enron's balance sheet. On 31 October, Andrew Fastow, former Chief Financial Officer, was accused of 78 charges of fraud. This trial resulted in Fastow confessing his crime on 14 January 2004, for two accusations of fraud; this confession resulted in an agreed sentence of ten years' imprisonment in return for collaboration with justice.[61] In February that year, the Justice Department filed 42 charges against Skilling.[62]

The former Chairman, Kenneth Lay, was accused of seven counts of conspiracy and fraud against the stock market. Jeffrey Skilling had 32 charges brought against him, which also included documentary fraud and use of information privileged. The third accused for the same charges, as well as for money laundering, was Richard Causey, Enron's Senior Account Manager, who pleaded guilty in December 2005 before the Federal Court of Houston. After his confession, Causey was sentenced to seven years behind bars and a fine of US$1.25 million, and could produce a significant about-turn in the trial.[63] Kenneth Lay obtained more than US$200 million in an allegedly fraudulent manner, according to the prosecution, and Skilling obtained more than US$100 million, of which he had spent US$20 million by the end of 2005 in legal defence fees.[64] Causey only obtained US$9 million illicitly, so the Court released funds totalling US$500,000 to allow him to cover his defence costs. In spite of everything, the trial against Enron's middle-ranking directors in the summer of 2005 ended with the absolution of five former employees. Apparently, the jury was unable to understand the complex financial and accounting operations on which the prosecution based its case.[65]

In the trial against the senior executives, the defence claimed that Enron was a victim of the panic that ravaged the markets in 2001, and not of accounting fraud.[66] The prosecution, to avoid confusing the jury with guilty technicalities, focused on the abuse committed by the directors, which included their enormous wages and salaries in a period immediately prior to Enron's bankruptcy, and particularly because they lied to investors, a sign of their guilt according to the prosecution. For example, according to statements by the former Investor Relations Manager, Paula Rieker, Lay instructed personnel in her department to remove a reference to a reduction in equity of US$1,200 million as a result of an asset value adjustment 'because it had nothing to do with profits'.[67] The prosecution also accused Lay of lying to Andersen in Autumn 2001, when he stated that its British subsidiary, Wessex Water Services, was not going to be sold and that many investments would be carried out within the company, in order to avoid this actual value adjustment, as established in accounting standards, since this totalled between US$4,000 million to US$5,000 million, whereas the book value was US$9,000 million. A similar adjustment would have caused Enron to lose its 'investment grade' rating, essential for it to be able to pursue its derivatives business.[68]

In the trial, the confession of the company's former Investor Relations Director, Mark Koenig, was crucial, when he declared that the problems of the retail and networks divisions were known in Enron but were not notified to investors. The earnings of the networks subsidiary were obtained by selling parts of the company, but the message to the outside world was that the revenues came from customers using the network: 'I was instructed not to discuss details in public'. By the beginning of

2001, the retail division had accumulated losses amounting to US$230 million but in the many announcements to analysts it was claimed that business was thriving and, to avoid disclosing information on these numbers, the division was merged with the wholesale business division. On 25 January, Enron celebrated its day with investors and Skilling did not mention these losses, stating that Enron should trade at US$126. In April, Skilling declared that 'we had an excellent first quarter, and the retail division had an extraordinary quarter as well', concealing the losses. Internal documents revealed losses in June 2001 of US$726 million that were not communicated, according to Koenig, because 'it would have been a very big and bad surprise'.[69]

Enron's former Chief Financial Officer, Andrew Fastow, declared that Skilling, the company's former General Manager, encouraged him to set up the SPVs off the balance sheet and that he had explained the firm's bad position to its Chairman Kenneth Lay, who nevertheless lied to investors. According to Fastow, Skilling ordered him 'to get me as much of that juice as you can', so these off-balance-sheet companies created to conceal losses in 1999 were maintained. In Fastow's words, 'the only purpose of these off-balance-sheet entities was to make Enron's numbers appear the way he wanted them to appear'.[70] Ben Glisan, the former Treasurer, supported these declarations; he also recognized having created another off-balance-sheet company, Raptor, to conceal investment losses.

Sentences were announced at the end of May 2006. Lay and Skilling were declared guilty of 6 and 19 charges, respectively, including accounting fraud. The sentence included prison terms of up to 45 years for Lay and 185 years for Skilling, but Lay's death in July precluded his imprisonment.

The Dean of the Faculty of Law at Texas University, William Powers, was commissioned by the North American Congress to analyze the Enron case. In his report, Powers concluded that the hedging operations arranged by the company were not real because, in practice, Enron was hedging its risks with itself. Powers accused the firm's directors of creating the income statement 'from top to bottom', Andrew Fastow of getting rich at Enron's expense and Kenneth Lay as the person ultimately responsible for the scandal, either through abuse or neglect, and of having promoted a culture within the company that later proved to be suicidal. The Powers Report concludes by stating that 70 per cent of Enron's profits generated between the third quarter of 2000 and the third quarter of 2001 were false.[71] Today, Enron has no more than 300 employees responsible for resolving the 1,000 legal proceedings it has open.[72]

What better epitaph for this chapter than the declarations of the then North American Deputy Attorney General, Paul J. McNulty, after hearing the guilty verdict in the Enron case:

Our criminal laws will be enforced just as vigorously against corporate executives as against street criminals. This verdict encourages us to continue to combat corruption wherever we find it.[73]

8
Conclusion

The financial fraud in Comptronix Corp. began in 1989, around the time the company lost a sizable customer. Rather than report disappointing results, management instituted a profit-increasing scheme that entailed collusion among several members of the management team. Basically, inventory was increased and cost of goods sold was reduced for a fictitious amount, boosting current sales and gross profit. This adjustment, for varying amounts, was recorded on a regular basis, typically monthly. To hide the adjustment from analysts, portions of the bogus inventory were moved to the equipment account, as it was easier to hide the overstated amounts there. Fake invoices were prepared to support the increases to equipment, making it appear that actual purchases of equipment had been made. Inventory was also reduced through the recording of fictitious sales, phoney accounts receivable were recorded. To show collections of these accounts receivable that did not really occur, the company wrote checks to vendors supposedly in payment for its equipment purchases. These checks, which were not endorsed by the bogus equipment-vendor payees, were then deposited in the company's own bank account, resulting in a simultaneous increases and decrease to its cash account. While not changing the cash balance, the complicated arrangement gave the appearance of cash activity, of collection of accounts receivable and payment of amounts due. This last step required participation by the company's bank. A bank spokesperson said the deposit arrangement was put in place 'to accomplish a legitimate business purpose'... The alleged financial fraud of Comptronix Corp. may have begun small. By the time it was uncovered, however, it had grown to immense proportions and involved many individuals.

Charles W. Mulford, in *The Financial Numbers Game*

Table 8.1 Money paid to investors as a consequence of litigation

Case/date	Entity	Millions of dollars
Enron		
August 2005	CIBC	2,400
June 2005	JP Morgan Chase	2,000
	Citigroup	2,000
October 2004	Lehman Brothers	225
June 2004	Bank of America	69
Total Enron		6,694
Worldcom		
May 2005	Citigroup	2,580
March 2005	JP Morgan Chase	2,000
	Bank of America	460
	Deutsche Bank	325
	ABN Amro	278
	West LB	75
	Tokyo Mitsubishi	75
	Lehman Brothers	63
	Caboto Holding	37
	BNP Paribas	37
	Mizuho	37
	CSFB	12
	Goldman Sachs	12
	UBS	12
Total WorldCom		6,003

Source: *The Wall Street Journal*, 23 December 2005.

Total fines imposed by the SEC on companies for accounting fraud in the period 2002–2005 were greater than those imposed since its creation in 1934.[1] Creative accounting is not an entertaining, academic or folkloric subject. Creative accounting is not just about going to prison, it is about money, as the Table 8.1 shows.

Substantial amounts of money were also paid to the SEC in out-of-court settlements: AIG paid over US$1,500 million; ten investment banks paid US$1,400 million to settle investigations into the lack of impartiality in their stock market analyses; North American investment funds paid US$3,000 million to settle investigations into abuse committed against minority investors through instructions to liquidate funds; and Time Warner paid a fine of US$300 million for inflating its advertising revenue figures.[2]

Harvey Pitt, President of the SEC in 2002, recommended that, to prevent future 'Enron's, accountants should include the following recommendations to client companies for consideration in their communications to investors:

1. Provide financial data at current value and their trend;
2. Use clear language, and not dark financial terms;
3. Identify the three or five most critical standards for corporate accounts.

For some considerable time, accountants have been asking for uniform accounting standards, and this uniformity must also apply to the way accounts are presented, classified and evaluated.[3] The plethora of accounting standards worldwide increases the likelihood of subjective accounting treatment that could lead to accounting fraud. International accounting standards have reduced opportunities for such fraud, and a merger of North American and international reporting standards, championed by distinguished financial experts such as the SEC's Chief Accountant Donald Nicolalsen,[4] would further diminish the opportunities for companies to commit accounting fraud, although time is still required to implement the, as yet, volatile accounting standards before undertaking a full blown merger of standards.[5]

In the US, financial reporting to the investment community has been regulated by legislation since 1934. Nevertheless, the implementation of the Sarbanes–Oxley Act in 2002 was a revolutionary step in cleaning up company accounts and structurally changing the way accounts are prepared. This law required, among other things, the reconciliation of any earnings metrics used by companies with book income as regulated under the North American system. This provision attempted to limit the abuse committed by numerous firms, which used 'pro forma earnings' to reflect only recurrent items, and in practice it meant that only positive aspects were reflected in these truly *sui generis* earnings, while negative aspects were left out. It also forced companies to attribute the same mediatic importance to both profit figures. For example, in communications to investors, if a specific size of letter was used to indicate 'pro forma' earnings, the same size letter had to be used to reflect book income. This provision was essential because the market was obsessed with 'pro forma' earnings, which normally excluded extraordinary and other vague items. In the period 1991–2001, these earnings represented 84 per cent of book income. However, in 2001 they only represented 55 per cent, and, in 2002, 47 per cent. In other words, the quality of 'pro forma' earnings reported by the market had decreased considerably. The Sarbanes–Oxley Act forced companies to increase the level of information provided on exceptional expenses, which had become a type of jumble box for the mess caused by the crazy policy of acquisitions between 1998 and 2000. If the action generating the exceptional cost took place within a period of 24 months immediately before the expense was incurred, it could not be treated as 'extraordinary'. Section 404 of the Sarbanes–Oxley Act also established the legally binding condition for companies to implement adequate internal control systems to review accounting, since, as the advertising agency Interpublic admitted, 'weak internal controls lead to accounting errors'; at the same time, Section 404 recognised accounting errors in acquisitions, income and leases.[6]

As a consequence of the application of the Sarbanes–Oxley Act in 2005, the number of accounting reclassifications rose sharply: from 613 in 2004 to 1,195 in 2005; the number of 'errors' in the recognition of expenses increased from 167 to 443; errors in the classification of assets, from 167 to 318; the manipulation of corporate equity, from 133 to 235; readjustments due to incorrect revenue recognition, from 122 to 160; and accounting entry errors from 72 to 142. The number of foreign enterprises with securities listed in New York markets, and therefore obliged to present their financial statements to the SEC, that were forced to reclassify their accounts increased from 27 to 100.[7] This is not surprising because now many international firms, particularly Russian companies, prefer to float their shares on the London market instead of New York. This has fuelled a debate within the SEC on whether it should regulate the standards established in the Sarbanes–Oxley Act,[8] which already suggests the advent of a new cycle of accounting surprises.

In Europe, the adoption of IFRS was like a breath of fresh air in accounting systems, since it cleaned up the image of financial reporting after the notorious scandals and allowed extremely diverse national accounting systems to be harmonized worldwide. Although the IFRS standards have thrown light on accounting black boxes, such as the pension funds deficit and the market value of derivatives contracts, criticisms of the standards are increasingly virulent. There is concern that the obsession with valuing each asset and liability at actual market value could introduce excessive volatility in company profit and loss accounts. Existing reporting standards are now so complex that people might begin to think they are becoming ineffective. Finally, it has been stated that the IFRS over-regulate; for example, in relation to the comments that directors must include to accompany accounts.[9] In fact, there have long been calls to develop an 'alternative bookkeeping system'. This would allow companies to use the footnotes in annual reports to present their discerning opinions on official accounting statements, as well explanations for this discernment. This alternative accounting system would complement information provided to the investment community, and also offer a vision on the optimism or pessimism with which the firm looks to the future.[10]

Corporate governance is another key area in which accounting abuse must be stamped out. The principle of 'what you don't know can't harm you' is no longer applicable. The key principle in question is ensuring that company managers do not have to report to those responsible for auditing their accounts. The best way to substantiate this principle is through an audit committee formed by independent directors with relevant experience in accounting and in the capital markets. This committee should be responsible for appointing external auditors, as well as for hierarchically supervizing internal corporate audits. The risks assumed by members of the board of directors are clearly increasing, as are the problems facing Thierry Breton, the former French Minister of Economy and Finance, due to his past position as director of the chemical company Rhodia.[11] It is therefore essential for directors to be very familiar with the accounting systems used by the company where they work. Their knowledge and understanding should not only focus on financial accounting, it should also cover tax accounting. This information must be requested particularly from the members of audit committees. As mentioned above, in line with the most advanced rules of good governance these committees must be formed by independent directors with experience in accounting and responsible for appointing auditors.[12] However, a smile still comes to my face whenever I hear political parties insisting that companies appoint 'independent' directors on their boards of directors to protect 'minority' shareholders. And I smile for one very simple reason: how many 'independent' directors are there on the National Securities Market Commission or in the Bank of Spain, or in the Council of Ministers itself, all bodies where the protection of 'minority shareholders' is possibly even more important than in companies? Unfortunately, we can once again only look on at another frustrating case of the double standards in politics, where political authorities appoint their 'directors' in administrations that have a crucial role to play for our country based on 'shares' assignable to each political party, while demanding corporate governance practices from private companies that it does not apply to itself.

The regulatory bodies, led by the SEC in North America, is taking firm steps to promote transparency by making it obligatory for companies to provide full details of the remuneration received by directors, covering all items, including bonuses, contributions to pension funds and even loans to directors and board members guaranteed by the shares and options of these directors, a common ploy to prevent directors from selling their shares, since these sales are looked upon enviously by institutional investors.[13] Thus, the recently bankrupt securities agency REFCO granted a US$430 million loan to its former Managing Director, Philip Bernett, without mentioning this in its accounts, which were audited by Grant Thorton.[14] REFCO suspended payments two months after being floated on the stock market.

Regulation tends to force listed companies to provide information on all types of remuneration received by directors, including stock options, variable wages and salaries, social benefits and retirement contributions. This trend began after the General Electric and Tyco scandals. In the General Electric scandal, the famous former Chairman, Jack Welch, received benefits upon retirement such as an apartment in New York, the use of the corporate jet or a bodyguard; in Tyco, the company's former Director, Frank Walsh, received a commission of US$20 million for his participation in an operation in 2001. Shareholders were never informed of these payments, and both companies agreed out-of-court settlements to conclude litigation without admitting they had acted wrongfully.[15] In the US, regulatory pressure remains at its highest levels. At the end of 2005, the SEC announced that companies had to inform investors of the value of pension funds and stock option programmes set up for the five most senior directors in the company, in order to achieve more transparent measurements of remunerations and not limit these to salaries and bonuses.[16]

Financial statements are not designed for persons unfamiliar with accounts. They can only be properly interpreted with the help of expert advisers. Two financial statements can only be compared if it is considered that both companies are comparable. Accounting principles must be uniform, but the results of this uniformity can differ in each particular case.[17] The Eighth European Directive, approved on 22 June 2005, will regulate the audit profession in the European Union. The Directive regulates the independence of auditors, the obligation of companies to set up audit committees in countries where there are no rules governing this aspect, and the elimination of corporate rotation, which is replaced by a key audit partner rotation system (audit partners firms are rotated every seven years).[18] This directive was the result of intense lobbying by European business organizations, who managed to convince the EU

to reduce some of the stricter aspects of the initial drafts of the directive which, for example, proposed making audit committees obligatory
without restrictions and rotating key audit partners every five years.[19]
External auditing services should always be permitted, provided that
they do not undermine the independence of auditors.

Corporate pressure to meet analysts' forecasts has often been a factor determining companies to overstep the mark and use creative
accounting. We have also seen how many companies choose to sacrifice
decisions that would be positive for them in the medium term simply to meet forecasts. Thus, 80 per cent of the executives interviewed
in a study stated that they would reduce expenses in important areas
such as research, development or contracts in order to achieve the figures expected by the market. These circumstances have meant that the
number of North American firms presenting forecasts diminished from
75 per cent in 2003 to 50 per cent in 2006. McKinsey, the management
consulting firm, performed a study of 4,000 companies and showed
how there was no empirical evidence to confirm that presenting forecasts to the market would improve share multiples, increase returns for
shareholders or reduce stock volatility.[20]

Remember that the quality of accounting income is determined by
its recurrence, the percentage of these benefits that are transformed
into cash, and the percentage of income generated by the company's
main business lines. In general, research has shown that companies
with better quality assets usually perform better on the stock market in
the medium term.

Although this book examines the main accounting scandals, it is
important to remember that these are singular and exceptional incidents
within the overall business fabric. A strong and independent accounting
system, efficient good governance systems and solid ethical principles
can help consolidate this trend in the future.

Finally, we should not lose sight of the ultimate consequences of
criminal responsibility deriving from the falsification of financial doc-
umentation. Although the former Managing Director of HealthSouth,
Richard Scrushy, was absolved of 36 charges relating to accounting fraud
in the HealthSouth accounting scandal in 2003, others did not escape so
lightly. The CEO of WorldCom was sentenced to 25 years' imprisonment
in 2005; Martha Stewart, former Chairwoman of Martha Stewart, spent
five months in prison and five months under house arrest; John Rigas,
the 80-year-old Chairman of Adelphia Communications, was sentenced
in 2004 to 15 years behind bars and his 49-year-old son Tim to 20 years;
the former Chief Executive of Tyco, L. Dennis Kozlowski, was sentenced

to between eight and 25 years in jail;[21] Jeffrey Skilling, former Managing Director of Enron, faced more than 20 years in jail for 19 charges of which he has been found guilty, as was Kenneth Lay, former Chairman of the firm, who was guilty of six crimes, but his death in June 2005 prevented his imprisonment. European legislation has achieved similar, albeit modest, results. Cees van der Hoeven and Michiel Meurs, former Managing Director and Chief Financial Officer of Ahold, respectively, were sentenced in May 2006 to nine months' imprisonment for fraud associated with concealing accounting documents from the company's auditor, Deloitte & Touche, during the period of their mandate, in relation to a consolidation operation. Paradoxically, had they been tried for this crime in the US they would have been imprisoned for up to 30 years.[22] On 6 June 2006, the trial began against 64 former managers of Parmalat, including the former Chairman, Calisto Tanzi, and the former Financial Director, Fausto Tonna. In the words of Tanzi's lawyer, 'Tanzi obviously cannot have very high expectations in this trial ... what he is waiting for is a point-to-point reconstruction. He doesn't expect to be declared innocent'.[23]

So, in periods of economic prosperity accounting fraud will diminish but, as we move into a phase of lower economic growth and larger debt issues, the following statement will once again ring true: 'Human beings have few basic needs: find enough food, find a place to live, and keep debt off balance sheets'.[24]

Notes

Introduction

1. Securities and Exchange Commission, a body created in 1934 by the North American government after the 1929 recession to supervise proper market conduct. The equivalent body in Spain is the *Comisión Nacional del Mercado de Valores* (CNMV – National Securities Market Commission).
2. According to Levitt, the five techniques used most were:
   (i) *'Big Bath' charges to clean up balance sheets*
       This practice consisted of recording huge extraordinary charges, reducing the value of certain assets only to restate them later as ordinary income, thus generating greater income growth;
   (ii) *Creative acquisition accounting*
       The use of the pooling system to simulate mergers that were really acquisitions is another common accounting gimmick. Companies have also often treated acquired patents as goodwill and not as intangible assets, in order to write them off in twenty years and not in four or five as intangible assets should be amortized, normally in the case of research and development expenses;
   (iii) *Cookie jar reserves*
       These were overstated charges to generate reserves that were used in difficult years to mitigate earnings fluctuations;
   (iv) *Premature recognition of revenue*; and
   (v) *Reporting potential losses* as a specific percentage of possible losses and then reporting that their net income impact was too small to be relevant. Cf. http://www. sec.gov/news/speech/speecharchive/1998/spch220.txt

1   Revenue Recognition

1. http://www.lucent.com/investor/financialreports.html
2. 'Accounting Games Companies Play', *Wharton*, 14 July 2004. Article available at knowledge.wharton.edu
3. 'Revenue Recognition or the Software Industry', *Salomon Smith Barney*, May 2001.
4. Report issued by the SEC in January 2003, developing section 704 of the Sarbanes–Oxley Act of 2002.
5. 'Valuation and Accounting: Fire in Ahold: Accounting for Vendor Rebates', *Salomon Smith Barney*, 26 February 2003.
6. Following examples in 'Revenue Recognition, Underestimated Issue in Equity Analysis', *UBS*, 28 October 2003, pp. 20 *et seq.*
7. http://www.rolls-royce.com/investors/reports/2002

8. If, for example, Rolls-Royce earns 10 excluding 3 corresponding to launch aids, and EADS earns 10 including these launch aids, and both companies have a stock market value of 100, both would have PERs of 10. The multiple, not adjusted due to the different accounting systems, indicates that both companies are at the same relative price when, if the adjustment were performed (reducing Rolls-Royce's profits by 3 or increasing those of EADS by 3) the answer is clear: EADS has a lower stock price. 'Footnotes', *UBS*, 10 March 2003.

9. Regulated by IFRS 2 and 11.

10. The 2004 Annual Report can be consulted at: http://www.gamesa.es/gamesa/index.html

11. International Financial Accounting Standards, previously known as IAS, or International Accounting Standards. The issued standards are known as IFRS (International Financial Reporting Standards) plus the number of the standard, and in English IAS or IFRS (depending on the time of issuance) plus the standard number. Political pressure in the preparation of the accounting standards was greater than expected. The Presidency of the International Accounting Standards Board (IASB), the body responsible for issuing the IFRS, valid in the European Union, passed from Paul Volcker, the former President of the North American Federal Reserve, to Tomasso Padoa-Schioppa, not without a certain amount of influence from the EU. Cfr. *Financial Times*, 27 December 2005.

12. http://www.fifa.com/en/media/index/0,1369,74717,00.html

13. 'Footnotes', *UBS*, 20 April 2004.

14. We do not know the current values, so to simplify we have used the example.

15. 'Footnotes', *UBS*, 7 September 2004.

16. http://www.sec.gov/Archives/edgar/data/108772/000095013002002336/0000950130-02-002336.txt

17. In December 2005, it was US$13.

18. 'Revenue Recognition, Underestimated Issue in Equity Analysis', *UBS*, 28 October 2003.

19. http://www.vodafone.com/section_article/0,3035, CATEGORY_ID%253D404%2526LANGUAGE_ID%253D2%2526CONTENT_ID%253D230864,00.html

20. 'Revenue Recognition: Underestimated Issue in Equity Analysis', *UBS*, 28 April 2003.

21. In North American accounting, Statement of Financial Accounting Standard (SFAS) 48 establishes that if this right exists and its impact cannot be estimated with certainty, the revenue must not be recognized until the sale is collected.

22. http://www.ahold.com/index.asp?id=855

23. http://www.ahold.com/index.asp?id=855

24. Financial Accounting Standards Board, created in 1973, currently based in Connecticut. It is an interdisciplinary accounting body with seven members which the SEC recognizes as the authority for establishing the accounting criteria to be followed by listed companies in the US by issuance of the

Statements of Financial Accounting Standards, more popularly known as SFAS, followed by the regulation number.

25. 'Valuation and Accounting: Fire in Ahold: Accounting for Vendor Rebates', *Salomon Smith Barney*, 26 February 2003.

26. http://www.parmalat.com/en/fset.html?sez=dc

27. http://www.heinekeninternational.com/pages/article/s2/12230000000050-13660000000045/financialinformation.aspx

28. http://www.heinekeninternational.com/pages/article/s2/12230000000050-13660000000045/financialinformation.aspx

29. 'Footnotes', *UBS*, 15 September 2003.

30. Quotes from Schilit (2002), pp. 63 *et seq.*

31. Schilit (2002), p. 72.

32. *Expansión*, 2 June 2005.

33. In this case, the techniques are almost completely fraudulent. These techniques are taken from Schilit (2002), pp. 83 *et seq.*

34. 'Software Industry: Enterprise Software Accounting Issues', *ING*, 6 October 1998.

35. SAB 101 Standard, December 1999, to be applied by all North American companies.

36. 'Footnotes', *UBS*, 18 November 2003.

37. EITF 00-21, in force since 1 July 2003. EITF means 'emergency issues task force'. These are decisions to clarify the practical implementation of accounting standards adopted by the FASB, which must ratify the EITF in order for it become an accounting standard. The reference number refers to the year and number, hence 00-21 refers to the twenty-first decision of 2000.

38. 'Revenue Recognition of the Software Industry', *Salomon Smith Barney*, May 2001.

39. 'Footnotes', *UBS*, 16 June 2003.

40. 'Jam Today: Revenue Recognition and Cash Flow at IT Services Companies', *West LB*, February 2004.

41. 'Revenue Recognition of the Software Industry', *Salomon Smith Barney*, May 2001.

42. 'Jam Today: Revenue Recognition and Cash Flow at IT Services Companies', *West LB*, February 2004.

43. 'Revenue Recognition of the Software Industry', *Salomon Smith Barney*, May 2001.

44. 'Can You Trust the Numbers', *UBS*, March 2002.

45. 'Footnotes', *UBS*, 12 May 2003.

46. Schilit (2002), pp. 70 *et seq.*

47. In any case, it is important to highlight that although international and North American accounting standards require companies to present cash flow statements, many firms use the 'indirect' method (based on net income) and not the 'direct' method (based on operating income); hence, it may be very difficult to calculate the latter until the presentation of cash flow statements by the direct method becomes obligatory.

48. Unbilled receivables.
49. 'Jam Today: Revenue Recognition and Cash Flow at IT Services Companies', *West LB*, February 2004.
50. 'Jam Today: Revenue Recognition and Cash Flow at IT Services Companies', *West LB*, February 2004.
51. 'Revenue Recognition of the Software Industry', *Salomon Smith Barney*, May 2001.
52. SEC, SB 101, 1999.
53. International Financial Accounting Standard.
54. IFRS 18, issued in 1993.
55. Stock market capitalization, plus net debt, plus minority interest, plus other financial liabilities not reflected in the balance sheets.
56. 'Can You Trust the Numbers?', *UBS*, March 2002.
57. *Expansión*, 31 October 2005.

2 Stock Options: The Great Accounting Fallacy

1. Price earnings ratio: stock market capitalisation divided by corporate profit.
2. 'The Art of Accounting: Counting the cost of option expensing in capital goods', *Deutsche Bank*, 7 January 2003.
3. 'Footnotes', *UBS*, September 2004.
4. 'Can You Trust the Numbers?', *UBS*, March 2002.
5. *The Wall Street Journal*, 12 October 2005.
6. Federal Accounting Standard Board.
7. 'Heads up on Current Accounting Issues & Trends', *Credit Suisse First Boston*, 18 March 2003.
8. 'Accounting for Stock-based Compensation', *Bear Stearns*, July 2003.
9. 'The Art of Accounting: Counting the Cost of Option Expensing in Capital Goods', *Deutsche Bank*, 7 January 2003.
10. For this purpose, North American accounting standards consider that stock options must be recognized as soon as the employee is notified that he/she has been granted these stock options, regardless of the date on which the Board of Directors takes the decision.
11. 'Footnotes', *UBS*, 4 May 2005.
12. For example, if a company changes to the new system in 2003, and in 2002 and in 2003 it issued shares valued at US$90 for a period of three years, it would recognize US$30 of cost in 2002 and US$60 in 2003.
13. 'Multinational Valuation, Pensions, Economic Profits', *UBS*, 1 June 2005: 14.
14. 'The Art of Accounting: Counting the Cost of Option Expensing in Capital Goods', *Deutsche Bank*, 7 January 2003.
15. 'Footnotes', *UBS*, August 2003.
16. 'Accounting Practices in the Semiconductor Industry', *Deutsche Bank*, 4 September 2003.

17. *The Wall Street Journal*, 12 October 2005.
18. 'Can You Trust the Numbers?', *UBS*, March 2002.
19. *Financial Times*, 29 December 2005.
20. 'Option Backdating: Is it Really Wrong?', *UBS*, 30 June 2006.
21. *Financial Times*, 28 July 2006.
22. *The Wall Street Journal*, 7 August 2006.
23. *Financial Times*, 29 December 2005.
24. *The Wall Street Journal*, 1 June 2006.
25. *The Wall Street Journal*, 1 June 2006.
26. *Financial Times*, 31 May 2006.
27. *The Wall Street Journal*, 13 June 2006.
28. Different documents by the management consultancy firm Towers Perrin supported Enron's remuneration schemes in the trial that determined the guilt of the company's managers. Consult the committee's report at www.gpoaccess.gov
29. *The Wall Street Journal*, 15 February 2006.
30. Schilit (2002): 144.
31. 'Footnotes', *UBS*, 1 March 2005.
32. *The Wall Street Journal*, 3 May 2006.
33. 'Footnotes', *UBS*, February 2004.

3   Off-balance-sheet Financing

1. These included REPOS, interest rate SWAPs, collateralized mortgage obligations, debt without recourse, purchase and sale options, unusual preferred shares and financial guarantees.
2. Shelvin (1987).
3. Sever and Chroeder (1988).
4. Khambata (1989).
5. Such as operating leases, renting, factoring and vendor financing.
6. 'Adelphia, Addressing Off-balance-sheet', *Salomon Smith Barney*, 27 March 2002.
7. 'US Wireless', *Bernstein Research*, 14 November 2001.
8. http://www.ericsson.com/investors/financial_reports/1999-2002/12month 00en.pdf
9. 'Raytheon', *Bear Stearns*, 16 August 2001.
10. 'Footnotes', *UBS*, July 2004.
11. Burns, Jaedicke and Sangster (1963).
12. Profits slightly less for tax reasons.
13. 'Footnotes', *UBS*, December 2003.
14. Bianco, David, 'Analysis of Operating Leases', *UBS*, 18 October 2004.
15. 'Airlines Accounting', *Morgan Stanley*, 1998.
16. 'Off-balance-sheet Issues in Restaurants', *Credit Suisse First Boston*, 19 April 2002.

17. 'Can You Trust the Numbers?', *UBS*, 2002.
18. 2005 annual report, page 2, available at: http://grupo.iberia.es/content/ GrupoIberia/Documentos/memoria per cent20Informe per cent20anual per cent202005.pdf
19. It is common practice in the finance sector to capitalize financial lease payments by multiplying same seven or eight times in order to estimate the total volume of obligations under these contracts.
20. *Expansión*, 4 May 2005.
21. *Expansión*, December 2004.
22. 'Hotel Operating Leases', *UBS*, 10 December 2002.
23. *The Wall Street Journal*, 10 May 2006.
24. Telefónica, 2001 annual report, available at: http://informeanual.telefónica. es/upload/esp/memorias/2001.pdf
25. Bauman (2003).
26. 'Off-balance-sheet Finance', *UBS*, 31 June 2002.
27. 'Off-balance-sheet Debt at Dow and Dupont', *Salomon Smith Barney*, 13 May 2002.
28. Casabona, Patrick: 'Off Balance Sheet Finance: A Second Look', *Practical Accountant*, February 2004.
29. 'FAS 150', *UBS*, 5 November 2003.
30. 'Accounting Implications of Enron', *UBS*, 17 January 2002.
31. 'It Services Off-balance-sheet Financing: Win, Win, Win', *Bernstein Research*, 2003.
32. Telefónica, 2001 annual report, available at: http://informeanual.telefónica. es/upload/esp/memorias/2001.pdf
33. 'Thai Banks: Off-balance-sheet Guarantees', *Schroeders*, 30 May 1997.
34. The company sells its accounts receivable to another company. This vehicle obtains the necessary liquidity to perform the purchase of these receivables by issuing A-1+/P-1 rated commercial paper, through a channel, which normally performs issues for different SPVs. Cash flows sold to the SPV will enhance as its credit rating improves, so that the credit rating of the financial assets sold by the SPV is better than the credit rating of the company that has generated those assets (and which avoids becoming indebted thanks to the SPV). This credit enhancement of cash flows can be performed using overcollateralization mechanisms, the letter of credit facility (provided by a financial entity) and a partial guarantee from a company (for example, parent company), the minimum rating being 'investment grade'.

      However, the most common and economical form of credit enhancement is overcollateralization. For example, if accounts receivable are sold amounting to US$100, the 'SPV' will pay the entity selling the assets a specific amount of money in cash today, for example US$90. The remaining US$10 will only be paid to the company if the income obtained from the accounts receivable in terms of accounts sold exceeds the amount necessary to repay the first US$90. The SPV will have obtained funds to finance the first US$90 through the issue of asset-backed securities. The US$10 corresponding to overcollateralization is subordinate to the repayment of the previous US$90. Before the securitization programme starts, the customer portfolio management systems are checked; their intrinsic credit rating and all the other elements that might influence cash flow quality are studied. This analysis is performed by both the agent bank and by recognized rating agencies. Then, monthly sale operations are carried out. If the balance of the customer portfolio grows during a given month, the company obtains additional finance. Since commercial paper is issued monthly in the total amount of the portfolio, if this increases, the liquidity obtained is sufficient to pay off the maturing debt corresponding to the issue of the previous month, and the company will receive easily sufficient liquidity.

35. For example, leverage, liquidity, profitability or cash flows, own from traditional bank financing.

36. The credit risk, US$147,000 million, is not equivalent to the notional value of the contracts, US$4.6 trillion, since credit risk is calculated as the cost of replacing all the profitable contracts at year-end, while the notional value would be equivalent to the non-payment of all the interest by the counterparty with a company for a nominal value of US$10 million during five years and the position at year-end in the bank's favour is US$500,000, the notional value will continue to be US$10, but the credit risk will be only US$500,000. From the notional value of US$4.6 trillion, it was calculated that 3.9 was the position on interest rates, 0.5 on currency, and 1 on other risks, mainly variable income.

37. 'Bond Insurance: What if the FASB Off-balance-sheet Crackdown Goes Through?', *Credit Suisse First Boston*, 7 March 2002.

38. *Financial Times*, 16 June 2005.

39. The strict North American standards governing the consolidation of SPVs is FIN 46. *Vid.* 'Heads Up on Current Accounting Issues & Trends', *Credit Suisse First Boston*, 18 March 2003.

40. 'Global Accounting: Off-Balance Sheet Finance', *UBS*, 31 January 2002.

41. 'If Off-balance-sheet Becomes a Taboo it is an Opportunity', *Credit Suisse First Boston*, 1 February 2002.

4   Risk Management, Derivatives and Hybrid Instruments

1. *Financial Times*, 6 February 2006.
2. 'Footnotes', *UBS*, 7 September 2004.
3. 'Accounting Issues', *Bear Stearns*, 5 February 1998.
4. 'Footnotes', *UBS*, 17 February 2004.
5. 'Footnotes', *UBS*, 29 June 2004.
6. 'The Changing Use of Derivatives: More Hedging, Less Speculation', *Wharton*, 12 February 2003. Article available at knowledge.wharton.edu
7. ED 7.
8. 'Footnotes', *UBS*, 8 September 2004.
9. 'Footnotes', *UBS*, December 2003.
10. 'Footnotes', *UBS*, 11 May 2004.

11. 'Gearing & Hybrid Securities', *UBS*, March 1999.
12. 'Footnotes', *UBS*, 15 September 2003.
13. Contingent convertibles or mandatory convertibles.
14. Which must be calculated, according to North American accounting standards (FAS 128) and IASs, based on shares issued, reducing the number of treasury stock and increasing by the dilution expected when stock options are exercised on shares, warrants and other convertibles. For more information, see 'EPS: Towards a Common Denominator II', *Bear Stearns*, 25 March 1996 and 'At The End: A Common Denominator', *Bear Stearns*, 7 April 1999.
15. Trigger price.
16. 'Contingent Convertibles', *UBS*, 1 October 2004.
17. 'CSFB Travel & Leisure: Accounting Watch', *Credit Suisse First Boston*, 13 July 2004.
18. 'Footnotes', *UBS*, 21 October 2003.
19. 'Footnotes', *UBS*, December 2002.
20. 'Heads Up on Current Accounting Issues and Trends', *Credit Suisse First Boston*, 18 March 2003.

5   Recognition of Expenses, Balance Sheet Fluctuations, Cash Flow and Quality of Earnings

1. 'Earnings Quality: The Winning Tortoise', *UBS*, 3 February 2004.
2. 'The Economic Implications of Corporate Financial Reporting', *NBER*, Working Paper no. 10550, June 2004.
3. *Financial Times*, 8 and 9 March 2006, citing a report by McKinsey.
4. 'Accounting Games Companies Play', *Wharton*, 14 July 2004. Article available at knowledge.wharton.edu
5. 'Heads Up on Current Accounting Issues and Trends', *Credit Suisse First Boston*, 18 March 2003.
6. Under the FIFO (first in, first out) method, the first items to enter a warehouse are the first to leave from a cost accounting standpoint; in times of rising inflation, this method increases company profits, but also raises its tax bill. The LIFO (last in, first out) method consists of precisely the opposite; the last items to enter the warehouse are the first to leave; hence, in a context characterized by rising prices, this method reduces profits *and* the corporate tax bill. The mean weighted cost analyzes the mean price of purchased produces, and applies this price to products leaving the warehouse.
7. *The Wall Street Journal*, 8 August 2006.
8. 'When an Asset is not an Asset', *UBS*, 20 June 2002.
9. Public announcement published on 23 January 2003; without the adjustment, the company's pre-tax profit would have been reduced by US$3 million, in the announcement it increased by US$27. *Vid.* 'Heads Up on

Current Accounting Issues and Trends', *Credit Suisse First Boston*, 18 March 2003.

10. For the following classifications and impact of IAS 37, 'Provision Accounting' is very useful, *UBS*, December 1998.
11. IAS 22 limits this practice.
12. *The Wall Street Journal*, 10 May 2006.
13. 'Footnotes', *UBS*, 19 January 2005.
14. 'Footnotes', *UBS*, 22 June 2004.
15. 'Spanish Banks: Are They Really That Efficient?', *UBS*, 11 July 2006.
16. 'Footnotes', *UBS*, 26 May 2004.
17. 'Footnotes', *UBS*, 1 February 2005.
18. *The Wall Street Journal*, 2 September 2005.
19. International Accounting Standards Board: accounting body responsible for issuing international accounting standards.
20. 'Footnotes', *UBS*, 24 February 2004.
21. 'Heads Up on Current Accounting Issues and Trends', *Credit Suisse First Boston*, 18 March 2003.
22. 'When an Asset is not an Asset', *UBS*, 20 June 2002, p. 3.
23. For this section's comments, *vid.* 'Deferred Tax Assets: A New Cookie Jar?', *UBS*, 24 October 2003.
24. *Expansión*, 29 January 2006.
25. 'A New Deferred Tax Liability – Pernod Ricard', *UBS*, 12 April 2004.
26. Current ratio.
27. Harrison–Horngren, *Financial Accounting*, p. 221.
28. *Expansión*, 19 April 2006.
29. 'Heads Up on Current Accounting Issues and Trends', *Credit Suisse First Boston*, 18 March 2003.
30. *The Wall Street Journal*, 18 January 2006.
31. *The Wall Street Journal*, 5 October 2005.
32. 'Motion Picture Industry', *Schroeder Wertheim & Co.*, 24 August 1994.
33. *Financial Times*, 10 February 2006.
34. *Financial Times*, 24 July 2006.
35. 'Accounting Issues', *Bear Stearns*, 7 December 1998.
36. Koller (2003).
37. 'Does Earnings Quality Matter?', *UBS*, 21 January 2004.
38. 'Reg G. The Squeeze on Pro Forma', *UBS*, 11 February 2003.

6   Subjectivity in the Consolidation of Companies

1. *Expansión*, 1 December 2005.
2. *Financial Times*, 17 October 2005.
3. 'Can You Trust the Numbers?', *UBS*, p. 10,.
4. 'Footnotes', *UBS*, 9 July 2003.
5. *Financial Times*, 29 November 2005.

6. 'Heads Up on Current Accounting Issues and Trends', *Credit Suisse First Boston*, 18 March 2003.
7. 'Accounting Games Companies Play', *Wharton*, 14 July 2004. Article available at knowledge.wharton.edu
8. 'Accounting Impact of Builder Performance Analyzed', *Deutsche Bank*, 5 August 2003.
9. 'Heads Up on Current Accounting Issues and Trends', *Credit Suisse First Boston*, 18 March 2004.
10. 'Heads Up on Current Accounting Issues and Trends', *Credit Suisse First Boston*, 18 March 2003.
11. 'IFRS 3: Business Combinations', *UBS*, 19 April 2004.
12. http://www.gamesa.es/img/pdf/accionista/gobierno_corporativo/informe_Gobierno_2000.pdf
13. 'Footnotes', *UBS*, 10 February 2004.
14. 'Earnouts & contingent considerations', *UBS*, 4 July 2002.
15. Bauman (2003).
16. *Expansión*, 20 July 2005.
17. *Expansión*, 30 May 2006.

7 Creative Accounting in Public and Private Entities

1. *Expansión*, 6 October 2005.
2. *Expansión*, 15 February 2006.
3. *Expansión*, 19 May 2006.
4. *Financial Times*, 10 May 2006.
5. *France Presse*, 23 January 2006.
6. *Expansión*, 2 August 2006.
7. *Reuters*, 25 November 2005.
8. *Financial Times*, 13 January 2006.
9. One level below the maximum credit rating.
10. *Financial Times*, 9 March 2006.
11. *The Wall Street Journal*, 11 January 2006.
12. *Expansión*, 10 July 2006.
13. *Expansión*, 29 August 2005.
14. *The Wall Street Journal*, 29 May 2006.
15. *Financial Times*, 10 May 2006.
16. *The Wall Street Journal*, 8 June 2006.
17. *Financial Times*, 29 May 2006.
18. 'Parmalat. Chairman & CEO Calisto Tanzi Replaced by Enrico Bondi', *Citigroup*, 17 December 2003.
19. 'Parmalat. Chairman & CEO Calisto Tanzi Replaced by Enrico Bondi', *Citigroup*, 17 December 2003.
20. One hundred base points is equivalent to 1 per cent.
21. Note that the notional value exceded the investment value.

22. B. Cova, 'The Parmalat fraud has generated too little reform', *Financial Times*, 7 November 2005.
23. 'How Parmalat differs from US Scandals', Knowledge@Wharton, 28 January 2004. Available at: knowledge.wharton.upenn.edu
24. *Financial Times*, 23 February 2006.
25. *Financial Times*, 1 March 2006.
26. *Financial Times*, 8 July 2005.
27. *The Wall Street Journal*, 28 April 2005.
28. *Financial Times*, 8 March 2006.
29. *The Wall Street Journal*, 17 June 2008.
30. *Expansión*, 29 June 2005.
31. *The Wall Street Journal*, 29 December 2005.
32. *Financial Times*, 10 May 2006.
33. *Financial Times*, 7 October 2005.
34. A. Micklethwait, 'Worldcom: the Downfall of a Giant', *IMD*, 2004.
35. H. Prasad Sharma, 'The Worldcom Accounting Scandal', *ICFAI*, 2003.
36. A.Micklethwait, 'Worldcom: the Downfall of a Giant', *IMD*, 2004.
37. A. Micklethwait, 'Worldcom: the Downfall of a Giant', *IMD*, 2004.
38. A. Micklethwait, 'Worldcom: the Downfall of a Giant', *IMD*, 2004.
39. *Expansión*, 2 March 2005.
40. *Financial Times*, 12 August 2005.
41. *The Wall Street Journal*, 12 August 2005.
42. *Expansión*, 31 January 2006.
43. *The Wall Street Journal*, 7 February 2006.
44. K. Bong, 'Enron Corp.', *Richard Ivey School of Business*, 2003.
45. 'The Enron Odyssey (A): The Special Purpose of SPEs', *Harvard Business School*, 23 August 2004.
46. K. Bong, 'Enron Corp.', *Richard Ivey School of Business*, 2003.
47. K. Bong, 'Enron Corp.', *Richard Ivey School of Business*, 2003.
48. K. Bong, 'Enron Corp.', *Richard Ivey School of Business*, 2003.
49. C. Edwards, 'Beyond Enron. The fate of Andrew Fastow and Company casts a harsh light on off-balance-sheet financing', *CFO*, February 2002.
50. *Expansión*, 30 January 2006.
51. *The Wall Street Journal*, 30 January 2006.
52. F. Grabowski, 'Enron', *Universitat Pompeu Fabra*, p. 11, 2002.
53. *The Wall Street Journal*, 18 February 2006.
54. M. Shashidhar, 'Coca-Cola: Questionable Accounting Practices', *ICFAI University Press*, 2004.
55. S.L. Schwarcz, 'Enron, and the Use and Abuse of Special Purpose Entities in Corporate Structures', *The Financier*, 9, 1–4, 2002.
56. *The Wall Street Journal*, 30 January 2006.
57. 'Credit Risk Transfer in a post-Enron world', *UBS*, March 2003.
58. *Expansión*, 1 June 2005.
59. 'Enron & Andersen: Bad Apples or Bad Barrel?', *Wharton*, 4 May 2005. Article available at: knowledge.wharton.edu
60. *The Wall Street Journal*, 13 December 2005.

61. *The Wall Street Journal*, 12 August 2005.
62. 'Enron Corporation: May 6, 2001 Sell Recommendation', *Harvard Business School*, 18 May 2004.
63. *The Wall Street Journal*, 29 December 2005.
64. *The Wall Street Journal*, 27 December 2005.
65. *Financial Times*, 29 December 2005.
66. *The Wall Street Journal*, 13 February 2006.
67. *Financial Times*, 24 February 2006.
68. Declarations by Mr. Hannon, who confessed, and former manager of international assets at Enron. *The Wall Street Journal*, 7 March 2006.
69. *The Wall Street Journal*, 3 February 2006.
70. *Financial Times*, 9 March 2006.
71. 'Testimony of William C. Powers, Jr. Chairman of the Special Investigative Committee of the Board of Directors of Enron Corporation before the Committee on Commerce, Science and Transportation, United States Senate', 12 February 2005.
72. *The Wall Street Journal*, 1 February 2006.
73. *The Wall Street Journal*, 29 May 2006.

8 Conclusion

1. *Financial Times*, 22 December 2005.
2. *The Wall Street Journal*, 7 February 2006.
3. SIMMONS, John K.: 'A Concept of Comparability in Financial Reporting' *The Accounting Review*, October 1967.
4. *Financial Times*, 3 November 2005.
5. *Financial Times*, 3 November 2005.
6. *Financial Times*, 16 December 2005.
7. *The Wall Street Journal*, 3 March 2006.
8. *Financial Times*, 15 December 2005.
9. *Financial Times*, 29 December 2005.
10. LI, David H.: 'Alternative accounting procedures and the entity concept', *The Accounting Review*, January 1963.
11. *The Wall Street Journal*, 28 June 2005.
12. 'Board members: Facing public scrutiny', Wharton, 18 June 2003. Article available at: knowledge.wharton.edu
13. *The Wall Street Journal*, 2 February 2006.
14. *Financial Times*, 20 December 2005.
15. *The Wall Street Journal*, 18 January 2006.
16. *Financial Times*, 29 December 2005.
17. KEMP, S., PATRICK, 'Controversies on the Construction of Financial Statements', *The Accounting Review*, January 1963.
18. *Expansión*, 23 June 2005.
19. *Financial Times*, 22 June 2005.
20. *Financial Times*, 24 July 2006.

21. Tyco had to pay a 50 million dollar fine in spring 2006 to the SEC to settle this 1,000 million dollar accounting fraud case. This manipulation included increasing profits by 500 million dollars by reducing the value of the assets of the acquired firms, in order to reduce amortization and exaggerate general provisions to smooth profits by reducing provisions. Tyco also exaggerated its operating income by 567 million dollar for fees charged to distributors of its subsidiary ADT Security Services Inc. *Wall Street Journal*, 18 April 2006.
22. *Financial Times*, 23 May 2006.
23. *The Wall Street Journal*, 6 June 2006.
24. Greene, Richard: *The Joys of Leasing*, November 1980, p. 51.

References

Bauman, Mark (2003) 'The Impact and Valuation of Off-balance-sheet Activities Concealed by Equity Method Accounting', *Accounting Horizon*, December.

Bianco, David (2004) 'Analysis of Operating Leases', *UBS*, 18 October.

Bong, Karen (2003) 'Enron Corp.', *Richard Ivey School of Business*.

Burns, Joseph, Jaedicke, R.K. and Sangster, J.M. (1963) 'Financial Reporting of Purchase Contracts used to Guarantee Large Investments', *Accounting Review*, January.

Casabona, Patrick (2004) 'Off Balance Sheet Finance: A Second Look', *Practical Accountant*, February.

Cova, Bruno (2005) 'The Parmalat fraud has generated too little reform', *Financial Times*, 7 November.

Edwards, C. (2002) 'Beyond Enron. The fate of Andrew Fastow and Company casts a harsh light on off-balance-sheet financing', *CFO*, February.

Grabowski, F. (2002) 'Enron', *Universitat Pompeu Fabra*, p. 11.

Greene, Richard (1980) 'The Joys of Leasing', *Forbes*, 24 November: p. 51.

Harrison, Walter T. and Horngren, Charles T. (2005) *Financial Accounting*, 6th edn, p. 221.

Kemp, Patrick S. (1963) 'Controversies on the Construction of Financial Statements', *Accounting Review*, January.

Khambata, Dara (1989) 'Off-balance-sheet Activities of US Banks: An Empirical Evaluation', *Columbia Journal of World Business*, summer.

Koller, Timothy M. (2003) 'Accounting: Now for Something Completely Different', *McKinsey on Finance*, summer.

Li, David H. (1963) 'Alternative accounting procedures and the entity concept', *Accounting Review*, January.

Micklethwait, A. (2004) 'Worldcom: the Downfall of a Giant', *IMD*.

Prasad Sharma, H. (2003) 'The WorldCom Accounting Scandal', *ICFAI*.

Schilit, Howard (2002) *Financial Shenanigans* (New York: McGraw Hill).

Schwarcz, S.L. (2002) 'Enron, and the Use and Abuse of Special Purpose Entities in Corporate Structures', *Financier*, 9, 1–4.

Sever, Mark and Chroeder, R. Harold, Jr. (1988) 'How Much Disclosure?', *ABA Banking Journal*, March.

Shashidhar, M. (2004) 'Coca-Cola: Questionable Accounting Practices', *ICFAI University Press*.

Shelvin, Terry (1987) 'Taxes and Off-balance-sheet Financing: R&D Limited Partnerships', *Accounting Review*, July.

Simmons, John K. (1967) 'A Concept of Comparability in Financial Reporting' *Accounting Review*, October.

Articles

'A New Deferred Tax Liability – Pernod Ricard', *UBS*, 12 April 2004.

'Accounting for Stock-based Compensation', *Bear Stearns*, July 2003.

'Accounting Games Companies Play', *Wharton*, 14 July 2004. Article available at knowledge.wharton.edu

'Accounting Impact of Builder Performance Analyzed', *Deutsche Bank*, 5 August 2003.

'Accounting Implications of Enron', *UBS*, 17 January 2002.

'Accounting Issues', *Bear Stearns*, 5 February 1998.

'Accounting Issues', *Bear Stearns*, 7 December 1998.

'Accounting Practices in the Semiconductor Industry', *Deutsche Bank*, 4 September 2003.

'Adelphia, Addressing Off-balance-sheet', *Salomon Smith Barney*, 27 March 2002.

'Airlines Accounting', *Morgan Stanley*, 1998.

'Board Members: Facing Public Scrutiny', *Wharton*, 18 June 2003. Article available at: knowledge.wharton.edu

'Bond Insurance: What if the FASB Off-balance-sheet Crackdown Goes Through?', *Credit Suisse First Boston*, 7 March 2002.

'Can You Trust the Numbers', *UBS*, March 2002.

'Contingent Convertibles', *UBS*, 1 October 2004.

'Credit Risk Transfer in a post-Enron world', *UBS*, March 2003.

'CSFB Travel & Leisure: Accounting Watch', *Credit Suisse First Boston*, 13 July 2004.

'Deferred Tax Assets: A New Cookie Jar?', *UBS*, 24 October 2003.

'Does Earnings Quality Matter?', *UBS*, 21 January 2004.

'Earnings Quality: The Winning Tortoise', *UBS*, 3 February 2004.

'Earnouts & Contingent Considerations', *UBS*, 4 July 2002.

'Enron & Andersen: Bad Apples or Bad Barrel?', *Wharton*, 4 May 2005. Article available at: knowledge.wharton.edu

'Enron Corporation: May 6, 2001 Sell Recommendation', *Harvard Business School*, 18 May 2004.

'EPS: Towards a Common Denominator II', *Bear Stearns*, 25 March 1996 and 'At The End: A Common Denominator', *Bear Stearns*, 7 April 1999.

'FAS 150', *UBS*, 5 November 2003.

'Footnotes', *UBS*, Note 19, Ch. 4, December 2002.

'Footnotes', *UBS*, 10 March 2003.

'Footnotes', *UBS*, 28 April 2003.

'Footnotes', *UBS*, 12 May 2003.

'Footnotes', *UBS*, 16 June 2003.

'Footnotes', *UBS*, 9 July 2003.

'Footnotes', *UBS*, Note 15, Ch. 2, August 2003.

'Footnotes', *UBS*, 15 September 2003.

'Footnotes', *UBS*, 21 October 2003.

'Footnotes', *UBS*, 18 November 2003.

'Footnotes', *UBS*, Note 13, Ch. 3, December 2003.

'Footnotes', *UBS*, Note 33, Ch. 2, February 2004.

'Footnotes', *UBS*, 10 February 2004.
'Footnotes', *UBS*, 17 February 2004.
'Footnotes', *UBS*, 24 February 2004.
'Footnotes', *UBS*, 20 April 2004.
'Footnotes', *UBS*, 11 May 2004.
'Footnotes', *UBS*, 26 May 2004.
'Footnotes', *UBS*, 22 June 2004.
'Footnotes', *UBS*, 29 June 2004.
'Footnotes', *UBS*, July 2004.
'Footnotes', *UBS*, 7 September 2004.
'Footnotes', *UBS*, 8 September 2004.
'Footnotes', *UBS*, Note 3, Ch. 2, September 2004.
'Footnotes', *UBS*, 19 January 2005.
'Footnotes', *UBS*, 1 February 2005.
'Footnotes', *UBS*, 1 March 2005.
'Footnotes', *UBS*, 4 May 2005.
'Gearing & Hybrid Securities', *UBS*, March 1999.
'Global Accounting: Off-Balance Sheet Finance', *UBS*, 31 January 2002.
'Heads up on Current Accounting Issues & Trends', *Credit Suisse First Boston*, 18 March 2003.
'Hedging & NIC 39', *UBS*, September 2005.
'Hotel Operating Leases', *UBS*, 10 December 2002.
'How Parmalat differs from US Scandals', Knowledge @ Wharton, 28 January 2004. Available at: knowledge.wharton.upenn.edu
'If Off-balance-sheet Becomes a Taboo it is an Opportunity', *Credit Suisse First Boston*, 1 February 2002.
'IFRS 3: Business Combinations', *UBS*, 19 April 2004.
'Industrials and Materials: The Art of Accounting', *Deutsche Bank*, 7 January 2003.
'It services Off-balance-sheet Financing: Win, Win, Win', *Bernstein Research*, 2003.
'Jam Today: Revenue Recognition and Cash Flow at IT Services Companies', *West LB*, February 2004.
'Motion Picture Industry', Schroeder Wertheim & Co., 24 August 1994.
'Multinational Valuation, Pensions, Economic Profits', *UBS*, 1 June 2005: 14.
'Off-balance-sheet Debt at Dow and Dupont', *Salomon Smith Barney*, 13 May 2002.
'Off-balance-sheet Finance', *UBS*, 31 June 2002.
'Off-balance-sheet Issues in Restaurants', *Credit Suisse First Boston*, 19 April 2002.
'Option Backdating: Is it Really Wrong?', *UBS*, 30 June 2006.
'Parmalat. Chairman & CEO Calisto Tanzi Replaced by Enrico Bondi', *Citigroup*, 17 December 2003.
'Provision Accounting', *UBS*, December 1998.
'Raytheon', *Bear Stearns*, 16 August 2001.
'Reg G. The Squeeze on Pro Forma', *UBS*, 11 February 2003.
'Revenue Recognition or the Software Industry', *Salomon Smith Barney*, May 2001.

'Revenue Recognition, Underestimated Issue in Equity Analysis', *UBS*, 28 October 2003.

'Revenue Recognition: Underestimated Issue in Equity Analysis', *UBS*, 28 April 2003.

'Software Industry: Enterprise Software Accounting Issues', *ING*, 6 October 1998.

'Spanish Banks: Are They Really That Efficient?', *UBS*, 11 July 2006.

'Thai Banks: Off-balance-sheet Guarantees', *Schroeders*, 30 May 1997.

'The Art of Accounting: Counting the Cost of Option Expensing in Capital Goods', *Deutsche Bank*, 7 January 2003.

'The Changing Use of Derivatives: More Hedging, Less Speculation', *Wharton*, 12 February 2003. Article available at knowledge.wharton.edu

'The Economic Implications of Corporate Financial Reporting', *NBER*, Working Paper no. 10550, June 2004.

'The Enron Odyssey (A): The Special Purpose of SPEs', Harvard Business School, 23 August 2004.

'US Wireless', *Bernstein Research*, 14 November 2001.

'Valuation and Accounting: Fire in Ahold: Accounting for Vendor Rebates', *Salomon Smith Barney*, 26 February 2003.

'When an Asset is not an Asset', *UBS*, 20 June 2002, p. 3.

'When an Asset is not an Asset', *UBS*, 20 June 2002.

Magazines

Expansión, December 2004.
Expansión, 2 March 2005.
Expansión, 4 May 2005.
Expansión, 1 June 2005.
Expansión, 2 June 2005.
Expansión, 23 June 2005.
Expansión, 29 June 2005.
Expansión, 20 July 2005.
Expansión, 29 August 2005.
Expansión, 6 October 2005.
Expansión, 31 October 2005.
Expansión, 1 December 2005.
Expansión, 29 January 2006.
Expansión, 30 January 2006.
Expansión, 31 January 2006.
Expansión, 15 February 2006.
Expansión, 19 April 2006.
Expansión, 19 May 2006.
Expansión, 30 May 2006.
Expansión, 10 July 2006.
Expansión, 2 August 2006.
Financial Times, 16 June 2005.
Financial Times, 22 June 2005.

Financial Times, 8 July 2005.
Financial Times, 12 August 2005.
Financial Times, 7 October 2005.
Financial Times, 17 October 2005.
Financial Times, 3 November 2005.
Financial Times, 29 November 2005.
Financial Times, 15 December 2005.
Financial Times, 16 December 2005.
Financial Times, 20 December 2005.
Financial Times, 22 December 2005.
Financial Times, 27 December 2005.
Financial Times, 29 December 2005.
Financial Times, 13 January 2006.
Financial Times, 6 February 2006.
Financial Times, 10 February 2006.
Financial Times, 23 February 2006.
Financial Times, 24 February 2006.
Financial Times, 1 March 2006.
Financial Times, 8 March 2006.
Financial Times, 9 March 2006.
Financial Times, 10 May 2006.
Financial Times, 23 May 2006.
Financial Times, 29 May 2006.
Financial Times, 31 May 2006.
Financial Times, 24 July 2006.
Financial Times, 28 July 2006.
France Presse, 23 January 2006.
Reuters, 25 November 2005.
The Wall Street Journal, 23 December 2003.
The Wall Street Journal, 1 February 2006.
The Wall Street Journal, 1 June 2006.
The Wall Street Journal, 10 May 2006.
The Wall Street Journal, 11 January 2006.
The Wall Street Journal, 12 August 2005.
The Wall Street Journal, 12 October 2005.
The Wall Street Journal, 13 December 2005.
The Wall Street Journal, 13 February 2006.
The Wall Street Journal, 13 June 2006.
The Wall Street Journal, 15 February 2006.
The Wall Street Journal, 18 April 2006.
The Wall Street Journal, 18 February 2006.
The Wall Street Journal, 18 January 2006.
The Wall Street Journal, 2 February 2006.
The Wall Street Journal, 2 September 2005.
The Wall Street Journal, 27 December 2005.
The Wall Street Journal, 28 April 2005.
The Wall Street Journal, 28 June 2005.

The Wall Street Journal, 29 December 2005.
The Wall Street Journal, 29 May 2006.
The Wall Street Journal, 3 February 2006.
The Wall Street Journal, 3 March 2006.
The Wall Street Journal, 3 May 2006.
The Wall Street Journal, 30 January 2006.
The Wall Street Journal, 5 October 2005.
The Wall Street Journal, 6 June 2006.
The Wall Street Journal, 7 August 2006.
The Wall Street Journal, 7 February 2006.
The Wall Street Journal, 7 March 2006.
The Wall Street Journal, 8 August 2006.
The Wall Street Journal, 8 June 2006.

Websites

http://grupo.iberia.es/content/GrupoIberia/Documentos/memoria per cent 20 Informe per cent20anual per cent202005.pdf
http://informeanual.telefonica.es/upload/esp/memorias/2001.pdf
http://www.ahold.com/index.asp?id=855
http://www.ericsson.com/investors/financial_reports/1999-2002/ 12month00en.pdf
http://www.fifa.com/en/media/index/0,1369,74717,00.html
http://www.gamesa.es/gamesa/index.html
http://www.gamesa.es/img/pdf/accionista/gobierno_corporativo/informe_ Gobierno_2000.pdf
http://www.heinekeninternational.com/pages/article/s2/12230000000050-13660000000
045/financialinformation.aspx
http://www.lucent.com/investor/financialreports.html
http://www.parmalat.com/en/fset.html?sez=dc
http://www.rolls-royce.com/investors/reports/2002
http://www.sec. gov/Archives/edgar/data/108772/000095013002002336/00009 50130-02-002336.txt
http://www.vodafone.com/section_article/0,3035, CATEGORY_ID%253D404 %2526
LANGUAGE_ID%253D2%2526CONTENT_ID%253D230864,00.html
www.gpoaccess.gov

Bibliography

'Accounting Games Companies Play', *Wharton*, 14 July 2004.

ACCID (2003) *Comprender las Normas Internacionales de Contabilidad* (Barcelona: Gestión 2000).

AECA (1981) *Principios y Normas de Contabilidad en España* (Madrid: AECA).

Amat, Oriol and Blake, John (1996) *Contabilidad Creativa* (Barcelona: Gestión 2000).

Bauman, Mark (2003) 'The Impact and Valuation of Off-balance-sheet Activities Concealed by Equity Method Accounting', *Accounting Horizon*, December.

Bereenson, Alex (2003) *The Number: How the Drive for Quarterly Earnings Corrupted Wall Street and Corporate America* (New York: Random House).

Bong Karen (2003) 'Enron Corp.', *Richard Ivey School of Business*, p. 17.

Burns, Joseph, Jaedicke, R.K. and Sangster, J.M. (1963) 'Financial Reporting of Purchase Contracts used to Guarantee Large Investments', *Accounting Review*, January.

Cano Rodríguez, Manuel (2001) *La Contabilidad Creativa* (Madrid: Pearson Educación).

Cowan, T.K. (1965) 'Are Truth and Fairness Generally Acceptable?', *Accounting Review*, October: 188–94.

Edwards, Charles (2002) 'Beyond Enron. The Fate of Andrew Fastow and Company Casts a Harsh Light on Off-balance-sheet Financing', *CFO*, February.

Giner, B. (1989) 'De los Principios Contables Generalmente Aceptados a los Legalmente Establecidos', *Técnica Contable*, March: 125–38.

Gonzalo, J.A., Castro, E. and Gabás, F. (1985) 'Los Principios Contables Fundamentales en al Actualidad', *Congreso de Censores Jurados de Cuentas*, March, Vigo.

Graham, John R., Harvey, Campbell R. and Rajgopal, Shiva (2004) 'The Economic Implications of Corporate Financial Reporting', *NBER*, Working Paper 10550, June.

Kemp, S., Patrick (1963) 'Controversies on the Construction of Financial Statements', *Accounting Review*, January.

Khambata, Dara (1989) 'Off-balance-sheet Activities of US Banks: An Empirical Evaluation', *Columbia Journal of World Business*, summer.

Koller, Timothy M. (2003) 'Accounting: Now for Something Completely Different', *McKinsey on Finance*, summer.

Laínes, J.A. and Callao, S. (2002) 'La Información Contable como Herramienta Corportativa', *Economistas*, 93: 85–92.

Lee, G.A. (1981) *Modern Financial Accounting* (Walton on Thames, Surrey: Nelson).

Li, David H. (1963) 'Alternative Accounting Procedures and the Entity Concept', *Accounting Review*, January.

Mulford, Charles W. and Comiskey, Eugene E. (2002) *The Financial Numbers Game, Detecting Creative Accounting Practices* (New York: John Wiley & Sons).

Naser, K. (1993) *Creative Financial Accounting: Its Nature and Use* (London: Prentice Hall).

Rojo, L.A. (1993) 'Tendencias de Contabilidad y Contabilidad Creativa', *AECA*, 36: 4–7.

Schilit, Howard (2002) *Financial Shenanigans* (New York: McGraw Hill).

Schwarcz, Steven L. (2002) 'Enron, and the Use and Abuse of Special Purpose Entities in Corporate Structures', *Financier*, 9 (1–4).

Sever, Mark and Chroeder, R. Harold, Jr. (1988) 'How Much Disclosure?', *ABA Banking Journal*, March.

Shelvin, Terry (1987) 'Taxes and Off-balance-sheet Financing: R&D Limited Partnerships', *Accounting Review*, July.

Sherman, H. David, Young, S. David, and Collingwood, Harris (2003) *Profits You Can Trust* (Upper Saddle River, NJ: Financial Times/Prentice Hall).

Simmons, John K. (1967) 'A Concept of Comparability in Financial Reporting', *Accounting Review*, October.

Túa, J. (1985) 'Algunas Precisiones Adicionales en Torno al Principio de Imagen Fiel', *Técnica contable*, December: 441–84.

Tweedie, D. (1988) 'Imagen Fiel v. the Rule Book: Which is the Answer to Creative Accounting' *Pacific Accounting Review*, December: 1–21.

Index

Note: page numbers in **bold** indicate entire chapters devoted to a subject.